Gender Discrimination and Human Rights

Gender Discrimination and Human Rights

Vijay Kumar Gupta

MD Publications Pvt Ltd
New Delhi
www.mdppl.com

Published by
MD Publications Pvt Ltd
"MD House", 11, Darya Ganj,
New Delhi-110002
Ph. : +91-11-41563325, 41562846
E-mail : **contact@mdppl.com**
Website : **www.mdppl.com**

ISBN : 978-81-7533-124-2

PRICE : Rs. 795.00

Published and Printed by
MD Publications Pvt Ltd at Printext,
D2/149A, Jeewan Park, Uttam Nagar, New Delh.

Preface

Gender Discrimination can be generalized as a subtype of essentialism. Discrimination can be partitioned as consisting of sexism against the female sex, sexism against the male sex, sexism against the intersex (hermaphrodite and pseudohermaphrodite), and sexism against the transsex (transmale and transfemale). Each type of sexism has its own history and form of intolerance to counter.

Sexist beliefs, as a species of essentialism, holds that individuals can be understood or be judged simply based on the characteristics of the group to which they belong in this case, their sexual group, as males or females. This assumes that all individuals "fit" into the category of "males" or "females" and does not take into account of intersexed people who are born with both sexual characteristics. This also assumes a homogeneous characteristics of all males in the "male group" and all females in the "female group" and does not take into account the huge differences within a group. There are also XX males and XY females who are genetically one sex but have developed the sexual characteristics of another sex at fetal stage.

Gender discrimination refers to differential treatment based on sex. Gender, the meaning attached to being male or female, carries different connotations of value in different cultures. Traditionally in Indian culture a higher value has been given to whatever is defined as male. Anglo colonists brought with them the ancient English custom of coverture, by which a married woman's civil identity was "covered by" or absorbed into her husband's for virtually all purposes except crime. Therefore, all of the personal property she brought to the marriage became her husband's as well as any earnings or income thereafter. Unable to sign a legal contract, she had to be a widow in order to make a will. With voting rights initially tied to property ownership, blocking women's access to economic resources also meant denying their political rights.

For minority women, sex discrimination in employment compounded racial and ethnic discrimination, relegating them to jobs at the very bottom of the economic scale. Occupational segregation and lower wages, as well as unrecognized, uncompensated labor for those doing housework, left most women economically dependent on men. As a result, the feminization of poverty long predated the twentieth century.

Although some women found new employment opportunities during the nineteenth century as secretaries, librarians, and school teachers, feminization of jobs once held by men resulted in a decline in pay and prestige. For those educated women seeking advanced training that could provide them entrée into better paying, male-dominated professions, universities served as gate keepers, barring their entry.

I have consulted various authors and derived much from their thinking and thoughts. I am grateful to them and record my thanks. Also, I thanks my family for extending wholehearted support during the compilation of this book. And finally, my thanks are due to Mr. Parnav Gupta, M/s. MD Publications Pvt. Ltd. Delhi for bringing out this book in a pleasing and attractive manner.

Editor

CONTENTS

	Preface	*v*
1.	Discrimination against Women in the Professions	1
2.	Discrimination against Women with Children	16
3.	Role of Family in Gender Discrimination	28
4.	Sex Discrimination in Today's Workplace	39
5.	Theories of Social and Gender Justice	76
6.	Consideration of Care and Justice	108
7.	Psychobiosocial Perspective to Understand Cognitive Sex Differences	148
8.	Women's International Human Rights Law	172
9.	Role and Function of Women's International Human Rights	205
10.	Domestic Violence as an International Human Rights Issue	227
11.	Proving Sex Discrimination in Court	242
	Bibliography	257
	Index	261

1

Discrimination against Women in the Professions

Introduction

Early in the nineteenth century, law schools generally excluded two groups of applicants felons and females. Among the many reasons advanced for the rejection of women "were the dangers of unchaperoned intellectual intercourse in the libraries, and the diversion of male attention in the classroom ." Even late in the century, women were still barred from practicing law in many states. As one judge pontificated while endeavoring to justify his decision to deny the admission of female candidates to the Wisconsin bar, "The peculiar qualities of womanhood, its gentle graces, its quick sensibility, its tender susceptibility," were surely not qualifications for "forensic strife."

As late as the middle of the twentieth century, female attorneys were openly discriminated against. As noted earlier, when Supreme Court justice Sandra Day O'Connor graduated near the top of her Stanford Law School class, the only offer of employment she received was for the position of legal secretary. As recently as 1965, major Wall Street law firms could point to only three female partners in their midst.

The legal profession has also long denied equal status to minorities. Of the forty thousand law firm partners listed in the 1997–98 *National Directory of Legal Employers,* only 1 percent were African American, and all minorities comprised less than 3 percent. A survey conducted in 1999 by the *American Bar Association Journal* and *National Bar Association Magazine* revealed that 75 percent of the black lawyers participating in the survey believed that law firms engage in tokenism rather than in genuine diversity and equality in advancing blacks to partnerships. Sixty-seven percent of black lawyers believed that minority female lawyers are treated less fairly than white female lawyers. Nonetheless, women, black and white, in ever increasing numbers, have entered this hostile environment. In 1975, 23 percent of the nation's law school students were women; by 1992, the number had risen to 42 percent, by 1996 to 44 percent, and by 1999 to 46 percent. The entering class in 2001 was comprised of more women than men.

Although obstacles to women entering the profession have gradually diminished, barriers still keep them from advancing to higher positions. In this regard, the law profession differs little from others: Women are underrepresented in the top positions and overrepresented in those at the bottom.

When Candace Krugman Beinecke was named chair of Hughes Hubbard & Reed in 1999, she became the first woman ever to head a major New York City law firm. At the time, only two other large firms in the country were led by women. Although nearly half the students then sitting in law school classrooms were female, only 15 percent of the partners in law firms of 140 or more lawyers were women. Obviously, no direct correlation exists between the increased numbers of women in the profession and their ascension to positions of power.

Women teaching in law schools face similar conditions. In 1999, they accounted for only 20 percent of the full professorships in the country's law schools and for 10 percent of law school deans. Moreover, at the eleven most selective law schools in 1997, only 18.6 percent of the faculty was female; at the fifteen least selective law schools, the number was 24.9 percent. Harvard Law School's faculty that year was only 15 percent female.

The number of women holding general counsel positions in Fortune 500 firms increased from six in the late 1980s to forty-four in

1999. Still, only 9 percent of top corporate legal positions are filled by women. Only 16 percent of corporate legal departments of between fifty-one and one hundred lawyers are directed by women, while more than one-half of the legal departments with twenty-five and fewer lawyers are headed by females.

Clearly, the legal profession has its own glass ceiling. Myriad factors have led to its continued existence, but one appears to stand out: Young male attorneys have always been encouraged to focus on career development, while female lawyers are expected to focus on home and family, as well as on their careers. Thus, the law firm role of the male lawyer differs significantly from that of the female attorney, and the contribution to the firm made by the single-focused male lawyer carries the greater value. Thus, more law firm partnerships go to men than to women.

In 1989, the Association of the Bar of the City of New York created a committee to study, monitor, and then address issues confronting the city's women lawyers. The committee focused first on the issues thought to be affecting the advancement of women in the city's largest law firms. Committee members assumed that a glass ceiling either existed or was perceived to exist in these firms, and they undertook to determine why. They concentrated on two issues. First, since both family and career are established during the years immediately following graduation from law school, to what extent do a woman's family responsibilities constitute a hindrance to law firm advancement? Second, do glass ceilings exist at various points in a female attorney's career?

The committee selected Cynthia Fuchs Epstein, a professor of sociology at City University and author of a work on the difficulties confronting women in the legal profession, entitled *Women in Law,* to design a study to explore these issues. Over the next several years, Epstein studied eight large city firms and the positioning of women lawyers in them. She presented her report to the committee in 1995.

Epstein's study showed a steady upward trend in the proportion of women hired by New York City law firms, to the point where their numbers were nearly equal to men. An upward trend in the number of female lawyers elevated to partner also occurred, but not at an equal rate. Although the proportion of female lawyers at these firms increased from 26 to 40 percent from 1980 through 1994, the proportion of female partners never exceeded 12 percent. Epstein concluded that sex stereotyping and the perception of differences in motivation between men and women constituted serious obstacles to women's mobility in these firms.

Many of the female lawyers reported to Epstein that after giving birth to a child they were denied the more coveted work and case assignments. Moreover, an expectation seemed to form in the firm that now that they were mothers they would withdraw from the partnership track, and this attitude tended to discourage women's full participation and commitment to their firms. Women, moreover, were often categorized as "outsiders" and perceived to be less committed to the firm. Sex stereotyping and the treatment of women as a category rather than as individuals provided serious obstacles to advancement. Some women, however, lowered their partnership aspirations when they found the pressure of work too difficult to reconcile with family responsibilities.

Although motherhood was usually considered a deterrent to career mobility, three-quarters of the women who did achieve partnership status were married with children. Epstein also observed that female lawyers were working in all specialties of the law instead of clustering in a few as in the past. Few women, however, headed practice groups or held management positions in their firms.

Epstein also reported that women faced prejudices emanating from stereotypical assumptions that often led to the selective assignment of women in connection with certain of the firm's matters. Women lawyers also confronted a "double-bind." If they did not exhibit behavior based on male models, they were branded as not tough enough or insufficiently aggressive, but if they were perceived as tough and aggressive, they were regarded as impaired women who acted like men. This "damned if you do, damned if you don't" attitude acted as a significant deterrent to the acceptance of women for partnership.

As committee members had anticipated, Epstein confirmed the existence of a number of glass ceilings that barred or limited the advancement of women at different career levels. Some of these ceilings were imposed by senior partners who issued the standards that structured their firms and who were responsible for decisions regarding promotion and the paths leading to it. Some glass ceilings were the product of conscious decision making, and others of general firm practices that adversely affected women. Glass ceilings, in some instances, were imposed by women themselves, based on pressures internal to their firms, as well as on pressures emanating from their familial responsibilities.

The law firms Epstein studied generally fell into two categories: the firm with established traditions in which partners were committed to replicating the firm as they knew it, and the market-driven firm where the financial bottom line effectively determined the firm's structuring. In the latter, decisions relating to partnership revolved around profitability; therefore, the ability to develop business was thought to be a sufficient, if not the only, reason for promotion.

Women were disadvantaged in both types of firms. The traditional firms replicated themselves as white male institutions. In the market-driven firms, expectations for business development were largely based on subjective criteria susceptible to the influence of stereotypes relating to the roles, motivations, and preferences of women.

Epstein's study demonstrated conclusively that Title VII has not eliminated sex discrimination from the legal profession. The statute's strict equalopportunity policy fails to take into account that most female lawyers are mothers, and that working mothers are required by the profession to accede to a male model of competition at a time in their lives when it is not possible for them to compete on that basis. In addition, although Title VII has been generally successful in rooting out overt acts of workplace sex discrimination, it has more often failed to provide female lawyers with adequate protection from more subtle acts of discrimination, usually based on false stereotypical assumptions about female workers and women in general.

Title VII has given female attorneys little protection from discriminatory denials of partnership status, as Nancy Ezold learned when her firm denied her a partnership. Ezold sued Wolf, Block, Schorr and Solis-Cohen, a Philadelphia law firm, alleging that the firm intentionally discriminated against her because of her sex when it decided not to admit her to partnership.

Wolf, Block had hired Ezold as an associate on a partnership track. Before entering law school, Ezold had accumulated thirteen years of administrative and legislative experience, first as an assistant to Maine's senator Edmund Muskie, later as a contract administrator for the Model Cities Program, and finally as an administrator in the Office of a Special Prosecutor of the Pennsylvania Department of Justice. She had graduated from the Villanova University School of Law in the top third of her class and had then worked at two small law firms in Philadelphia. After Wolf, Block hired Ezold, it assigned her to its litigation department, where she worked for the next six years.

Throughout her tenure with the firm, Ezold's performance was reviewed regularly, as was that of each of Wolf, Block's associates, in accordance with commonly accepted standards of legal performance, such as legal analysis and research, negotiation, and advocacy skills, and in accordance with ten categories of personal characteristics, such as reliability, attitude, and the ability to work independently. These evaluations were recorded on standard forms that were later used by the firm's partners in deciding whether to offer partnership status to an associate.

Ezold received positive evaluations from nearly all the partners for whom she had done any substantial amount of work, but two of her later evaluations questioned her ability to analyze legal issues. Subsequently, the firm's partners voted to deny Ezold promotion to partner. Ezold then resigned and sued Wolf, Block for sex discrimination.

After the trial court reviewed the evidence, including the associate evaluation forms, it determined that Ezold had been held to a higher standard of performance than the firm's male associates, and that she was at least as capable, if not more so, than the male associates who had been offered partnership positions. Wolf, Block, the court ruled, was not entitled under the law to apply its promotion standards more severely to female associates, and it concluded that the firm's differential treatment of female lawyers constituted discriminatory conduct the real reason for Ezold's rejection for partnership.

Ezold's victory was short-lived, as the appellate court reversed the trial court's decision. The appellate court ruled that Wolf, Block's partners were entitled to exercise their business judgment in deciding whether Ezold possessed the legal analytical skills sufficient to meet the firm's standards. It rejected as "immaterial" the trial court's finding that Ezold excelled in other areas, and it held that the trial court should not have interfered with Wolf, Block's evaluation process: "Wolf's articulated reason for refusing to offer Ezold a partnership was its belief, *based on a subtle and subjective consensus among the partners,* that she did not possess sufficient legal analytic ability to handle complex litigation. We have cautioned courts on several occasions to avoid unnecessary intrusion into subjective promotion decisions".

Only five of Wolf, Block's 107 partners were women. Thus, when the appellate court gave its approval to the firm's denial of partnership to Ezold, a denial based on a "subtle and subjective consensus among the partners," the court was relying upon a "consensus" fashioned primarily by men. In these circumstances, female candidates for partnership are required to fit a cast or model subjectively formulated by men; in essence, the court ruled that even though this model may disadvantage female candidates for partnership, it is not a matter of concern for the court, which must avoid intruding upon the subjective evaluative process designed by the male members of the firm.

The Ezold case reflects the difficulties women lawyers meet when they contest decisions denying them partnership status. It is next to impossible to win such a case without evidence of overt and blatant acts of sex-discriminatory conduct, which usually is not available. In the view of many lawyers, the appellate court's opinion in this case "cemented the glass ceiling in place" in the legal profession.

A glass ceiling also exists in our colleges and universities. The American Association of University Professors (AAUP) reported in 1998 that the gap in salaries between male and female faculty members widened between 1975 and 1998, even though greater numbers of women moved into the profession during that period. Although some of the salary differences may be explained by seniority as well as by life-style choices of women with family responsibilities, gender bias continues to generate substantial disparities in university salaries. Further, women, more often than men, are forced to accept appointments in lower-paying institutions. Accordingly, women are more likely to hold positions in community colleges than in research universities. The largest salary disadvantages reflect the relegation of women to less remunerative positions.

Disparities in rank and tenure also persist. Although women are more likely to hold professorial positions, disproportionate numbers continue to work as lecturers and instructors. Even among women professors, relatively few are elevated to full professorship. The increasing numbers of women entering the profession have not culminated in any improvement in the positions they are assigned. In fact, the proportion of women who achieve tenure is declining. A glass ceiling is fully in place in academia.

Despite disparities in salary, rank, and tenure, female participation in the profession has continued to increase. The expansion of college and university faculties is largely attributable to increasing numbers of women in the profession; the number of men entering academia is barely sufficient to sustain current participation rates. The AAUP reported that the female share of college and university faculty positions had increased from 23 percent in 1975 to 34 percent in 1998. It appears likely that more women will aspire to professorial positions as ever increasing numbers of women earn Ph.D. degrees. Of the more than 42,000 research doctorates granted by U.S. universities in 1997, more than 40 percent were awarded to women.

With more women entering the professorial ranks, the problems experienced at MIT are likely to occur in educational institutions with increasing frequency. A case in point is Christine Sweeney's. Sweeney earned a bachelor of education degree at Keene State College, a small liberal arts college that is part of the University of New Hampshire. She later acquired master's and Ph.D. degrees at Catholic University. After teaching for three years at Emmanuel College, Sweeney was appointed associate professor of education at Keene State. Three years later, she sought promotion to full professor.

Sweeney's department chair had recommended her for promotion, but an all-male Faculty Evaluation Advisory Committee unanimously voted against the promotion, and, subsequently, her dean concurred with that decision. Shortly thereafter, Sweeney charged the school with sex discrimination. Pending the trial of her lawsuit, Sweeney again sought promotion, again the all-male faculty committee voted against her, and again the dean concurred. The president of the college told Sweeney that she lacked the qualifications required for promotion, that she held narrow, rigid, and old-fashioned views, that she tended to personalize professional matters, and that she emphasized to her students the importance of maintaining her classroom window shades at an even height.

A few months after the president's criticisms, Sweeney tried for full professor a third time and succeeded. Thus, the issues in her discrimination suit were limited to whether the college had discriminated against her on her first two attempts.

Sweeney submitted statistical evidence supporting her claim that sex bias undermined her first two attempts at promotion, and that a glass ceiling had barred her and other women from moving up. Only four women in the entire history of Keene State had achieved the rank of full professor, while in the seven years before Sweeney filed her sex discrimination suit, the number of male full professors had increased from ten to twenty-three. In fact, more men held full-professor positions than instructor positions, despite the school's insistence that entry to full-professor rank was a significant achievement reserved for the excellent few. Sweeney also showed that each of the four women who achieved full professorship had first attained a Ph.D., while several male professors had not. The court held that this evidence supported a finding that Keene State applied a double standard in promotion decisions. The court could have relied on other evidence that also indicated that Keene State had engaged in sex-discriminatory conduct. The reasons given Sweeney for denying her a promotion on her first two attempts were pretexts. If Sweeney was unqualified for promotion, as the president alleged, because of her narrow and old-fashioned views (including her views on window shades), what explanation did Keene State have for promoting her a few months later? Why was Sweeney deemed unqualified on the first two occasions but qualified on the third? The position taken by the school to justify the promotion denial was simply not believable. In these circumstances, courts frequently rule that if the reason given by the employer for its actions is not credible, then the court may assume that the employer proffered a false reason to cover up or mask its true reason, namely, that it had engaged in discriminatory conduct. One aspect of academia's glass ceiling that has been the subject of much litigation, beginning soon after the inception of Title VII, is the failure to grant tenure to women on the same terms it is granted to men. This is an area of the law of sex discrimination that the courts are reluctant to enter, and when they do, they rarely overturn a tenure decision. When four women assistant professors at Cornell University alleged they had been denied tenure because of their gender, the court listed six reasons why contested tenure decisions must be set apart from other types of Title VII claims:

- Tenure contracts, unlike the ordinary employer-employee relationship, entail lifetime commitments and collegial relationships.
- Tenure decisions are generally noncompetitive in the sense that a decision to grant or not grant tenure to a particular person does not necessarily affect the future of other tenure candidates.
- A tenure decision is usually highly decentralized in that the decision is made at a departmental level by many persons rather than by a single person or small group of individuals, as in other employment decisions.
- The number of factors considered in a tenure decision is quite extensive.
- Tenure decisions are often a source of great disagreement, as strongly held views are common.
- Tenure decisions involve conflicting views of scholars working in specialized academic fields. The courts cannot hope to master these areas of academic scholarship, even though they may need to do so to resolve differences in these scholars' opinions.

Although tenure decisions are not exempt from Title VII review, the reluctance of the courts to consider them has led to a judicial attitude that requires the submission of particularly strong evidence of discriminatory conduct for the claimant to have any reasonable hope of success.

In denial-of-tenure cases, the plaintiff often relies upon evidence that demonstrates that her college or university held her to a stricter standard of performance than that required of male faculty members. Although, as noted, the litigation success rate among tenure claimants has not been great, Connie Rae Kunda was an exception.

Kunda was an instructor in the Department of Physical Education at Muhlenberg College in Allentown, Pennsylvania. At the time of her hiring, she had a bachelor's degree in physical education, and although she had not earned a master's degree, college administrators had not advised her that one would be required for advancement at Muhlenberg. Five years later Muhlenberg rejected her for promotion to assistant professor. Nothing was said to Kunda indicating that the college had denied her the promotion because she lacked a master's degree, nor was she told that a master's degree was mandatory for promotion or for tenure consideration. Two years later, the college's Faculty Personnel and Policies Committee unanimously recommended Kunda for promotion to assistant professor, but the dean of the college disagreed: "I cannot recommend that she be promoted because she holds only a Bachelor's degree. If she held a Master's degree I would certainly recommend her promotion on the strength of the known excellence of her work at the College. She is an outstanding teacher in her area, has made fine contributions within the Physical Education Department, and has been a dedicated and loyal member of the faculty." The following year, the committee again unanimously recommended her promotion and, in addition, urged that she be granted tenure. Again, the dean rejected the recommendations. Kunda then sued the college for sex discrimination.

Kunda first brought to the court's attention particulars pertaining to the promotions of other faculty members in the physical education department, some of whom had not earned master's degrees. In fact, the department chair had been promoted to full professor although he held only a bachelor's degree. Kunda then submitted evidence demonstrating the differences in the counseling the college extended to male members of the physical education department and that extended to Kunda during the process leading to the tenure decision. Male candidates were advised that a master's degree would strengthen an application for tenure. On one occasion, the dean initiated a meeting with one of the male faculty members, a candidate for tenure at about the same time as Kunda, and specifically advised him that he should obtain a master's degree. The dean also encouraged two other men in the department to obtain master's degrees. Kunda, however, never received similar counseling. She was not made aware of the importance of a master's degree to the tenure process. This evidence clearly showed that the college favored male faculty members over Kunda. She had been subjected to disparate treatment; the college treated female faculty less advantageously than male faculty.

Kunda also submitted evidence of procedural irregularities in the tenure approval process. First, the dean spoke against Kunda's tenure candidacy at a meeting of the Faculty Personnel Policies Committee, although in the past he had declined to appear at committee meetings that considered matters pertaining to tenure or promotion. Second, earlier in the process, the dean had failed to advise the committee that Kunda was a candidate for promotion, and thus on that occasion her application was not acted upon. With evidence of this type at hand, together with evidence of disparate treatment, the court had little difficulty in concluding that Kunda had been a victim of sex discrimination.

Sex discrimination is not limited to the legal profession and academia. We have already seen an example of the type of discriminatory conduct women experience in the accounting profession. In another case, after Brenda Smart obtained a bachelor's degree in economics, she worked as an analyst for Columbia Gas System Service Corporation in Wilmington, Delaware. Smart, under the supervision of the assistant controller, prepared cash-flow forecasts and analyzed SEC reports and regulatory disclosures. When she expressed interest in a newly created senior analyst position, she received conflicting advice; one supervisor told her she would need a bachelor's degree in accounting, while another advised her that her degree in economics was sufficient. To be on the safe side, Smart began taking evening accounting courses at the University of Delaware.

After some delay, Columbia Gas decided to fill the senior analyst position, and the task of selecting the person to fill that position fell principally to Donato Furlano, Smart's direct supervisor. Subsequently, on three separate occasions, Furlano offered the position to a male employee, each of whom rejected the offer. The personnel department then assembled a list of employees who appeared to meet the minimum qualifications for the position, and Smart and four other women were on the list. Furlano rejected out of hand all of the women on the list, and then offered the position to a newly hired male worker who was not on the list. Furlano's choice for the position had an accounting degree and five years of accounting experience.

When Smart later charged Columbia Gas with sex discrimination, company officials claimed that Smart was not promoted to the senior analyst position because she lacked accounting experience and the requisite analytical skills, though they admitted that with appropriate training, she would have been capable of performing the duties of the position even without an accounting degree.

Smart claimed that she was as qualified as the male employee selected, that the company had failed to consider any women for the position, and that Columbia Gas's method of promoting employees to middle- and upper-management positions favored men. The trial court found that the five women that Furlano had rejected out of hand were at least as qualified, if not more so, as the male candidates that he had not rejected, and that Smart was as qualified as the worker chosen by Furlano. At the conclusion of the trial, the court ruled that gender had been a determinative factor in the decision not to promote Smart, and thus it awarded judgment in her favor.

Physicians rarely appear as claimants in sex discrimination cases, in part because many doctors are self-employed or practice as members of small medical teams. But discrimination against women exists in medicine just as in the other professions. The *New England Journal of Medicine* recently reported that female doctors are more likely than their male peers to teach at medical schools but are less likely to be promoted to senior medical positions: Women are 26 percent less likely than men to be promoted from junior faculty positions to associate professor, and still fewer advance from associate to full professor.

Jean Jew's case reflects these conditions. Jew obtained her medical degree from Tulane University, and later the University of Iowa's College of Medicine appointed her an associate professor in its Department of Anatomy, headed by Terrence Williams. Previously, Williams had been at Tulane University, where Jew had conducted research under his supervision. Throughout her employment at the University of Iowa, Jew worked closely with Williams as a research collaborator, and they coauthored several articles for scientific publications. The professional relationship between Jew and Williams was close, and she was a friend of his wife, also a professor at the College of Medicine.

Not long after Jew's appointment to the Department of Anatomy, rumors began to circulate suggesting that a sexual relationship existed between Jew and Williams. The ongoing rumors accused her of using her sex as a tool for advancement in the department. Thereafter, sexually suggestive cartoons and sex-based graffiti referring to Jew appeared on the wall of the men's room and at other places in the department. One of the male faculty members repeatedly speculated aloud about a sexual relationship between Jew and Williams, and he told faculty, graduate students, and staff that Jew had been observed having sexual intercourse with Williams in his office, that she was a "slut," and that she had received preferential treatment based on her sexual relationship with Williams. Another male doctor referred to Jew as a "slut," a "bitch," and a "whore."

Jew complained to the dean of the College of Medicine, advising him of the conduct of the male doctors in her department, and charged the college with ignoring the existence of a pattern of sexual harassment intended to discredit her professional and personal reputation. College officials advised her that nothing could be done, that a single woman commonly encountered these kinds of difficulties in a small-town, goldfish-bowl type of environment.

Jew continued to author and coauthor with Williams a number of articles that were published in prominent medical journals. She received two grants from the National Institute of Health and another from the National Science Foundation. In due course, the medical school considered her for promotion from associate professor to full professor. In accordance with established procedures, school administrators placed the proposed promotion before the entire faculty of the Department of Anatomy for approval or rejection.

The same faculty members who had verbally harassed Jew were among those called upon to evaluate her work and vote on her promotion. Two of the doctors who voted against her promotion were those who had called her a "slut" and a "whore." Another doctor who voted no commented that Jew had received many more advantages than he. All the voting faculty had heard the rumors, and, not surprisingly, they voted against her promotion. Those who voted no gave as their reason their belief that Jew had not established her "independence" in the areas of research and publication.

When Jew later sued the university for sex discrimination, the court, citing the conduct she had endured, ruled in her favor: "The ongoing rumors, which were false, accused her of physically using her sex as a tool for gaining favor, influence and power with the

Head of the Department, a man, and suggested that her professional accomplishments rested on sexual achievements rather than achievements of merit. The sexual relationship rumors, of course, also implicated Dr. Williams. Unlike the import of the rumors with respect to Dr. Jew, however, there was no suggestion that Dr. Williams was using a sexual relationship to gain favor, influence and power." The court held that Jew's rejection for promotion flowed directly from the harassing and discriminatory conduct of the male doctors in her department and directed the university to promote Jew to full professor.

Female lawyers, university professors, accountants, and doctors continue to be victimized by sex-discriminatory conduct, as are women in all the professions even in the world of astronomy. For more than a century, women have earned at least 10 percent of the doctorates awarded in astronomy, and women currently account for 25 percent of these degrees. At a meeting of the American Astronomical Society in early 2000, researchers presented the results of a survey on the status of women in the profession: Women at the highest levels of the profession remain a rarity. Only 5 percent of the country's professors of astronomy are female. Among the elite universities, more male than female graduate students win postdoctoral appointments to the schools from which they received their graduate degrees. For women in the field of astronomy, the glass ceiling reaches to the sky.

❑❑❑

2

Discrimination against Women with Children

Introduction

Public opinion has produced a widespread belief that woman's physical structure and the functions she performs in consequence thereof, justify special legislation restricting or qualifying the conditions under which she should be permitted to toil. That woman's physical structure and the performance of maternal functions place her at a disadvantage in the struggle for subsistence is obvious. This is especially true when the burdens of motherhood are upon her." Nearly a century later, such sex stereotypes remain prevalent, albeit modified in form. Working mothers remain subject to significant restrictions on advancement to higher positions in the workplace.

Shortly after World War II, for example, the Edwin L. Wiegand Company in Pennsylvania initiated a policy of discharging female employees upon marriage and of refusing to hire women who were married. The policy was necessary, according to Wiegand's management, to provide jobs for male "bread winners" returning from the war. At the time, the policy was lawful, and it remained lawful until July 2, 1965, the effective date of Title VII.

The EEOC later adopted regulations providing workplace protection specifically for married women: "The Commission has determined that an employer's rule which forbids or restricts the employment of married women and which is not applicable to married men is discrimination based on sex prohibited by Title VII of the Civil Rights Act." An employer policy or practice, even if not directed against all female employees, is nevertheless discriminatory if a subgroup, such as married women, is singled out for treatment different from that extended to male employees. Similarly, an employer may not select unmarried women with children for adverse treatment.

Over the past four decades, the number of married women with children employed outside the home has increased significantly. In 1960, approximately 6.6 million married women with children were employed in the workplace, and by 1997, this number had grown nearly threefold to 18.2 million. The workplace participation of women with very young children has also greatly increased. In 1960, the labor force participation rate of married women with children under six years of age was 18.6 percent, but by 1997, it had increased to 63.6 percent. In that year, 77.6 percent of married women with children between the ages of six and seventeen were gainfully employed. Statistical studies forecast the continued presence of working women with children in the workplace, even while at home they continue to be the major child-care givers.

With this marked growth in the employment of married women with children has come an increased reliance of working mothers upon Title VII protections against workplace discriminatory policies and practices. In Hot Springs, Arkansas, Martha Coble applied for the position of director of the school district's new teachers' center, designed to improve teacher skills, revise curricula, and experiment with new teaching methods and materials. In her thirteen years with the school district, she had accumulated a wide variety of classroom experience and was certified as an elementary school teacher, an elementary school principal, an elementary school supervisor, and a curriculum specialist for grades kindergarten through high school. Bill Nipper, the other applicant for the director's position, was similarly qualified. After the school district superintendent interviewed each candidate, he selected Nipper.

Coble then charged the superintendent and the school district with sex discrimination.

At the trial, Coble argued that her status as a working mother had been the primary reason for the superintendent's decision not to select her as the director of the teachers' center. Coble testified that during her interview, the superintendent noted her absences attributable to the illnesses of her children, questioned her about her children's ages, and asked her whether, in light of her family obligations, she could handle the long hours the director's position demanded. When the superintendent later notified Coble that he had selected Nipper for the position, he noted that although Coble was as qualified as Nipper, she had a family and he did not. Thus, it was clear that the superintendent's choice was influenced by his assumption that Coble's family responsibilities would interfere with her performance.

The superintendent rebutted none of this evidence, and the court concluded that his decision to reject Coble was largely based on the false premise that a mother's performance of child-care responsibilities necessarily interferes with her workplace functions. The court's ruling was buttressed by the failure of the school district to offer any evidence demonstrating that marital or parental status had been a factor in filling other administrative positions presumably as demanding as the director's position, and most of those positions had been filled by men with children. Clearly, women with children, as compared with men with children, faced substantial barriers to advancement in the Hot Springs school district.

Joann Trezza, also a working mother, was an attorney in the legal department of Hartford, Inc., an insurance company with offices in New York City. Working alongside Trezza in the department was a female attorney, unmarried and without children. When an opening occurred for a management position in the legal department of one of Hartford's suburban offices, the unmarried attorney was appointed to the position, even though Trezza was senior to her. When Trezza asked why Hartford had not considered her for the post, the managing attorney of the legal department told her that it was assumed that because she had a family she would not be interested in the position.

A year or so later, Trezza was in line for promotion to an assistant managing attorney position, but Hartford again rejected her in favor of a female attorney who was unmarried and childless. At the time, Hartford also elevated a male attorney, married with children, to an assistant manager post. After Trezza complained to one of Hartford's senior vice presidents that she felt she had been denied the promotion solely because she was a married woman with children, Hartford finally ordered her advancement to an assistant managing attorney position.

Four years later, the managing attorney of the legal department decided to retire. Since Trezza was then the second most senior attorney in the office and had consistently earned excellent performance evaluations, she believed she was the logical choice to be the retiree's successor. Rather than naming Trezza, however, Hartford appointed a thirty-eight-year-old female attorney with no children. The appointee had considerably less experience than Trezza, had never practiced law in New York, and, in fact, was not admitted to practice law in the state. Trezza sued Hartford for sex discrimination.

When Hartford asked the court to dismiss Trezza's case, her attorneys submitted an abundance of evidence supporting her claim that during the course of her employment Hartford had discriminated against her merely because she was a married woman with children and that male employees with children were not similarly treated. First, they showed that only seven of the forty-six managing attorneys employed by Hartford nationwide were women, and of these seven, four were employed in East Coast offices, and none of the four had school-age children. On the other hand, many of the men serving in managing attorney positions had children. Second, on three occasions Trezza's supervisor disparagingly commented on "the incompetence and laziness of women who were working mothers." In addition, on another occasion, a senior vice president of the company declared that it was his opinion that working mothers cannot simultaneously be both good mothers and good workers, remarking to Trezza, "I don't see how you can do either job well." Based on this evidence, the court denied Hartford's motion to dismiss Trezza's claims, and thus they were required to proceed to a trial of the ultimate issue did Hartford discriminate against Trezza because she was a working mother? A trial was avoided, however, when Hartford agreed to resolve Trezza's claims.

If the matter had not been settled prior to the trial, it appears highly likely that Trezza would have prevailed.

Both Coble and Trezza submitted evidence that their employers favored their male employees who had children over female employees with children. This type of evidence is typical of sex discrimination cases based on allegations of disparate treatment, that is, men and women similarly situated are not similarly treated. What would have been the result in these cases if evidence of disparate treatment had not been available? We turn to Andrea Bass's sex discrimination claim against Chemical Bank for the answer.

Bass's responsibilities as assistant vice president and product manager at the bank included the development of marketing plans for new cash management products. Given her success in this position, Bass anticipated promotion to vice president. Chemical, however, declined to promote her. Subsequently, Bass gave birth to her first child, and on her return from maternity leave, Chemical relieved her of certain of her responsibilities, making it less likely she would be promoted. Three years later, after Bass had her second child, Chemical reassigned virtually all of her remaining responsibilities as product manager. Not long after, Chemical promoted a single woman with no children to the vice presidency position that Bass had long anticipated being awarded. At this juncture, Bass sued Chemical for sex discrimination, claiming she had been denied promotion only because of her status as a working mother.

Bass was passed over for promotion in favor of another woman, not a man. She was unable to produce any evidence comparing the treatment afforded her by Chemical with its treatment of married men with children. Thus, the basic piece of evidence that would have established discriminatory conduct was missing; Bass could not prove that Chemical's decision to deny her promotion to vice president was based on gender. The most that Bass could show was that she was discriminated against because of her parental status, but that type of discrimination is not prohibited by Title VII.

Coble, on the other hand, demonstrated that she was discriminated against not only because she was a parent, but also because she was a woman. Trezza's initial concerns with the failure of her company to promote her were based on allegations that women without children were being favored over her, but ultimately she also produced evidence that the company's failures to promote her were based on her gender as well as her parental status. Missing from Bass's claim was any evidence that she was discriminated against because she was a woman, and thus her claim was doomed to failure.

Melissa Fuller's sex discrimination case against GTE Corporation was similarly deficient. Fuller claimed that GTE discriminated against her because of her status as a mother of young children. She alleged that her department supervisor continuously made negative comments about her children, suggesting that Fuller needed to get her priorities straight, as her job came before her family. On one occasion, the supervisor suggested a pet carrier as a cage for Fuller's children. Despite this apparent animus toward working mothers, thirty-five of the forty-four employees subordinate to the department supervisor were women, twenty-two with children. Of the nine males in the department, only one had children. The court dismissed Fuller's case because she had failed to prove that she was treated differently from men, and more specifically, she failed to show that she was treated differently from male workers with children.

Some working mothers, among them Susan McGrenaghan, have attempted to extend the scope of the protections of Title VII to smaller subgroups of married women with children. McGrenaghan charged the St. Denis School in Philadelphia with having discriminated against her because she was the mother of a disabled child. After the birth of her son, the school transformed McGrenaghan's full-time teaching position to one requiring her to work a half day as a teacher and a half day as a resource aide. This constituted a demotion, as it involved significantly diminished job responsibilities. McGrenaghan alleged that the reduction in her job responsibilities was based on unfounded stereotypes concerning the adequacy of the work performance of mothers having disabled children, and that a similar employment decision would not have been made either for a woman without a disabled child or for a father of a disabled child. In support of her claim, McGrenaghan offered evidence that she was replaced in her full-time teaching position by a less qualified woman who was not the mother of a disabled child. She also introduced testimony that the principal of the school had expressed animus against working mothers of disabled children. Even though McGrenaghan's claim extended only to a very small subclass of women, the court ruled that she had a valid Title VII claim.

The court in this case adopted a broader view of Title VII proscriptions. The school argued that it could not be held liable for sex discrimination because McGrenaghan had failed to produce any evidence that she was treated less favorably or differently on the basis of her gender as she failed to prove that she was treated differently from its male employees. Moreover, her replacement was a woman. This argument tracked that asserted in the Bass case. In rejecting the school's position, the court relied on the "sex plus" doctrine. McGrenaghan was a member of a subclass of women who have children with disabilities, and she alleged that her job transfer was based on unfounded stereotypes concerning mothers of disabled children, that a similar decision would not have been made of a woman without a disabled child or of a father with a disabled child. She also charged the school with discriminatory animus against working mothers with disabled children. These allegations, according to the court, were sufficient to establish a valid Title VII claim.

We turn now to a different type of sex discrimination often encountered by women with children. Title VII provides for a strict equal employment opportunity policy for women; women must be treated no less favorably than similarly situated men. But enforcement of this policy does not inevitably lead to equality. Although men are now more likely than in the past to assume a larger share of family and child-rearing responsibilities, women remain the primary caregivers in the home. Many working mothers must fulfill their family responsibilities while employed in a work environment designed by men with far fewer family obligations. Since men have traditionally relied on their wives to take on most child-rearing and other family responsibilities, they could structure a work environment that demanded nearly total commitment to the job, ignoring in greater part the impact such commitment had on their families. But a married woman with children cannot adequately fulfill her responsibilities at home while working in such an environment. Thus, providing women with treatment equal to that extended to male workers fails to produce equality: A strict equal opportunity policy holds mothers to a male model of competition in which they cannot equally compete.

The failure of employers to afford workplace equality for working mothers appears under many guises, one of which condemns women who leave the workplace for relatively long periods of time to raise their children. Men who have made their jobs the central priority in their lives often find it difficult to accept on equal terms co-workers who have not. These men and on occasion, even some women are unwilling to accommodate working mothers who, because of their responsibilities to their children, cannot and will not be guided by such priorities. The refusal to accommodate working mothers is an attitude that too often culminates in job-related decisions adverse to them.

The courts have struggled with these workplace problems. On some occasions, courts have viewed charges of workplace inequality from the perspective of a working mother, but on other occasions, they have been blind to that perspective, regarding it as irrelevant or inappropriate to determining whether workplace discrimination exists.

When women return to the workplace after a lapse of several years, they often discover that their employers perceive them differently from workers without career interruptions. After Arlene Coopersmith graduated from law school, she practiced law for about four years before giving birth to her first child. Except for some part-time work, for the next fifteen years she was primarily engaged in raising her children, and she returned to full-time employment only after her youngest child turned twelve. After working in nonattorney positions for a few years, Coopersmith applied for an attorney-advisor position with the Veterans Administration in Washington, D.C. The VA rejected her application, primarily on the ground that she could not point to any recent legal experience relevant to the type of work she would be required to perform if the VA hired her.

Coopersmith then charged the VA with sex discrimination, arguing that its preference for applicants with recent legal experience discriminated against women. She contended that since women are more likely than men to interrupt their careers to raise children, they would less likely have recent legal experience. When Coopersmith's charges of discrimination reached the court, her attorneys submitted statistical data showing that a large portion of women in the general labor force interrupts employment for child rearing. Based on these data, they argued that many women would be rejected for positions that called for recent experience. The court rejected this statistical evidence because it failed to demonstrate that female attorneys, as distinguished from female workers in general, similarly interrupt their legal careers. In effect, the court said that Coopersmith was comparing apples with oranges, and that the statistical data failed to support her position.

But even if Coopersmith had submitted statistical evidence demonstrating that female attorneys also interrupt their careers to raise their children, the court stated, it would have rejected those statistics since they would fail to disclose whether male attorneys temporarily leave their practices to fulfill family responsibilities. From the court's perspective, Coopersmith had not submitted data that would permit a comparison of the treatment extended to women with children with that extended to men with children. In the court's view, Coopersmith had failed to demonstrate that the VA's preference for applicants with recent experience disadvantaged female more than male applicants. Although Coopersmith's case was weak, it is nonetheless clear that the court assumed a very narrow and restrictive view of the measure of proof necessary to establish her case. A similar viewpoint led to the demise of Cynthia Fisher's claims against Vassar College.

In her sex discrimination case, Fisher claimed she was denied tenure when Vassar discriminated against her because of her absence from academia for eight years while she was raising her young children. She won a resounding victory in the trial court, only to encounter defeat on appeal.

At the time of the trial, Fisher was married with two adult daughters. She held a bachelor's degree from the University of Wisconsin and a master's degree and a Ph.D. from Rutgers University. She had also engaged in postdoctoral studies at Rutgers Medical School, and after the eight-year hiatus, had taught biology at Marist College. At that point, Vassar hired Fisher as a member of its Biology Department faculty. After teaching nine years at Vassar, Fisher was denied tenure; that was when she sued the college for sex discrimination.

In the thirty years prior to Fisher's tenure review, no married woman had ever achieved tenure at Vassar in the hard-science departments, that is, in biology, mathematics, physics, chemistry, geology, and computer science. All women tenured in the hard-science departments during that thirty-year period had been unmarried when they were hired and still unmarried when they were granted tenure. Evidence submitted to the trial court showed that while married women in the hard sciences were discouraged from advancing to tenure, single women without children were not. In fact, at the time of Fisher's denial of tenure, Pinina Norrod, an unmarried female, was granted tenure. But while Norrod had not taken any breaks from her career, the Department of Biology professors reviewing Fisher's credentials and qualifications for tenure were very much aware that she had interrupted her career to raise her children. During the tenure review process, the Biology Department focused on this hiatus in Fisher's career, criticizing her for being "out of the field for eight years" and being "out of date." The "out of date" reference, which implied that Fisher's scholarship was obsolete as a result of the time spent at home with her children, did not square with the facts. While Fisher was caring for her children, she kept abreast of developments in her field. At the time of her tenure review, seven of Fisher's papers had been accepted for publication in prestigious journals, and she also had written a book that was later published. Her record of publication was superior to that of three male assistant professors who had just been granted tenure. In addition, she had received several grants that would not have been awarded if her knowledge of her field were deficient or out of date.

In examining the evidence submitted in support of Fisher's claim, the trial court focused its attention on Vassar's grant of tenure to the unmarried Norrod, who, unlike Fisher, had not experienced a break in her career. Norrod had taught in the Biology Department six fewer years than Fisher, had a much lighter teaching load, and was considered for tenure after she had served as an assistant professor for two years, while the normal period of service was seven years.

Ultimately, the court ruled that the Biology Department's apparent obsession with a married woman's family choices reflected its acceptance of the stereotype that a married woman with child-rearing responsibilities cannot be a productive member of its faculty: "The persistent fixation of the Biology Department's senior faculty on a married woman's pre-Vassar family choices reflects the acceptance of a stereotype and bias; that a married woman with an active and on-going family life cannot be a productive scientist and, therefore, is not one despite much evidence to the contrary." The court ruled, despite Vassar's protest that it had historically advanced the cause of women, that the college had consistently demonstrated prejudice toward its married female faculty members, and it awarded Fisher damages in the sum of $627,000.

On the appeal of the trial court's ruling, the appellate court noted that the trial evidence supported an inference that Fisher's eight-year absence from academia had diminished her chances for tenure, and if the Vassar professors and administrators involved in the tenure process equated that absence with child rearing, then a sex-based animus may have underlain the entire process. But for such a claim to succeed, the appellate court ruled, Fisher would have to submit evidence comparing the tenure experience of women who had taken extended leaves of absence from work with the tenure experience of men who had taken such leaves. That is to say, Fisher would have to prove that women who left the workplace to fulfill child-rearing responsibilities were treated differently from, and less favorably than, men who took extended leaves of absence, and that these men were more likely to be granted tenure than the women. This type of statistical data, however, was unavailable to Fisher or, for that matter, anyone else. Nevertheless, from the perspective of the appellate court, her claim had to be rejected.

This narrow-minded and parochial approach to the issue was highly criticized by three dissenting judges: "The predominant reason that working women take absences from work is to bear and raise children; there is no persuasively comparable reason for absences among working men, and it is fatuous to suggest that Dr. Fisher is to be faulted for not producing evidence of the tenure experiences of men who took absences. With rare exception, men do not take extended absences from work to raise children (or for any other reason). The trial court was entirely correct: the Biology Department's 'persistent fixation on Dr. Fisher's pre-Vassar family choices reflects the acceptance of a stereotype and bias.'" It was clear to the dissenting judges that the majority's position called for an exercise in futility.

Vassar was entitled to deny Fisher tenure if her extended absence had left her deficient in knowledge of the developments in the field of biology. But, her publications and grant awards demonstrated the timeliness of her knowledge. The trial court was entirely justified in considering the Biology Department's adverse views of Fisher's hiatus as constituting evidence of bias against married women. Unfortunately, the appellate court's position prevailed.

Despite the generally unfavorable reception given by the courts to cases that raise these issues, some employers have altered their position regarding the workplace role of working mothers. In recognition that women with children confront problems in the workplace unique to them, some employers have initiated special career paths, commonly called "mommy tracks," designed specifically to accommodate working mothers. Flex-time, part-time, extended maternity leaves, and job sharing are some of the workplace variations that typical mommy-track plans offer. Many women, however, object to special career paths designed solely for working mothers. Acceptance of the mommy track as a normal workplace fixture is in effect an acknowledgment that women with children require special consideration to succeed. Opponents of the mommy track fear that its existence will only buttress the stereotype that working mothers, regardless of the efforts they exert on behalf of their employers, are less committed to their jobs and their employers. Others fear that women who accept the mommy track remove themselves from the center of activity; they become second-string players, confining themselves to positions of lesser power. Indeed, some of my fellow lawyers have confirmed those fears, noting a recent trend among employers to withhold promotions from mommy-track participants.

The elimination of the workplace problems that working mothers have long experienced does not appear to be close at hand. Sex bias will continue to corrupt the workplace whenever employers question the appropriateness of the presence of working mothers. Unhappily, the courts give increasing evidence that their views of the protections provided by Title VII for working women with children may not be sufficiently expansive to bring about meaningful change.

❑❑❑

3

Role of Family in Gender Discrimination

Introduction

Women have continued to experience improvement in working conditions, employment discrimination against women persists in various forms in at least three distinct categories: overt sex discrimination, sex stereotyping, and disparate treatment.

Overt and Blatant Forms of Sex Discrimination

For the most part, employers who discriminate against women endeavor to conceal their conduct. Others, however, have so little regard for the anti-discrimination laws that they openly flout them. Their conduct is overt and blatant, as Gendra Sennello found when she moved from Michigan to Florida and went to work as a sales agent with Reserve Life Insurance Company in Ft. Lauderdale. The following year, Reserve Life promoted her to a management position, and during the next seven years she gradually moved up the ranks to district manager of the company's Ft. Lauderdale office. Sennello's record at Reserve Life was exemplary. She effectively managed three offices, was often promoted, and was highly regarded by her colleagues. Then, suddenly, she was demoted and, shortly after, terminated.

The demise of Sennello's career at Reserve Life coincided with the arrival of a new regional manager. For many years, William Ebert worked for Reserve Life in regional manager positions throughout the country, and at this time he was appointed regional manager for Florida. Immediately after assuming his new duties, Ebert conferred with Sennello's direct supervisor, advising him that "we can't have women in management because women are like Jews and Niggers; they hire like themselves, and the trouble with that is that when they leave they take the workers they hired with them." Ebert criticized Sennello because in his eyes she had hired too many women. He was not happy with the "gender make-up" of her offices. He pressured Sennello to resign her management position, but to remain with the company as a sales agent. Sennello decided to accept the demotion, returning to the position she had filled when hired seven years previously. Six weeks later, Ebert fired her.

Ebert was not the only highly ranked employee at Reserve Life who expressed discriminatory animus toward women in management. At a company sales conference, Reserve Life's president, Douglas Pierce, while commenting on a critical letter Sennello had written, derisively remarked that he had not realized Sennello "was so high on the women thing." On another occasion, Pierce, responding to a comment of a woman employee, crushed out a cigarette with his shoe, stating, "That's why I don't like women in management they keep grinding and grinding."

Remarkably, neither Ebert nor Pierce attempted to conceal his bias against women in management; apparently, they felt they had little to fear from openly sexist behavior. They simply acted as if the laws barring discrimination in employment did not exist. Their conduct was unlawful, it was overt, and it was blatant. In the end, after Sennello sued the company for sex discrimination, Reserve Life suffered the consequences of their conduct.

A similarly blatant display of overt discrimination occurred in the case of Irene Spears, who taught in an elementary school in Pike County, Kentucky. Although she was consistently rated by her supervisors as a superior teacher, Spears's main interest was elevation to a principal's position. Two years after starting her teaching career in Pike County, Spears obtained a master's degree, and four years later a degree as an educational specialist. Subsequently, she attained the highest professional rating a teacher could achieve in Kentucky a Rank I classification and at that point the state certified her as qualified for an elementary-school principal position. Spears immediately sought promotion to an administrative role in the Pike County school system.

During the succeeding five years, nine administrative positions became available in the system, and in each instance the superintendent of schools appointed a man to the vacancy, while not considering Spears for any of them. Later, during the trial of Spears's sex discrimination suit against the county, the court ruled that in each instance Spears had been better qualified than the male employee who had received the appointment.

Statements made by the superintendent of schools in connection with the nine appointments were viewed by the court as discriminatory; they disclosed an illicit frame of mind. On one occasion, the superintendent commented that he wanted to appoint a man as principal of one of the county's high schools because he wanted someone who would instill "the discipline of a football coach." On another occasion, after Spears inquired about a vacant elementaryschool principal's position, the superintendent told her he "needed a man up there."

Although not as offensive as the discriminatory remarks made by the Reserve Life officials, the superintendent's statements nevertheless were blatant, clearly demonstrating a discriminatory animus toward women. It may appear surprising that a person in his position could be so insensitive to the demands of the anti-discrimination law, but such occurrences are common. In the case reports that follow, the prohibition against sex discrimination often is the farthest thing from the minds of employers, and in such circumstances, female workers inevitably are the targets of discriminatory behavior. Dana Throgmorton's story is a case in point.

United States Forgecraft Corporation, located in Arkansas, hired Throgmorton as a quality control clerk and, soon after, promoted her to coordinator of a computer system that Forgecraft used for production data. Throgmorton remained in the coordinator position until Forgecraft decided to discontinue use of its computer system, and at that point she was terminated. Forgecraft then eliminated some of Throgmorton's former job responsibilities and assigned others to a male employee.

Throgmorton sued Forgecraft, alleging that her termination occurred as a consequence of a general gender bias on the part of management, and that if she had been a man, she would have been transferred to another position rather than terminated. In support of her allegations of sex bias, Throgmorton testified that the company's chief operations officer had told her that women did not belong in management. This attitude appeared to reflect the views of the company's owner, whose testimony sounds as if it comes out of another century:

Here she was a little old girl, a country girl, up there that didn't know anything from come sic' em and here he wanted her to help him implement a very complex system. And so all she could do is follow one, two, three, four and, you know, what can you do with a girl who is nothing but a clerk and all she did was run copies.I guess a man could have done that job, but it's more suited to a woman.

Shuffling paper and punching a keyboard is most women have better dexterity than men and you see more women clerks than you do men clerks. That's our history in business, isn't it?

If this attitude sounds as if women at Forgecraft were relegated to second-class status, that is precisely how it was described by a consultant for the company: "Women in that company were second class citizens, treated like cattle, different than any company I've ever been in. Women appeared to understand that they were subservient to the men. No women could ever make a decision." Based on this testimony, the court ruled that Throgmorton's termination was gender related, as Forgecraft would have found another position for her had she been a man.

A more egregious example of blatant sex discrimination may be difficult to find, and yet Forgecraft's owner freely testified to his sex-biased attitudes. He denigrated and ridiculed the company's female workers, disclosing a company bias against women. His decision to testify in this fashion exhibited either a contemptuous disregard for the law, an arrogant belief that he was free to act without regard to it, or gross ignorance of it. In any case, sex discrimination at his company was overt and blatant.

Another blatantly discriminatory case was that of Maureen Barbano, a social welfare examiner for Madison County in upstate

New York. Responsible for determining the eligibility of individuals for public assistance, Medicaid, and food stamps, she was generally familiar with federal, state, and local laws pertaining to the operation of the public assistance programs in the county. After three years in this position, she learned of an opportunity for advancement at the Madison County Veterans Service Agency, which reported a vacancy for director of the agency, responsible for the supervision of veterans' welfare programs throughout the county. Barbano filed her application with the agency's six-man hiring committee and was scheduled for an interview.

Before entering the interview room, Barbano overheard one of the interviewers say, "Here are copies of the next resume," followed by the comment, "Oh, another woman." Early in the interview, one of the committee members, Donald Greene, told Barbano that he wanted to know what her plans were for having a family, since there were "some women" he was unwilling to consider for the position. As if this question were not sufficiently objectionable, he also asked Barbano whether her husband would object to her transporting male veterans around the county. Barbano responded that the questions were irrelevant and discriminatory. Greene demanded answers. When Barbano again declined to respond, Greene growled that the questions were relevant he did not want to hire a woman who would get pregnant and then quit. Barbano advised the committee that if she decided to have a family, she would take no more time off than medically necessary. Greene once again asked whether Barbano's husband would object to her "running around the county with men" and declared he would not want his wife to do it. Barbano retorted that she was not his wife, and on that note, the interview was concluded.

The committee interviewed several other candidates, determining that all were qualified, and awarded the position to Allan Wagner, who for the previous six years had been a school bus driver and part-time bartender at the local American Legion. In contrast to Barbano's experience with county public assistance programs, Wagner had no knowledge of federal, state, or local laws pertaining to veterans' benefits and services and was generally unfamiliar with the county's welfare agencies.

After the committee rejected her, Barbano sued Madison County for sex discrimination. The court later ruled that Greene's questioning of Barbano, constituting nearly her entire interview, was discriminatory. His queries about a possible pregnancy and Barbano's husband's feelings about her "running around the county with men" were totally unrelated to any qualification for the director position. Thus, the committee's weighing of the relative merits of Barbano's and Wagner's qualifications were necessarily tainted with discrimination.

Perhaps Greene's attitude was an outgrowth of a lifetime of antipathy to women in the workplace. Although this would not justify his treatment of Barbano, it would tend to explain his conduct at the interview. But what about the other five committee members? Although they must have known that Greene's questions were discriminatory in fact, Barbano told the committee they were none voiced any objection to Greene's queries. They went along with this charade of an interview. Whether they acted in contemptuous disregard for the law, or as the result of a belief that they were free to act without regard to it, or simply in ignorance of the law, we do not know. Regardless, they violated the law, and Madison County paid the price for their conduct.

Three of Olsten's senior vice presidents were determined to prevent Mary Ann Luciano's promotion to vice president. They revised her job description to ensure an unsatisfactory job performance rating so as to preserve the all-male status of senior management in their division of the company. They undertook to achieve their goals by openly discriminating against Luciano.

In another case, a woman applied for a vacant position on a small-town police force. In her interview with the police chief, he informed her that she was the most qualified of those applying for the position, but he also warned her that some of the town aldermen were opposed to women on the police force. Subsequently, the aldermen decided not to fill the vacancy. Even though the failure to fill the vacant position required other police officers to work substantial amounts of overtime, no new police officers were hired for the next eighteen months. The aldermen allowed these circumstances to prevail for a year and a half rather than place a woman on the police force.

Incidents of blatant and overt discrimination against women have decreased as employers have discovered they are able to achieve their ends by acting covertly. As employers have become more proficient in concealing their discriminatory intent, their conduct has become less readily identified as discriminatory. As a result, victims of discriminatory behavior have found it more difficult to prove to a court or jury that they were actually victims of discrimination.

Sex Stereotyping

Sex discrimination in the form of sex stereotyping is often closely allied with acts of overt discrimination, as was true in three of the cases just reviewed. In the *Sennello* case, the newly appointed regional manager assumed that women tend to hire other women. In the *Spears* case, the school superintendent assumed that female teachers were incapable of coping with situations he felt could be handled adequately only by someone with a football coach mentality in other words, solely by a man. In the *Throgmorton* case, the company owner assumed that women do not perform well as managers. As noted in the last chapter, the Supreme Court has repeatedly ruled that an employer may not lawfully make employment decisions based on stereotyped characterizations of the sexes.

Yet gender stereotypes persist in the workplace. Personal attributes presumed necessary for higher-level positions in the business world are often seen as incompatible with personality characteristics generally associated with women. For example, women are viewed as nurturing and sensitive traits often not looked upon favorably in the workplace. On the one hand, women are frequently perceived as lacking the aggressiveness and dedication necessary for success; on the other hand, women who are assertive and dedicated to their jobs are often viewed as overly aggressive, uncooperative, and unfeminine. Ann Hopkins confronted such a no-win situation.

Hopkins served as a senior manager in the accounting firm of Price Waterhouse. She had worked in the firm's Office of Government Services in Washington, D.C., for five years when the partners in that office proposed her as a candidate for partnership. They praised her character as well as her accomplishments, describing her as "an outstanding professional" who had a "deft touch," and a "strong character, independence and integrity." They also favored her for partnership because she had succeeded in obtaining major new clients for the firm, a record none of the other candidates for partnership could match.

When Hopkins was nominated, only 7 of the firm's 662 partners were female, and of the eighty-eight persons proposed for partnership, Hopkins was the only woman. When the partnership nominations were put to a vote, fortyseven of the candidates were admitted to partnership, twenty-one were rejected, and the remaining twenty including Hopkins were advised that their candidacies would be held for reconsideration the following year. One year later, all of the male candidates who had been placed on hold were renominated for partnership, but Hopkins was not. When she inquired about her rejection, she was told that difficulties she had experienced in interpersonal skills as well as her aggressive, tough behavior had contributed to the negative decision. Hopkins then sued the firm, alleging that stereotyped views of women and female behavior had played a substantial role in her rejection for partnership.

Evidence submitted to the court during the course of the litigation revealed that some of the firm's partners reacted negatively to Hopkins solely because she was a woman, and these partners had evaluated her on sex-based terms. Several partners criticized her use of profanity. One partner described her as "macho," another asserted that she "overcompensated for being a woman," and still another suggested that she take "a course at charm school." Hopkins was advised that if she wanted to improve her chances for partnership she should "walk more femininely, talk more femininely, dress more femininely, wear make-up, have her hair styled, and wear jewelry."

In previous years, Price Waterhouse had also evaluated female candidates for partnership on sex-based terms. These women were viewed favorably if they were perceived to have maintained their femininity while becoming effective professional managers. To be viewed as a "women's libber" was regarded negatively.

Ultimately, Hopkins's case reached the Supreme Court. In determining whether gender had played a motivating role in the decision to deny Hopkins partnership status, the Court first set out a rule of thumb to be followed in cases where it is necessary to decide whether a woman has been discriminatorily denied a job opportunity: "In saying that gender played a motivating part in an employment decision, we mean that if we asked the employer at the moment of the decision what its reasons were and if we received a truthful response, one of those reasons would be that [she] was a woman." As it would be somewhat naive to expect a totally truthful response to such a query, the Court examined the specific circumstances Hopkins confronted at the moment of Price Waterhouse's decision to reject her for partnership, and focused on the partners' stereotypical comments about her aggressiveness: "In the specific context of sex stereotyping, an employer who acts on the basis of a belief that a woman cannot be aggressive, or that she must not be, has acted on the basis of gender. An employer who objects to aggressiveness in women but whose positions require this trait places women in an intolerable and impermissible Catch–22; out of a job if they behave aggressively and out of a job if they don't. Title VII lifts women out of this bind."

The sex-based evaluations used by Price Waterhouse reflected negative stereotypes of female workers and, therefore, subverted the evaluation process of the female candidates for partnership. Price Waterhouse discriminated against Hopkins when it relied on these negative stereotypes to deny her partnership status.

Disparate Treatment

A third type of discrimination that women commonly encounter can be defined as second-class-citizen treatment. Some employers simply treat their male employees more advantageously than their female employees, paying them more and promoting them more frequently. These same employers relegate women to lower-paying, dead-end positions and generally refuse to promote them. An employer's different, or disparate, treatment of men and women constitutes the very essence of sex discrimination.

At the trial, the jury heard evidence that at the time that budgetary problems were said to underlie the reduction in Polacco's salary, the Department of Biochemistry had offered to hire a male professor at a salary twice the size of hers; when he declined to accept the offer, the department failed to reallocate any portion of those funds to pay Polacco's salary. Polacco claimed that this was discriminatory and that as the wife of a faculty member, she was consistently treated as a second-class citizen by the department. The jury agreed with those assessments and granted her substantial damages.

Polacco's lawsuit succeeded because she was able to show that the Department of Biochemistry treated her differently than it treated men. The inference the jury could, and probably did, draw from the department's behavior is that if Polacco had been born male, her salary would have remained intact. Disparate treatment of male and female workers may occur with respect to any aspect of the employment relationship. Linda Rodhe can testify to that. Rodhe was employed as a secretary by K. O. Steel Castings, Inc., in San Antonio, Texas. For some time, she had been engaged in a romantic relationship with a company foreman, Arnulfo Lopez. Management knew of the relationship, and apparently it had not been the cause of any problems. Those circumstances changed when Lopez struck Rodhe during an argument one evening in her apartment, and the following day she informed the company's personnel director that she was unable to report for work because of the injuries she had sustained. She returned to work the day after, only to be assaulted by Lopez again, this time on company premises. The company's president and vice president were on a business trip, but when they returned a few days later, one of their first orders of business was to resolve the matter between Rodhe and Lopez. Their solution was to fire Rodhe. Lopez was not released or even disciplined.

Even if company executives believed that both Rodhe and Lopez were guilty of offensive behavior although no evidence was offered showing that Rodhe was at fault they failed to consider their offenses in the same light. If company officials felt that they confronted a serious disruptive situation, why not dismiss both Rodhe and Lopez? Instead, they fired only one of the workers, the female rather than the male. But no legitimate, nondiscriminatory reason justified different treatment. Only gender could have been the basis for the disparity in treatment.

Elements of disparate treatment were present in some of the cases already reviewed. As an example, it played a significant role in Mary Ann Luciano's case against the Olsten Corporation. The evidence in that case showed that women generally were not promoted to management positions. The existence of a glass ceiling is a form of disparate treatment. Men are not confronted with glass ceilings; they simply do not encounter artificial barriers to advancement. While Olsten's female employees faced significant restrictions on promotion to upper-level management, male employees even those with poor performance records were regularly promoted to those positions. At the same time that Luciano was dismissed, supposedly because her position had been eliminated, Olsten created new positions for male employees who faced the elimination of their jobs. Disparate treatment of Olsten's female workers was rampant.

Over the long history of disparate treatment at MIT, male faculty were paid more than female faculty, male professors were allotted more research money than female professors, female faculty members were barred from department head positions and rarely appointed to important committee seats, women were assigned less office space than men, and fewer awards were granted to women, even though they attained professional status equal to their male colleagues. In such circumstances, disparate treatment of women was an everyday event.

Discrimination against women in the workplace assumes many forms, probably as many forms as there are employers, but as we proceed to examine cases of discrimination against specific groups older women, women of color, women in the professions, pregnant women, and women with children we will find that these cases, for the most part, fall within one of the three categories of sex discrimination just reviewed.

4

Sex Discrimination in Today's Workplace

Introduction

The treatment of sexual harassment and other forms of gender discrimination is a complex and challenging clinical task about which relatively little has been written. Victimized individuals enter treatment (1) at different stages of the discriminatory experience, requiring different intervention styles and focuses; (2) with differing levels of insight and motivation, requiring a variety of alliance-building techniques; and (3) with diverse and variable symptom complexes of different degrees of severity, requiring a broad range of treatment modalities. In general, the degree of psychological distress and psychiatric illness in the patient or client will depend upon (1) the nature of the experience, (2) the context in which it occurs, and (3) the preexisting condition of the victimized person with regard to both external and internal resources and vulnerabilities. For example, a severe response would be anticipated if a socially isolated, financially strapped woman with a past history of sexual abuse was exposed to prolonged discrimination involving both sexual assaults and severe work inequities from a respected mentor, in the context of a highly specialized, nontransferable career track, in which the woman was highly invested both financially and emotionally. In contrast, a mild response would be anticipated if a psychologically healthy, economically stable woman with a supportive family and coworkers was exposed to critical gender-focused remarks and negative differential treatment during quarterly public meetings with an off-site manager who had little impact on her job evaluations and with whom all contact would cease in 3 months, when she is being promoted to a new work station. The literature addressing the negative consequences of sexual harassment and gender discrimination has evolved from early accounts that focused primarily on economic and productivity losses, to more recent accounts that address medical and psychological consequences from multiple perspectives.

Despite the encouraging proliferation of the literature, there is still a limited amount devoted to treatment of victimized people This chapter will provide a multidimensional approach to treatment that integrates (1) the existing literature on the treatment of sexual harassment and discrimination; (2) relevant preexisting literature on psychopharmacology, psychodynamic therapy, cognitive behavioral therapy, group therapy, and trauma and grief therapies; and (3) my clinical experience. The model is a revision of an approach to sexual harassment that I initially developed and presented in Bernstein and Lenhart. This version incorporates new data and experiences appropriate to both sexual harassment and other forms of gender discrimination. It provides illustrative and related information necessary for proper case management, such as (1) available resources, (2) modes of resolution, (3) relevant legal issues, (4) types and styles of presenting symptomatology, (5) appropriate therapeutic stance for treaters, and (6) formats for initial evaluations. It can be utilized by a single treating clinician or a collaboration of treating clinicians such as an individual therapist, a medication doctor, a group therapist, an EAP counselor, and so on, who handle various stages of treatment according to their areas of expertise. The model can be outlined in nine steps or stages, as follows:

Multidimensional Treatment Model for Sexual Harassment and Gender Discrimination

1. Establishment of the appropriate therapeutic alliance and clarification of the clinician's role.

2. Assessment of the severity of the immediate crisis and appropriate validation and support regarding the challenges presented.
3. Evaluation and treatment of immediate physical and psychological symptoms presented and establishment of therapeutic contract for periodic monitoring of symptoms throughout treatment.
4. Ventilation of feelings and exploration of self-cognitions and goals.
5. Reestablishment of a sense of control via the development of effective coping strategies and formulation and enactment of a realistic plan of action.
6. Assessment of potential personal losses and retaliatory behaviors from others and institution of proactive protective measures.
7. Identification of and appropriate mourning of inevitable losses.
8. Reestablishment of investment in preexisting or newly formulated goals and activities.
9. Attention to long-term and other significant therapy and treatment issues.

This model is presented in sequential steps but is intended to be flexible and adaptable to the wide variation of patients, problems, points of entry into treatment, and constant changes in status with which clinicians must deal. This chapter will focus on issues related to the initiation of effective treatment: Steps 1-3. Chapter 7 will discuss approaches to helping the patient deal with both the internal psychological and the external situational challenges, Steps 4-6. Chapter 8 will explore issues related to aftermath, recovery, and reinvestment, Steps 7-9. It will also present issues related to specific populations.

STEP 1: Establishment of the Therapeutic Alliance and Clarification of the Clinician's Role

Managing the Initial Referral

Patients and clients enter treatment related to discriminatory experiences with differing levels of motivation and insight and from a variety of referral sources. Some may be unaware that their physical and emotional symptoms are related to a discriminatory experience, or they uncover the experience in the context of ongoing treatment that is focused on other issues. Others may be focused on issues of sexual harassment and unaware that other forms of discrimination or other psychological issues are a primary or a contributory cause of their distress. Some may already be involved in the litigation or complaint process, which often exacerbates symptomatology and blurs treatment goals. They may seek consultation for forensic or treatment objectives, or both, or be unclear regarding the distinction. A small group may enter treatment for unrelated problems or for problems such as marital discord and unresolved grief, which are the aftermaths of discriminatory and harassing events.

Referrals may also arise from a variety of outside sources. Physicians such as internists, primary care doctors, and obstetricians or gynecologists may refer patients for symptom management. Because many physicians still do not take work histories from woman, they may be unaware of the work or academic trauma that has transpired. Conversely, they may be the first professional in whom the woman confides. Employee Assistance Program (EAP) professionals may refer clients or patients when their symptomatology is severe, cannot be resolved within the time-limited period in which they are authorized to treat, or both. Mental health clinicians who are unfamiliar with this area of treatment or who are anxious about involvement with potential legal aspects of a case may seek consultation or referral. Attorneys may legitimately refer clients for a variety of issues: (1) treatment of psychiatric symptoms related to discrimination, (2) management of the stress involved in litigation, and (3) forensic assessment and expert testimony. Occasionally, attorneys unduly pressure the clinician to act as both therapist and expert witness, to maximize psychological injuries, or both. Employment and human resource personnel may make empathic and appropriate treatment referrals but may also attempt to intrude upon the treatment with institutional goals, such as discouraging litigation. In instances where the clinician is an employee of the work or academic institution where the incident occurred or when the evaluation or treatment is mandated or financed, or both, by that institution, the potential for a conflict of interest and the misuse of the clinician's role is further heightened unless the boundaries of confidentiality and disclosure are established at the outset with both the patient and the institution. Employee Assistance Program clinicians are often the first to evaluate a sexual harassment or discrimination client. They can play an invaluable role in addressing initial symptomatology, understanding the institution's complaint procedures, and making appropriate referrals for longer-term treatment when necessary.

Clarifying the Clinician's Role and the Boundaries of Treatment

Clarification of the clinician's role and disclosure of and discussion of any potential conflicts of interest or limits to confidentiality are essential first steps in treatment. This promotes the therapeutic alliance and affords the patient or client the opportunity to truly give informed consent for the treatment. If the patient or client is engaged in or would consider legal remedies for her situation, she should be informed of the possibility that her clinician, her treatment records, or both may be subpoenaed. If she realizes only later, in the context of treatment, that discrimination has occurred, these issues should be addressed at that time. Potential strategies for protecting confidentiality should be discussed and mutually agreed upon. Any preset limits to confidentiality, such as employment reports, conferences, and so on, should be disclosed. The treatment record should be kept in a concise medical and legal mode, free of speculation and other material that could be misused: (1) diagnosis and symptoms targeted for treatment, (2) rationale and type of treatment methods employed, and (3) treatment outcomes and changes in the patient's clinical status.

If the patient or client is already involved in litigation, the clinician should emphasize the critical need for the patient's attorney to retain a separate forensic evaluation by another professional to (1) document relevant historical information, (2) correlate discriminatory events with symptoms, (3) discuss the patient's symptoms relative to her pre-event character, (4) evaluate allowable issues related to credibility, (5) review the existing medical and psychiatric records, and (6) determine emotional damages and treatment needs. This provides the best, but not an absolute, safeguard that the clinician's views or the treatment record will not be unduly publicized or utilized in court in a manner that would compromise or destroy the therapeutic alliance. The vast differences and conflicts of interest between the role of the forensic expert and the treating clinician should be clarified with the referring attorney and the patient, along with an explanation as to why the treating clinician cannot accept both roles.

If the treatment is being financed or mandated by the involved work or academic institution, the following issues should be discussed with the patient: (1) the stated purpose of the institutional referral, (2) the type of reporting contract the clinician is expected to have with the institution, (3) the purpose of any mandated reports or discussions, and (4) the clinician's relationship and obligation to the institution. The patient and the clinician can agree to mutually discuss the contents of any verbal or written reports, records, or other communications with the institution prior to their disclosure and afterward. If the patient is initially too distressed to fully appreciate these issues, they should be reviewed again when she has stabilized. The clinician should seek consultation and, if necessary, refer the patient to another treater when conflicts of interest are interfering with proper treatment.

Assuming an Appropriate Therapeutic Stance

The most appropriate therapeutic stance for beginning treatment is that of empathic validation. It is important for the treater to take an actively supportive and educative position during the initial sessions. The patient will respond well if the clinician initially communicates a willingness to believe the following: (1) that her perspective has validity; (2) that she deserves help; (3) that she is not "crazy," and that any initial symptoms and impairment are more likely the result of her real experience than caused by any premorbid pathology; and (4) that she has suffered retaliation in some form if she has filed a complaint or taken legal action. Conversely, the patient or client may suffer secondary traumatization, with an exacerbation in symptomatology, if the clinician initially takes any of the following stances: (1) disbelief, vigorous questioning, or both of her report and credibility; (2) preoccupation with whether the experience meets legal criteria for discrimination, rather than focusing on the patient's distress level; (3) undue focus on sexual harassment and failure to elucidate other forms of discrimination; (4) a rigid analytic stance that fails to acknowledge the significance of real external events, that overemphasizes the contribution of internal psychological issues, and that implies the patient is to blame for her distress; or (5) minimization of the discriminatory event and attempts to identify other issues as the focus for treatment.

The clinician can better assess if the patient is distorting the events or exhibiting inappropriate or self-destructive behaviors and motives that are contributing to her suffering after an alliance has been formed, some stabilization has occurred, and more complete information is available. Documentation of false claims is rare, in comparison to underreporting of legitimate claims. It is true that some women distort, exaggerate, or engage in provocative or other destructive workplace behaviors (1) as a frequent result of earlier sexual traumas; (2) as a result of other characterological or affective pathology, and, occasionally, (3) as part of a psychotic delusion. Although it is important for the clinician to identify and treat these problems, it is essential that these issues are addressed in a supportive and timely manner. Early in treatment, they should be presented as a means of enhancing the woman's effectiveness in coping with her situation and preventing her from taking inappropriate steps toward resolution. Later in treatment, after her current situation has been resolved, they can also be presented as a preventative measure to help her avoid future distress and vulnerability. The patient or client can and should be asked if she feels that other psychological or external factors are contributing to her distress, but this should be done in a manner that communicates a wish to target all sources of stress, as opposed to questioning the validity of her perceptions.

Common counter transference reactions may also influence the formation of therapeutic alliance. Overidentification with the perpetrator's or the institution's viewpoint or lack of awareness of the prevalence of discriminatory events can lead to some common therapy errors: (1) denial/ disbelief regarding the abuse of power and/or irrational stereotyping inherent in these situations, or both; (2) overemphasis of the patient's pathology; (3) focusing undue concern on the legal definition of discrimination or the harasser's or institution's reputation, while denying or minimizing the patient's injuries; and (4) failure to identify, and to address the detrimental effects of lack of support from friends, coworkers, family, and the work/academic institution. Overidentification with the victimized person can result in (1) failure to address the patient's contributing behaviors, ineffective coping strategies or any underlying pathology; or (2) failure to assist in avoiding premature or suboptimal forms of action, based upon incomplete processing of anger and other affects.

Therapists should also be aware of any personal gender stereotypes and conflicts of interest that they are bringing to the treatment.

Providing the patient with a cognitive framework for treatment is helpful in forming an alliance for patients and clients who are in acute distress or confused. Marmar and Marmar et al. Present an overview of the therapist's role, based upon the trauma model, in which the therapist (1) assists in altering negative cognitive attributions, (2) assists with the modulation and the processing of affect, (3) assists the patient in identifying the unconscious meaning of the trauma, and (4) assists the patient in developing strategies to contain the trauma without resorting to maladaptive or avoidance behaviors. The clinician should describe these functions in lay terms at the onset of treatment. An example of what that information might be is as follows:

Experiences like the one you have just described to me are often harmful to people's mental health, their views of themselves, their relationships, and their work functioning. I can help you assess if you are being affected negatively in any way. If so, we can work together to reverse these changes. I can also help you to assess the possible ways in which you could deal with your situation so that you can choose the approach that best suits your needs. I can support you in enacting your plan and in dealing with any stress associated with your taking action. We can then review the outcome and deal with anything that is preventing you from reinvesting in your life and work. Your treatment will involve our reviewing your current situation, obtaining background history, and assessing how you are coping as you work on resolving your situation. If at any time you develop symptoms such as depression or anxiety, we can utilize medication or cognitive and behavioral techniques to help you so that you can feel your best and function at your best at all times. We can work on this at your own pace and continue to meet until the situation is fully resolved and your life and work have returned to "normal."

The following case example illustrates issues involved in clarifying the clinician's role and establishing a therapeutic alliance.

CASE VIGNETTE 4-1

Problems Related to Clarification of Clinician's Role

Janet Jones was a 26-year-old graduate student who entered treatment for symptoms of anxiety and depression after filing a formal, institutional sexual harassment complaint against her mentor-professor, an illustrious, internationally known scientist.

In the context of investigating her complaint, Janet had received excellent advice from the dean of the graduate school, who ultimately recommended treatment. The dean negotiated on behalf of Janet for the school to pay for the costs of her treatment. Janet's therapist legitimately discussed the nature of the treatment contract with the institution at the onset of therapy and received verification from both Janet and the dean that the treatment would be entirely confidential and that the only statements required from the therapist would be to certify that continued treatment was indicated and to submit bills. This agreement was satisfactory to the therapist, Janet, and the dean, who was authorized to represent the school. Treatment focused initially on containment of the anxiety and the depressive symptomatology by a combination of psychotropic medication and psychotherapy. The therapist focused on assisting Janet in assessing and implementing a transfer of her graduate work to another mentor, a move that was well supported by her dean. As both she and her therapist began to explore some residual depressive symptomatology, Janet became more resistant to the treatment, especially when they mutually identified conflicts with her father as the source of her residual symptoms.

Janet's father, himself a noted professor, had been killed unexpectantly in an auto accident 5 years earlier, leaving many unresolved issues between him and his daughter. Janet's father had always adopted a punitive, rigid, and devaluing stance toward his daughter, a position that was passively supported by Janet's mother. Although Janet had begun to address these issues with her father, his untimely death had abruptly terminated her attempts and enhanced problems related to the idealization of him by both her mother and herself.

Janet's therapist clarified that these were longer-term therapy issues but important ones in terms of her potential vulnerability to relationships with male authorities. Janet was asked if she wished to embark upon this segment of treatment or to conclude the therapy now that her presenting symptoms were greatly relieved and her immediate situation had been rectified. Janet informed her therapist that she wished to continue the treatment but after six sessions informed her therapist that an excellent opportunity to study abroad for 8 weeks had presented itself. She expressed the wish to temporarily discontinue her treatment and resume after her study abroad. She and her therapist agreed to a termination at that point, and the treatment was concluded after two additional sessions, to the satisfaction of both the therapist and Janet, who expressed great appreciation for the help she had received.

The therapist heard no further from Janet until 6 months later, when she received a call from an attorney representing Janet in a lawsuit against her institution. The attorney requested the therapist to testify on Janet's behalf. The therapist explained that she could not serve as an expert witness, given that she had already had a treatment relationship with Janet and her understanding was that treatment, though temporarily on hold, was still ongoing. She recommended that a forensic evaluation be performed by another clinician. The therapist also explained to the attorney that the initial treatment contract with Janet had included an understanding that she would never serve as an expert witness. The attorney remarked that Janet was well aware of the agreement but felt that her therapist was in the best position to help her, and she did not have money to support a forensic expert. The therapist suggested a joint conference between Janet, the attorney, and herself, but Janet refused the conference, again for monetary reasons.

Despite the therapist warning the attorney that she might have information regarding Janet that might prove detrimental, the attorney named the therapist as a factual witness, and she was subpoenaed for deposition. During the deposition, the defense attorney questioned the therapist regarding the reasons for Janet's termination of treatment, and the therapist responded by explaining the educational opportunity that had presented itself to study abroad. The defense attorney informed the therapist that Janet had not traveled abroad and asked how she, the therapist, could explain this. The therapist was circumspect but shocked. The case went to trial, and the therapist unwittingly became the defense's primary witness. The explanation Janet gave her therapist for discontinuing treatment was utilized in the service of diminishing her credibility with regard to her sexual harassment complaint. Janet was crushed and developed a depression, in which she expressed a deep sense of betrayal by her therapist, whom she idealized. She had great difficulties (1) in appreciating her unrealistic expectations that her therapist would rescue her, (2) in engaging with a new therapist, and (3) in properly placing her experience into perspective and completing her treatment regarding issues with her father.

CASE VIGNETTE 4-2

Nontherapeutic Stance by Clinician

Katherine Glid was a 32-year-old attorney who sought treatment for depression, which arose in the context of being involuntarily transferred, along with four other female colleagues, to what was derisively labeled "the dead end division" of her law firm. Katherine had entered the large urban firm with high hopes and excellent academic credentials. She had spent 7 years working intensively to develop a career in her chosen subspecialty. The lateral transfer would make it impossible for her to reap the benefits of her past work and pursue this specialty.

The problem had first surfaced during Katherine's maternity leave, which had occurred 2 years previously. Following her pregnancy, 3 months' maternity leave, and return to work, she had been treated as though she had no strong commitment to work and as though her potential was limited. This change of attitude greatly distressed her. She was assigned to less important cases and not put forward as a candidate for teaming with some of the firm's more illustrious partners.

As Katherine described these themes in her therapy, her therapist began to focus not on the disparate treatment in the external situation but rather on Katherine's denial of the problem as a major issue in her current situation. This stance caused Katherine to blame herself and become even more critical in her expectations of herself than she had been prior to her treatment. Without soliciting Katherine's ideas and wishes or reviewing possible options, her therapist focused on the unlikelihood of winning a lawsuit. The therapist considered this stance supportive, in the sense that it would save Katherine undo distress. Also intending to be helpful, the therapist suggested that this might provide an unexpected opportunity for her to get better acquainted with her new baby and to take advantage of her husband's sympathetic stance and ability to support the family financially without Katherine's income. By pursuing this theme, the therapist failed to identify that the primary cause of Katherine's distress was the loss of a potential career track with which she was highly identified and which she had worked hard to obtain. He also inadvertently heightened her conflicts regarding the demands of her work and family life. In addition, he took a rigid stance with regard to treatment hours, insisting on regular treatment hours with no changes. This situation created stress for Katherine, whose work often required that she travel out of state. The therapist further exacerbated the situation by frequently traveling himself to lecture at various locations throughout the country, without acknowledging the disruption this created for his patient or the contradiction in his messages.

When Katherine's symptoms failed to respond to treatment and her depression became more prolonged, the therapist became irritated and began to more directly blame Katherine for her situation. By mutual consent, a consultation was obtained. The consultant recommended terminating the treatment and switching therapists. The therapist initially agreed to the consultation but later attempted to undercut the transfer, further exacerbating Katherine's distress. Treatment with her next therapist progressed painfully. Much time and energy needed to be devoted to the misconceptions and internalized blame created by the first therapy, allowing little opportunity or energy in the therapy, to be devoted to Katherine's external situation. This caused her further frustration and self-blame, because her initial motivation for treatment was to obtain support in coping with and mastering the work situation.

STEP 2: Assessment of the Severity of the Immediate Crisis and Appropriate Validation

After the establishment of a therapeutic alliance, there needs to be an assessment of the nature of the immediate crisis in terms of (1) safety, (2) threats to employment or academic status, (3) severity of presenting somatic and emotional symptoms, (4) disruptions in important relationships, and (5) threats to financial viability. This assessment, combined with validation of the serious reality of the patient's or client's situation, is a good way to begin treatment. Starting in this context helps the clinician to ascertain areas of stress and begin to structure an appropriate course of treatment. This also encourages the patient to realistically assess, rather than deny the reality of, her external situation and to mobilize coping responses and problem-solving strategies, rather than regress to a depressed, helpless, and devalued state. Usually, some aspects of the patient's or client's story have already been reviewed, but it is important at this time to explain that some detailed information will need to be collected in order to plan treatment. This includes (1) a detailed account of the events; (2) a developmental family, marital, sexual, and work history; (3) a past medical and psychiatric history; and (4) a mental status exam. The evaluation should be conducted with emphasis placed on assessing the severity of the immediate crisis so that appropriate preventative interventions can be made regarding extenuating external circumstances, debilitating symptomatology, or both. It is important that the clinician not assume that the patient's current emotional state is the cause of her discrimination or harassing experience.

Sample Evaluation Format

Chief Complaint and History of Present Illness

1. Tell me your story regarding what has happened.
   A. Incidents of discrimination?
   B. When did they occur?
   C. Where did they occur?
   D. Who was present?
   E. Who has been informed?
   F. Has a complaint been filed or any other action taken?
   G. Have you kept a record of your experience?
2. What has brought you to the point of coming to see me?
3. How is this experience affecting you?
   A. Symptoms: emotional and physical
   B. Relationships: at work and in your personal life
   C. Work functioning: motivation, attendance, performance
   D. Economic situation
4. Do you have sick or personal time accrued?
5. Do you consider yourself to be in a crisis situation? If so, regarding what issues?
   A. Your safety
   B. Your family's safety
   C. Your job and career
   D. Your finaces

E. The status of your relationship with your spouse or other significant person

F. Thoughts of hurting self or others

G. Other

6. Do you consider yourself to be at risk in any way?
7. Who are the people whom you can count on for support?

A. At home

B. At work

8. Have you told any of these people about your situation? If so, what was their reaction? If not, why?
9. Have you told anyone else? What has been that person's response?
10. How long have you been in this situation?
11. Have you experienced any other instances of harassment or discrimination at this job?
12. Did you take any action?
13. Describe the action.
14. Have you consulted an attorney? Have you filed a lawsuit?
15. Do you know of anyone in your current work setting who is having similar experiences?
16. What actions has this person taken and what has been the result?
17. In the past, were you having any troubles at work unrelated to this situation?
18. In the context of this situation, have you been given an increased workload, been ostracized, skipped over for promotion, received a detrimental assignment or transfer, or in any other way suffered retaliation?
19. What evaluations or other evidence of your work performance is available prior to these events?
20. Have you been documenting your work performance since the events?
21. Are there any immediate changes you could make in your work or academics to alleviate the situation without cost to you?

A. Transfer job, stop seeing this client, customer, or colleague

B. Transfer reporting responsibilities

C. Transfer location
D. Drop courses
E. Other

Concomitant Stresses

1. Are there any other situations causing stress in your life at this time?
   A. Marital
   B. Parenting/family
   C. Health (physical and mental)
   D. Finances
   E. Legal
   F. Other

Relevant Past History

1. What other jobs have you held?
2. Have you experienced harassment and discrimination in any of these positions? If so, describe.
   A. How did you respond?
   B. What was the outcome?
3. What has been your previous work performance? Documentation?
4. Have you ever filed for Workmen's Compensation, filed a lawsuit or been sued?
5. Does this experience remind you of any other relationship in your life?
6. Does this harassment or discrimination experience remind you of any other experiences in your life?
7. Have you ever had any of the following experiences? (time, age, duration)
   A. Physical abuse (by a spouse or partner, date, parent, or family member, etc.)
   B. Emotional abuse
   C. Verbal abuse
   D. Childhood incest or molestation
   E. Rape or coercive sex, date rape
   F. Sexual exploitation by a professional such as a physician, a lawyer, clergy, and so on

G. How did you cope with this situation?

(A standard developmental and family history review should also be performed with the patient at this point.)

Medical and Psychiatric History

1. Have you ever experienced your current symptoms in the past? If so, when?
2. Past psychiatric treatment: when, what, outcome?
3. Current medical treatment and medications
4. Are your currently using alcohol or drugs? Has this increased in your current situation?
5. Have you used alcohol or drugs in the past?
6. What is your current medical symptomatology and what is its chronological relation to you work situation?
7. How do you feel about what has been happening to you?
8. Why do you think this is happening?
9. Do you think you have contributed to your situation? If so, how? What would you do differently?
10. Is anyone trying to make you feel guilty?
11. What would you consider to be the ideal outcome in this situation?
12. Do you think it will be possible to achieve this?
13. What do you hope to get from treatment?

Relevant Cultural and Economic Factors to Consider

The therapist must be familiar with relevant cultural and economic issues in order to collaborate properly with the patient or client in this preliminary assessment of her circumstances. The following factors are important to consider at this stage of the treatment.

1. Most women work out of economic necessity.
2. Most women are in junior or lower-status jobs, and their perpetrators are likely to have some authority or status advantage over them in the work hierarchy if a confrontation occurs. If a woman holds a higher-status position, she is likely to be outnumbered by male peers who might identify with the perpetrator or minimize the significance of her experience.
3. Cultural norms place women in a no-win situation. If a woman rejects a harasser's advances, she is challenging his

masculinity. If she tactfully ignores him, she may be misinterpreted as being coy, And he may increase his attentions. Similarly, if she challenges discriminatory behaviors, she may be labeled a troublemaker and be blackballed. If she is silent, she may lose any opportunity for promotion, salary equity, expert mentoring, and so on.

4. Culturally, women may still hold responsibility for controlling men's sexual behavior and are encouraged to internalize blame for any sexual misconduct. Similarly, they are socialized to accept nurturing subordinate roles and to internalize responsibility for maintaining relationships, even when those roles and relationships may be discriminatory toward them.
5. Women are expected to put families before jobs and may interpret sexual harassment and other forms of gender discrimination as a reminder that they should be at home with their families, even if they are working out of economic necessity.
6. Gender discrimination and sexual harassment reinforce the low self-confidence and difficulty in judging one's own abilities that most women bring to the workplace as a result of negative stereotypes they are taught at an early age.
7. Students and professional women may depend on the perpetrator of the discriminatory behavior for valuable education and training experiences, verbal or written evaluations and references, and opportunities for career advancement. Informal blackballing instigated by the perpetrator or another representative of the institution can be extremely difficult to combat effectually in this instance. Blue-collar and public service women breaking into traditional male occupations depend on their coworkers for safety, job training, support, and advancement, and they face similar difficulties.
8. Victimized people in highly specialized positions or with special training or women with significant financial needs and minimal work or educational backgrounds cannot easily transfer, change jobs, or find alternative tutors or mentors. In these circumstances the victimized individual may be forced to deal with the stress of continued interaction with the

perpetrator or suffer severe educational, economic, job, and career-development losses.

9. Victimized people from ethnic or racial minority groups may be subjected to withdrawal of support, community sanctions, or both, because of cultural mandates (1) not to speak publicly about sexuality; (2) to settle these issues privately within the community, rather than speak out publicly against one of her own (e.g., Anita Hill and Clarence Thomas); (3) to value domestic roles over work roles; and (4) to give advocacy against racism priority over advocacy against sexism.
10. Homosexuals and bisexuals may be vulnerable to the same community inhibitions as other minority groups and, in addition, may fear unwanted invasions of their privacy, negative reactions toward them, or both, due to exposure of their sexual preference.
11. Family and marital problems, losses, and other life stresses may complicate the patient's or client's work or academic situation.
12. Support systems vary with regard to family, coworkers, superiors, and friends. Problems with supports may contribute both to psychological symptoms and to difficulties with resolution of discriminatory events.
13. A significant number of victimized individuals will have histories of previous sexual traumas, increasing their vulnerability to severe symptomatology, flooding of repressed memories, or both.
14. Although sexual harassment has received the most public attention, other forms of gender discrimination are even more common and may accompany and complicate the resolution of harassment or may be the sole or main cause of the patient's distress.
15. Studies indicate that if a patient is complaining of harassment and discrimination, it is likely to have occurred because most workers are reluctant to complain. Although her institution may currently be alleging incompetence in the victimized woman's work and academic performance, it is likely to have been adequate or superior prior to the event. The longer her problem has persisted, the more likely her performance has deteriorated.

16. Disruption and conflict in significant relationships with spouse, family, friends, coworkers, mentors, and others are common, highly significant sequelae of harassment and discrimination situations.

Review of the complicated personal, economic, employment, and cultural circumstances helps both patient and clinician develop respect for the severity of the challenge. They can identify special areas of stress that are immediate and need to be targeted or are anticipated and may require attention in the future. This also helps them to avoid the following countertransference errors common at this stage of treatment: (1) devaluing a patient or client for an initial inability to take action, or (2) erroneously supporting the patient or client in taking immediate or impulsive action that may be ineffective or not in her best interest. It is also possible at this point for the clinician to identify victimized individuals who have minimal symptomatology, healthy coping skills, and good supports, who may require little or no treatment. They may be referred to self-help and education resources or seen supportively on an intermittent or an as-needed basis, to assist them in formulating or enacting a plan of action and dealing with any symptoms that arise. Informal grassroots support groups, as well as formal structured support groups, can be especially helpful in this respect. Additional resources are available from national organizations and agencies, some of which are listed as follows:

1. The Institute for Research on Women's Health, Suite 109, Washington, DC 20009-2530, (202) 483-8643
2. The National Council for Research on Women (NCRW), 530 Broadway, 10th Floor, New York, NY 10012-3920, (212) 274-0730
3. The Women's Legal Defense Fund, 1875 Connecticut Ave. NW, Washington, DC 20009-5728, (202) 986-2600
4. Legal Resource Kit: Employment Sexual Harassment can br ordered from NOW/LDEF, 99 Hudson St., New York, NY 10013-2815, (212) 925-6635.

Guidelines for Effective Individual Responses to Sexual Harassment and Gender Discrimination

1. Define the problem as clearly as you can and document the situation.

A. Is the problem disparate treatment, disparate impact, or a hostile environment? Is it sexual harassment, another form of gender discrimination, or both?

B. Could it be conceptualized as sexism, skewed group behavior, or micro-inequity?

C. Is it sexual harassment or another form of illegal gender discrimination, or is the behavior destructive but not illegal?

D. How severe is the impact on you?

E. Is the impact temporary or long term?

F. Is the behavior directed toward others, as well as you?

G. Have others witnessed the behavior?

H. Document all incidences in writing as completely and objectively as possible, including dates and any attempts you have made to remedy your situation.

2. Assess your emotional status.

   A. Have you developed depression, psychosomatic complaints, anxiety, panic, rage reactions, or post-traumatic reactions? If so, get professional help.

   B. Have you developed some problematic defensive reactions, for example, displaced anger, withdrawal, self-blame, isolation, chronic ambivalence, lowered goals? If so, try to contain these and work on a more effective response.

3. Get help and support. Don't isolate yourself. Discuss your situation with a trusted friend, a colleague, a peer, the AMWA hotline, a mentor, and so on. Be sure to check whether an institutional official must file a compulsory report or a complaint before you discuss the situation. You want to maintain control.

4. Maintain a high level of job or school performance and document this.

5. Clarify your goals in working out a solution.

   A. Do you want the behavior to stop?

   B. Do you want not to work with this person?

   C. Do you want a grade or an evaluation to be changed?

   D. Do you want financial reimbursement for losses?

E. Do you want institutional sanctions against the individual?

F. What were your original career, work, and personal goals and how can they best be served? (Revenge is not a productive goal and usually means your anger is not yet in perspective.)

6. What are your responsibilities, given your role within your institution? Do these conflict with your personal goals for resolution? If so, how could this conflict be resolved?
7. List all possible strategies for dealing with your situationn and list the potential risks and benefits of each strategy. Get input from others you trust.
8. Which strategy best fits your overall personal goals, without substantial risk to you?
9. What back-up strategy could you use if your first strategy fails?
10. What steps could you take to minimize the potential risks of your first-line strategy?
11. Proceed with your best strategy at your own pace, in a manner that protcets you from further losses.
12. Be prepared for a mourning period. Some loss is experienced with discrimination, no matter how well the situation is handled. Share your sadness and get support from others.

The following case example illustrates the importance of properly addressing the immediate crisis.

CASE VIGNETTE 4-3

Assessment of the Immediate Crisis and Special Cultural Challenges

Tamar Gregorian was a 25-year-old married woman referred by her family doctor for acute symptoms of agoraphobia and depression. Mr. Alexander Gregorian reported that his wife had abruptly refused to return to work, had sequestered herself in the bedroom, was eating and drinking very little, and would not speak to him about whatever was going on. The situation was exacerbated by the fact that the couple was greatly isolated and in a stressful situation.

Both Tamar and Alexander had recently come to the United States as immigrants from the Middle East. Their departure from their native country had been chaotic and traumatic, the result of major political and religious differences with their families of origin. Although both Tamar and Alexander had been schooled in the United States, their initial plan was to return to their homeland and to build a life there. This unexpected fracture from their family of origin had been greatly distressing to both of them and had precipitated a flight, which had not allowed them time to properly plan an appropriate move to the United States. Fortunately, Alexander, a scientist, had obtained a position in a computer startup company with the help of a colleague from school. Tamar had also been helped by this friend, who assisted her in obtaining a position in the supply division of the company.

The couple's economic situation was near crisis. Although both had obtained jobs with benefits, the cost of moving and the lack of possessions, combined with the lower-status jobs that they were able to obtain, had left the couple in need of both salaries, a factor that greatly concerned Tamar's husband.

The partners were also stressed over their abrupt and disruptive disconnection from their families of origin. Tamar, in particular, had many conflicts regarding the change in her role-specifically, the fact that neither she nor her husband were practicing the Moslem dress code and that she had broken strict family traditions in entering the workplace. Alexander was agitated by his wife's condition but freely acknowledged that the stress of the new move, the newness of the country, and his own economic worries were exacerbating his response to his wife's illness.

On initial evaluation, Tamar was quite constricted in affect and very reluctant to speak to her therapist. She did agree to antianxiety and antidepressant medication but was very reluctant to meet with the therapist. She did, however, at the insistence of her husband, acquiesce and arranged to be on sick leave for 1 week. The leave was accomplished with the assistance of the couple's friend. Alexander was especially anxious about the outcome, fearful that his wife would lose her job and that the relationship with their friend would be strained by this additional request for special treatment. Tamar agreed to several therapy meetings during the week of her leave. In the context of the frequent meetings she was able to give a more complete history, initially focusing on (1) the difficulties of the adjustment to the United States, (2) her sadness and anxiety with regard to her fractured relationships with her family, and (3) concerns for the couple's economic viability. She was initially unable to ascertain the reason for her agoraphobic stance.

In the context of discussing how the move had impacted on the marital, emotional, and sexual relationship, Tamar became agitated and ultimately revealed that a courier delivering laboratory supplies to the corporation had approached her sexually. Without her permission, he had fondled her breasts. This precipitated her abrupt departure from the workplace, as well as an intense sense of shame and guilt. She stated that in her country, such an act would bring dishonor upon the entire family and that she had been disobeying Moslem Law by not covering her body properly and by entering the workplace. Although she saw her husband as supportive and was consciously aware of his breach with the family religion, she nonetheless imagined that he would have a punitive reaction to her situation, as she was certain her father would have.

With her therapist, she identified the immediate goal of not losing her job or her relationship with her husband, who was her only source of support, both emotionally and economically. With her therapist's assistance, she was able to explain the situation to her husband in a joint conference and to name it as sexual harassment. Neither Tamar nor Alexander wished to jeopardize their positions within their new company by filing any type of complaint. With the assistance of their American friend, Tamar was able to transfer from the warehouse to the telecommunications section of the supply division and effectively remove herself from contact with the courier. After dealing effectively with the initial crises and challenges, she was able to continue her therapy at a less frequent pace and to address longer-term issues related to her family of origin and her immigration status.

STEP 3: Evaluation and Treatment of Immediate Symptomatology and Negotiation of a Therapeutic Contract

Physical and psychological symptoms of varying severity are common in people victimized by sexual harassment and other forms of gender discrimination and may vary or exacerbate at different stages of treatment, as the patient deals with prolonged litigation, traumatic confrontations, significant losses, withdrawal of support, and other commonly associated stresses. If the patient is in crisis at the time of the initial evaluation or has endured a prolonged experience, it is likely she will have some configuration of debilitating symptoms, requiring immediate attention. A small minority of patients may have or may acquire suicidal or homicidal symptoms.

Eliciting the patient's primary complaints and reviewing the most common symptomatology allow the therapist to identify the immediate problems that require treatment. It is also important at this time to educate the patient as to the need for continual monitoring of the common symptoms, given the likelihood that symptoms may change or exacerbate as the woman experiences stress and change over the course of treatment. Common symptoms to review include: distractibility, psychomotor agitation or retardation, appetite change, insomnia, hyperinsomnia, decreased libido, hypersexuality, impaired functioning (social or occupational), disorientation, memory loss, phobias, obsessions, compulsions, ruminations, hallucinations, delusions, racing thoughts, dysphoria, apprehensive expectations, anxiety, dyspnea, palpitations, chest pain, choking sensations, vertigo, feelings of unreality, paresthesias, sweats, fainting, trembling, suicidal or homicidal ideation, reexperiencing traumatic events (flashbacks), constricted affect, difficulty concentrating, hypervigilance, avoidance, psychophysiologic symptoms, exaggerated startle response, irritability, detachment, pessimism, social withdrawal, crying, depression, logorrhea, indecisiveness, guilt, feelings of worthlessness and inadequacy, loss of interest or ability to enjoy life, loss of energy, crying spells, drug and alcohol abuse, headaches, diarrhea, muscle spasm, nausea, panic attacks, headaches, diarrhea, or dyspepsia.

Some of the most common psychological problems requiring treatment include (1) anxiety or post-traumatic stress, along with depressive and substance abuse disorders; and (2) psychosomatic symptoms and complaints.

Problematic anxiety and depressive and post-traumatic symptoms can be treated effectively with adjunctive psychotropic medications selected on the basis of the most disruptive target symptoms. Although controlled studies are limited to general traumatic and depressive experiences, rather than harassment or discrimination, they provide some guidelines regarding choice of medication. Hamilton and Shrier recommend several approaches: (1) low-dose antianxiety medications can be helpful for daytime anxiety, panic, and agitation, provided they do not trigger dissociative states; (2) SSRIs (selective serotonin reuptake inhibitors) preferentially, but also tricyclic and MAO antidepressants, can reduce depression, mixtures of depression and anxiety, and obsessive ruminations; (3) mood stabilizers alone or in combination with antidepressants can be effective in patients complaining of hostility, irritability, and hyperactivity; (4) sleep medications are helpful for transient uncomplicated insomnia; and (5) meditation or a variety of behavioral relaxation techniques may also prove valuable.

Occasionally, patients or clients may present for treatment with these complaints but do not connect them with workplace or academic situations. In this case, it is important for the clinician to elicit further history, as the individual may be denying or minimizing her situation or may simply be unaware of the connection between her physical symptoms and her experience at work or school. Victimized individuals should be asked specifically about suicidal ideation and destructive feelings toward themselves, especially if they are depressed. Homicidal ideation should also be elicited. These behaviors are rare but have occurred in this context, especially in clients or patients with previous sexual traumas. Interventions for symptom relief should be placed in the context of enabling the client or patient to function optimally so that she can maintain credibility at work and devise the best strategy for resolution. The following case example demonstrates the importance of proper diagnosis and treatment of initial symptomatology and ongoing collaboration of monitoring of symptoms.

CASE VIGNETTE 4-4

Treatment of Initial and Ongoing Symptomatology That Is Key to Resolving Sexual Harassment

Cynthia Jones was a 35-year-old corporate executive who was referred for therapy by her attorney, for symptoms of anxiety and agitation that had exacerbated in the context of litigation proceedings involving her former company, against which she had filed a sexual harassment lawsuit. Cynthia had been recruited to the area to join a small start-up firm specializing in her area of technical expertise. Tom, one of the senior executives of the corporation, was especially helpful to her in negotiating her position and in assisting her move to a new city. Six months after Cynthia began work, Tom began to pressure her for dates. He became irritated when she persistently and firmly declined. He ceased asking and withdrew from contact with her. Worried about losing his valued patronship, Cynthia volunteered for extra work, agreed to overtime hours, and strove to become conciliatory. Despite her efforts, Tom criticized her work in public business meetings and pressured her immediate boss for a reevaluation of her performance. Tom's criticisms were reflected in her new evaluation, which occurred 4 months prior to the regular period. She also did not receive assignments to the types of work that had been promised her at her hiring.

Shortly thereafter, another senior executive approached Cynthia to report vague complaints from secretaries and various business clients regarding her attitude and deportment. She was told that she did not fit in with the company culture, and it was suggested that she seek another position. When she challenged this position, she was told that she left them no other choice than to document her significant deficits, which might jeopardize her in finding a new position.

Three months later she was fired and was read a list of shortcomings, most of which she felt were inaccurate. She was asked to remove her belongings from the premises and to vacate immediately. Stunned, she began to pack but was interrupted by Tom, who entered her office and smugly told her of his satisfaction in ruining her career. He then began to further devalue her work. Enraged, she attempted to pass by him and out the door. He pushed her back, stating that he was not finished with her and that she had a lot more coming to her. She retains no memory of the remainder of the conversation. Once at her apartment, Cynthia was obsessed with the memory of Tom's hands on her and was too furious and anxious to sleep. She invited a friend to stay with her, who also recommended that she consult an attorney specializing in discrimination. The following morning she visited the attorney and immediately filed suit. Although active and focused in her sessions with her attorney, Cynthia began experiencing panic attacks, explosive episodes, and sleep disturbance at home. She became so anxious when her attorney was preparing to file suit that he referred her for therapy.

On initial evaluation, Cynthia reported that she was extremely anxious at bedtime and often unable to fall asleep. During the day, she experienced panic attacks, combined with explosive outbursts of anger directed toward friends and occasionally toward her attorney. Initially, she was phobic regarding medication but was ultimately able to control her panic symptoms by using antianxiety medications and behavioral relaxation techniques. At the suggestion of her therapist, she instructed her attorney to postpone legal proceedings until she stabilized. Therapy initially focused on controlling her symptomatology, stabilizing her in a new job she had been offered, and creating a supportive network of friends in her new city. Her symptoms diminished, and she saw her therapist less frequently for medication monitoring and support at work.

Three months later, Cynthia became symptomatic again when her attorney reactivated her case. Although she permitted him to file the complaint, her fears escalated when she considered the necessity of giving a deposition. In the context of exploring these fears, she began having nightmares that she ultimately associated with being raped by a date at age 15, an experience she had tried not to think of. Over a 4-month period, she was able to explore the current harassment experience in the context of her parents' reaction when she told them about her date rape. Her mother had been ashamed and encouraged her to minimize the experience, and her father had accused her of being deliberately seductive and had instituted a punitive curfew. Integration of this material enabled Cynthia to give a deposition against her corporation and ultimately to receive a settlement.

This chapter has presented a conceptual model for the treatment of people victimized by sexual harassment and gender discrimination. The initial stages of treatment have been reviewed in detail: (1) establishment of a therapeutic alliance and clarification of the clinician's role, (2) assessment of the severity of the immediate crisis, and (3) evaluation and treatment of immediate symptoms and establishment of therapeutic contact for periodic monitoring of symptoms throughout treatment. These steps are necessary before the patient can effectively formulate an effective plan of action. Even if the patient has already taken action prior to entering treatment, these initial steps should still be reviewed. If she is symptomatic or in crisis, the action she has taken is not likely to be well thought out or effective or she may be in crisis related to retaliatory actions taken against her.

Sex Discrimination

In 1994, male members of the faculty of the School of Sciences of the Massachusetts Institute of Technology outnumbered women twelve to one. Of the 252 men on the MIT faculty, 194 were tenured; of the 22 faculty women, 15 were tenured. Nancy Hopkins, a prominent DNA expert and one of the tenured women, over a period of years had designed and taught a course very popular with MIT students. When the number of students enrolled in it exceeded one thousand, the School of Sciences administrators designated a male professor to assist her. Despite Hopkins's role in developing and teaching the course, MIT later informed her that they had designated her male assistant, not her, to turn the course into a book and a CD-ROM.Hopkins was bitter. While discussing the quality of her professional life with another female professor, she discovered that her colleague, like herself, felt that over the years she had been targeted for adverse treatment, and that MIT had not treated her nearly as well as men faculty. Discussion with a third female faculty member, who also acknowledged unhappiness with her life as an MIT professor, led the three to poll the tenured School of Sciences female professors and analyze their positions at MIT. To their amazement, their efforts disclosed the following:

- The School of Sciences paid male faculty members more than female faculty members.
- On average, research monies allotted to men exceeded those allotted to women.
- The School of Sciences had never appointed a woman to head a department.
- MIT assigned female faculty members less office space than their male colleagues. Although MIT insisted that office space was assigned equally, it later conceded that School of Sciences administrators had included lab space in their measurements of the office space assigned to women, but not in the measurements of that assigned to men.
- Male professors who received job offers from other institutions were given raises as inducements to remain with MIT; women were not.
- Women were rarely appointed to important committee seats. As a result, they felt marginalized and excluded from significant roles in their departments.

- Marginalization was often accompanied by fewer awards granted to women, despite professional accomplishments equal to or surpassing those of their male colleagues.
- Compared with fifty-five men, only seven women were then on a tenure track.
- For the past ten years, and perhaps longer, only 8 percent of the faculty of the School of Sciences had been female.

It became apparent to Hopkins and the other female professors that sex-based measures had long adversely affected women throughout the university. A longterm pattern of discrimination based on gender was indisputable. Based on their findings, the women were convinced that their gender, rather than their talents or abilities, had been the guiding force in the development of their professional lives lives substantially inferior to those of their male colleagues. They then resolved to effect changes. They charged the School of Sciences with discriminatory conduct and set forth a proposal to eliminate such conduct from the daily lives of the female faculty:

> *This proposal has been developed by the tenured women faculty in the School of Sciences. It speaks to our serious concerns about the small number of women professors at MIT, and about the status and treatment of the women who are here. We believe that unequal treatment of women faculty impairs their ability to perform as educators, leaders in research and models for women students.*

We believe that discriminatory attitudes operate at the time of hiring junior faculty and influence the experiences of the women who are hired.

Thus, we need to develop safeguards to prevent, detect, and promptly correct the experiences that together constitute gender discrimination.

We believe that unequal treatment of women who come to MIT makes it more difficult for them to succeed, causes them to be accorded less recognition when they do, and contributes so substantially to a poor quality of life that these women can actually become negative role models for younger women.

Lest there be any doubt that these women were charging MIT with unlawful discrimination, they made the charge explicit: "The heart of the problem is that equal talent and accomplishment are viewed as unequal when seen through the eyes of prejudice. Currently, a glass ceiling exists."

School of Sciences officials, without admitting that they had deliberately discriminated against female faculty, responded positively to the proposal. Their written response emphasized "our collective ignorance" as the basic cause underlying the long-standing discrimination against female faculty members. MIT's president, Charles M. Vest, remarked: "I have always believed that contemporary gender discrimination within universities is part reality and part perception but I now understand that reality is by far the greater part of the balance." The dean of the School of Sciences, Robert J. Birgeneau, commented: "I believe that in no case was this discrimination conscious or deliberate. Indeed, it was usually totally unconscious and unknowing. Nevertheless, the effects were real."

The faculty chair, Lotte Bailyn, was of a similar mind:

> *The key conclusion that one gets from the proposal is that gender discrimination in the 1990s is subtle but pervasive, and stems largely from unconscious ways of thinking.*

This makes the situation better than in previous decades where blatant inequities were endured but not spoken of. We can all be thankful for that. But the consequences of these more subtle forms of discrimination are equally real and equally demoralizing.

In subsequent remarks and statements issued by administration officials, the discrimination experienced by the MIT women was described as "unconscious and unknowing," neither "deliberate" nor "blatant," and although it was "subtle," it nevertheless was "pervasive." One wonders how several generations of MIT male administrators could have been unaware that the School of Sciences practices and policies adversely affected the professional lives of its women professors. Is "collective ignorance" an adequate explanation? How could these administrators not have known that they had assigned female faculty members less office space than their male colleagues, that the School of Sciences paid male faculty more than female faculty, that research monies allotted to men exceeded those allotted to women, that administrators had never appointed a woman to head a department, that women rarely were appointed to important committee seats, and that for ten or more years the proportion of women on the faculty had remained at approximately 8 percent? Even if MIT administrators had failed to realize the full effect and consequence of these practices and policies, is it conceivable that they could have been totally unconscious of their existence? MIT's written response to the women's claims is mostly silent in this regard, but one comment is revealing: "Some argued that it was the *masculine culture* at MIT that was to blame and little could be done to change that."

False assumptions regarding women's work ethic prevail in a masculine work culture, and thus men working in such a culture are likely to remain oblivious to the needs and concerns of female workers. Although males may remain insensitive to the adversities suffered by women employed in such a culture, and although they may at times remain largely unaware that practices and policies benefiting men at the same time negatively affect female workers, their conduct is no less pernicious. Acts of sex discrimination committed by men working in a masculine culture generally are subtly conceived and not readily discernable, and thus their existence may be difficult to establish. Consequently, discrimination committed in a masculine work culture, as at MIT, frequently remains unaddressed for extended periods of time.

Men working in a masculine culture tend to emphasize the differences between the gender-role expectations of men and those of women as they relate to child-rearing responsibilities, and they conclude that a woman's family obligations conflict with her work responsibilities, thus requiring the assignment of women to less-demanding positions. Still other false perceptions of working women lead to unrealistic conclusions regarding women's "proper" role in the workplace.

Such faulty perceptions and stereotypes distinguish sex discrimination from acts of discrimination based on race, national origin, or religion, which are grounded in emotional and subjective prejudice. Sex discrimination emanates from an acceptance of false stereotypes pertaining to characteristics thought to be common to working women. These false stereotypes arose in an era when brawn was apt to be more highly valued in the workplace than brains. Physically demanding jobs could often be better performed by men. The economy's shift in emphasis from manufacturing to service industries was accompanied by the expansion of white-collar positions at the expense of blue-collar jobs, and this led inevitably to an expanded role for women in the workplace. Service jobs, however, are filled on the basis of subjective judgments. Almost all upper-tier jobs, for example, require a subjective judgment of a worker's ability to make decisions in unanticipated conditions. As the court cases later reviewed show, subjective judgments in personnel decisions are often influenced, consciously or unconsciously, by false stereotypes relating to such attributes as aggressiveness, leadership ability, the capacity to adapt to unforeseen circumstances, and the ability to handle interpersonal relationships. Women are decidedly disadvantaged when hiring and other employment decisions are influenced by such stereotypes.

Furthermore, male managers still primarily responsible for most hiring and other workplace decisions are more likely to attribute to other men than to women the qualities and characteristics they deem necessary for a position. This attribution is based on what Rutgers University professor Alfred W. Blumrosen describes as a deep-rooted assumption that those whose backgrounds are similar to their own or familiar to them are likely to do a better job than those whose background and experience are different. This tendency to identify with persons "like ourselves" and to project upon them characteristics and attributes which we believe we have, is an important element in the necessarily subjective judgments which predict future performance. The higher the job level, the more visible will be the performance of the person selected, and the greater the pressures on the selecting personnel will be to demonstrate their acumen. This pressure increases the likelihood that a "bias toward the familiar" will occur in the selection process.

These same male managers, consciously or unconsciously, may accept as true any number of false assumptions pertaining to the traits, characteristics, and work habits of female workers. One of the most pernicious of these false assumptions undermines and devalues the work roles of mothers with young children.

Because women traditionally have assumed primary familial responsibility for the rearing of their children, men, relieved of such responsibilities, have performed well in jobs requiring a near total commitment to the workplace. An employer may structure a job description that demands an uncompromising work commitment, while ignoring the impact of such a commitment upon the (presumed male) worker's family, as the employer may safely assume that the worker's wife will accept all child-rearing responsibilities. This is no longer the case in our society. The male worker's wife is now more likely to be employed herself and thus is no longer available for full-time child care. But unenlightened employers persist in requiring the acceptance of a work ethic that establishes the job as the central, if not the sole, priority in a worker's life. Those who agree to function in such a capacity are sometimes referred to as "ideal workers."

A workplace structured on the ideal-worker concept is based on the assumptions first, that the ideal worker is a man, and second, that, if the ideal worker is married, he can depend on his wife to fulfill all, or nearly all, child-care responsibilities, thus freeing him to work extended days, maintain inflexible work schedules, travel frequently, and work unimpeded by any concerns for the daily welfare of his children. Because employers perceive working mothers as confronting a conflict of loyalty between home and work, they assume that these women, regardless of their circumstances, lack the commitment required of the "ideal worker," and thus they exclude women as candidates for positions structured for such workers.

A work environment grounded in the ideal-worker concept materially limits the employment role of the working mother. Mothers with young children, compelled to work in an environment designed for men without child-rearing responsibilities, are relegated to positions perceived as consistent with the fulfillment of family responsibilities, and these positions generally are inferior and lower paying. Because such a work environment adversely impacts women, an employer who fails to structure its workplace to accommodate the responsibilities of working mothers will likely, sooner or later, be charged with sex discrimination.

Because the devaluation of the workplace role of women is often subtle and thus difficult to establish, the courts have been slow to recognize this type of employer conduct as discriminatory. Except for issues pertaining to discrimination against pregnant women, the courts have rarely considered the concept of motherhood as it relates to sex discrimination. Yet this unequal treatment, built into the practices and procedures of male-dominated organizations, routinely disadvantage female workers, since the central features of these practices and procedures have been constructed by men according to norms that exclude or degrade the experiences and perceptions of women. In such an environment, women are generally subordinated and devalued. This is the essence of sex discrimination.

Although women have forced some employers to reevaluate the need for such male norms, other employers have rejected all efforts to restructure their workplaces to eliminate conditions and practices that adversely affect women. An attitude that denies the need for change an attitude based on an assumption of male superiority leads to even higher expectations of men's abilities, while women are categorized as fit for employment only in specified lowerpaying, lower-status positions.

Historically, employers have tended to categorize women as capable only of "women's work," positions that exist in relatively few occupations and rank among those with the lowest status and compensation. The assignment of women to such positions results in the segregation and stratification of women in the workplace. The consignment of women to occupations disproportionately female tends to extend their segregated and stratified roles.

Until recently, 95 percent of all secretaries, stenographers, and typists were women. Although a significant reduction in job segregation has occurred in professional positions, it continues in many other job categories. The Census Bureau statistics disclose some improvement in the hiring of women in some other job categories, women are still generally excluded from the male-dominated positions.

Undoubtedly, some women who anticipate that they will be called upon to fulfill family responsibilities freely choose to work in lower-paying and lowerstatus positions; they may be reluctant to make a significant investment in job training or to make the commitments necessary to attain higher-paying and higher-status posts. But women's careers are equally likely to be shaped by the job opportunities that employers historically have made available to women. Employers who falsely perceive women as exhibiting less commitment to their jobs feel justified in assigning them to high-turnover positions with low-turnover costs, and these jobs generally carry low pay and little status. Women who accept these positions are merely responding to employer expectations, rather than expressing a lack of interest in attaining better-paying positions. Relying on false stereotypical assumptions about working women's traits and characteristics, these employers shape women's work aspirations by creating a work environment that undermines the female work role.

In addition to encountering glass ceilings, male-dominated work environments, and job segregation and stratification, working women also confront other areas of discrimination in today's workplace discrimination against older women, against women of color, against professional women, and against women who are pregnant. To exacerbate matters, sexual harassment of women of all ages, of all skin colors, in all job categories, and in all occupations and professions pervades the workplace. In the workplace, women get "old" at a younger age than men. Age is as likely as gender to disadvantage older working women, and in many instances, an older woman faces discriminatory conduct on account of both age and sex. Some employers who prefer attractive female employees hold older women, but not men, to a standard of attractiveness equated with youth; such an employer may be guilty of age as well as sex discrimination against its older female workers.

Only 3 percent of female executives are African American. They are paid less, rated lower in performance evaluations, and subjected to biased promotion practices. More impenetrable than glass ceilings, African American women view barriers to promotion as "concrete ceilings" that bar them from advancement. As a consequence of these barriers, a large number of African American women remain in lower-paying clerical and sales positions.

Discrimination against women in all professions persists, but it remains particularly egregious in the legal profession. A recent survey of the Association of the Bar of the City of New York disclosed that glass ceilings had been consciously imposed by senior male attorneys to deter the elevation of women in their firms. Sex stereotyping and perceptions about motherhood and its incompatibility with the professional life of a lawyer were found to present serious obstacles to the upward mobility of female lawyers.

Pregnancy is often perceived by management as a disruptive event in the workplace and, as a consequence, women who announce their pregnancies often find they are less than welcome to continue in their positions. It is not uncommon for a woman returning to work after childbirth to find her job materially altered or even eliminated. The law requires employers to apply its policies relating to leave, seniority, compensation, and benefits to pregnant workers on the same terms as to workers with temporary disabilities. An employer who treats a pregnant worker less favorably than a similarly situated nonpregnant worker is guilty of sex discrimination. The law is clear, but employer compliance with the law remains less than complete.

Sexual harassment is particularly widespread and more likely than not will present a problem for nearly every working woman at some point in her life. Such harassment generally reflects an unequal relationship between a male manager and a subordinate female employee, with terms of employment that tend to create a hostile or offensive work environment for the woman. As Mona Harrington noted in her book *Women Lawyers:* "Sexual harassment of women by male co-workers expresses the ancient rule that women *should* be sexually available to men. And at the same time, it reminds the professional woman especially that while she appears in the workplace as the supposed equal of her male colleagues, she is not really an equal. It tells her that although she is gaining some economic independence, she is still subject to an old order in which she is ultimately subordinate to men, ultimately and naturally defined by her body as a male possession."

Sexual harassment denies equality. It conveys the message that a woman is not regarded as a respected colleague but rather as a sexual object. Even though sexual harassment cases often evolve into events of notoriety for the harasser, this conduct nevertheless widely persists in the workplace.

The case of the MIT professors raises another issue typical in sex discrimination cases women who are subjected to acts of discrimination often remain unaware that they have been victimized because of their gender. Although the MIT female professors eventually concluded that sex discrimination was the source of their plight, they endured several years of unhappiness with their professional lives before registering a complaint. How was it possible, especially in light of the adversities placed in the paths of these women, that they failed to realize that the mistreatment they experienced occurred on account of their gender? How could these women, obviously among the intellectual elite, have continued to endure this treatment for years without complaining or trying to eliminate its source?

Some female workers assume a "Don't rock the boat" attitude, consciously deciding to endure the adverse conditions of their employment. Others fail to act because they mistakenly believe that the adversities associated with sex discrimination in employment no longer exist, and thus their unhappiness with the circumstances of their employment must arise from another source. Other women realize they have been subjected to sex bias, but their personal circumstances or family responsibilities prevent them from devoting the time and effort necessary to effect a plan of action to eliminate the discrimination. Others simply lack the courage or energy to challenge their employer's conduct. All too often, women accept discriminatory conduct without complaint, and this usually leads to additional discriminatory conduct. Unless charged with discrimination and confronted with a lawsuit or the threat of a lawsuit, an employer is not apt to direct any of its resources to removing discrimination from its work site, since the costs of eliminating it may exceed the costs of permitting it to continue.

Women have the power to eliminate sex discrimination in the workplace, and they must avail themselves of the resources at hand the laws outlawing employment discrimination. Almost all employers contest any claim of discrimination. They put such a claim in the same category as charges of theft, fraud, or grand larceny. They resolutely contest all claims of discrimination. Thus, a woman who elects to enforce her right to work in an unbiased environment must be prepared for battle; she must be prepared to participate in an extended period of intense and bitter litigation.

On rare occasions, as in the case of MIT, an employer may agree to mend its ways, rendering litigation unnecessary. But even the actions MIT has agreed to undertake to eliminate sex discrimination from its campus will take years to fully implement. If MIT's School of Sciences continues to hire women professors at its current rate, which represents a significant increase since the charges were made, it will be 2040 before even as much as 40 percent of its faculty is female. A masculine culture does not die easily.

We have examined, in broad outline, sex discrimination in today's workplace. Before we look at the ways women have used and are now using the anti discrimination laws to contest workplace discrimination, we need to become familiar with those laws and follow their development in the courts over the last four decades.

5

THEORIES OF SOCIAL AND GENDER JUSTICE

Introduction

The employment and academic environments in which individuals work is essential for understanding not only the negative psychological consequences of sex discrimination but also how victimized people recover from these adverse experiences. Appreciating how the structural and environmental conditions of an individual's work or educational environment contribute to discriminatory events is clinically significant for several reasons. (1) It helps the clinician avoid the negative therapeutic consequences of the classic psychoanalytic bias by allowing the clinician to focus on external, as well as intrapsychic, factors in evaluating patients or clients with work-related complaints. (2) It helps the victimized person to avoid immobilization and internalization of guilt and shame. (3) It helps the therapist and the patient/client in collaborating to formulate an effective and adaptive coping plan.

This chapter will provide an overview of the clinically relevant aspects of the current employment and academic environments. Pragmatic information, theoretical concepts, and current trends will be discussed. Case examples will be provided to illustrate significant points.

Relevant Trends in Today's Work and Educational Environments

The impact of gender in the workplace and in academic settings has increased dramatically in the last 50 years. There have been both significant gains and significant areas of stagnation in regard to gender equity. In the early 1970s, women began to enter the employment market in significantly larger numbers, and since then their numbers have continued to increase. In 1970 43% of adult women were either employed or seeking employment. In 1998 that number had increased to 60%. During this same time period, the participation of men in the labor force decreased from 80% to 74%, resulting in an increased proportion of woman in the total labor force from 38% in 1970 to 46% in 1998. A similar gender equity has occurred in the distribution of men and women entering previously male-dominated professional schools, such as law and medicine. In addition, the proportion of woman managers has risen from 16% in 1970 to 44% in 1998. Among these increased numbers of employed women in general is an increase in the numbers of mothers of young children and single mothers. Along with shifts in numbers have come shifts in women's attitudes and expectations regarding work outside the home. As a result, career and salaried employment plays a more salient role in women's sense of themselves. In short, more women are impacted by the work environment, and this impact is of higher psychological significance.

Perceptions of men's and women's roles are also in great flux. Innumerable variations between traditional and egalitarian attitudes now exist between individuals, their families, and their workplace contacts. Thus two women with similar credentials, career attitudes, and goals may have very different experiences, depending on the attitudes of their colleagues, coworkers, mentors, bosses, and significant individuals in their personal lives. Of special importance is the lack of attitudinal change in CEOs and other high-level administrators. Current research indicates that these top policy and decision makers continue to demonstrate traditional gender stereotypes and stereotypical beliefs regarding men and women.

These individuals may either resist promoting women altogether or only help women who are significantly junior or subordinate to them.

Paralleling these significant changes for women are significant areas of stagnation. The average full-time female worker continues to receive less pay than the average full-time male worker does. Female-dominated occupations still receive lower pay than male-dominated occupations do, and women are still paid less than men are for the same occupation. Furthermore, the gender gap in earnings appears to be increasing, after a period of decline. In addition, sex segregation, although declining, remains a defining element of occupational structure, affecting choices for both men and women and still confining women to lower-paying and female-dominated occupations and positions.

Most significantly, the number of women in top management and administrative positions in work and educational organizations remains consistently and disproportionately low, around 10%. Gary Powell summarizes the recent research that documents the persistence of gender stereotyping that operates against women seeking top positions, despite changes in opportunity and attitudes for women at other levels. This makes it difficult for women to impact the policies and structures of their work and educational environments. In addition, support and resources for housework, child care, elder care, and other duties traditionally performed by women homemakers have not kept pace with the needs of the growing number of these women who are now employed or are students outside the home. Despite the increased involvement of men, women continue to carry out most domestic responsibilities, and many expect to continue to do so.

Emerging Trends in the Work Environment

Cooper and Lewis recently reviewed the gender implications of several new trends emerging in the workplace. Their discussion provides a framework for summarizing these trends. Beginning in the 1990s, globalization, recession, and advancements in information technology have resulted in (1) radical and continuous restructuring of work organizations, and (2) an information overload and accelerated work pace. The fundamental unspoken employer-employee contract promising long-term stable employment and advancement in the work hierarchy, in return for hard work, high performance, and loyalty, has been eroded. This has impacted morale, motivation, and employee loyalty but has also provided an opportunity for change. Work organizations, ranging from manufacturing companies to educational institutions, are relying more on a small core of permanent full-time employees working in-house, supplemented by a much larger pool of part-time and contract employees working on specific projects or tasks, oftentimes from their homes. Employees ranging from factory line workers to administrators, college professors, and physicians are having the experience of fewer people doing more work with less job security.

Several elements of this transition-namely, the flexible workplace, job insecurity, long work hours, and the existence of virtual organizations-have gender implications. Women have traditionally been part-time discontinuous workers with more flexible attitudes toward work. The question arises as to whether or not they will be more adaptable and therefore more preferred workers in this new environment. Women's career aspirations and management styles have traditionally focused on performance, achievement of expertise, and satisfaction within a job, rather than on promotion. Their management styles have included good communication and people skills, flexibility, a capacity to mentor others, and good transitional leadership skills. It remains to be seen whether careers of achievement in flat organizations in a culture of rapid change will be a better fit for women than men or whether for men will adapt more feminine styles.

Cooper and Lewis' discussion raised many questions with gender implications. Will career paths regress back to the traditional styles within these new organizations, with men still at the top of most organizations, or will men be willing to share or relinquish power in this time of change? Will job insecurity and the likelihood of unanticipated periods of unemployment force men and women to adapt more egalitarian roles in the home? Will the opportunity to partake in more flexible work structures lead to more sharing of gender roles in the home, or will this make it more likely that women will continue to shoulder the burdens of domestic responsibilities? If women at times are the sole providers for their families, will men become active at home, or will a woman's job be played down or be considered temporary? Will women continue the current norm of experiencing job stress not only for themselves but also on behalf of their spouses, or will men begin to be impacted by women's occupational stresses and share some of the emotional burden of family life? Will employees continue the trend toward working longer hours to guard against job loss, or will they rebel and become more assertive in moving from organization to organization in accordance with their needs? Will this create a new trend of horizontal, rather than vertical, movement? Will parents' working long hours to succeed create more stress at home, and will they then spend even more time at work to escape these tensions? Will families' stress spill into the workplace? Will couples have fewer children? Will men and women unite and adapt to the lack of work permanence by demanding a better balance between work and family, a higher quality of life? Will home-based work in virtual organizations allow more opportunities for caretakers to obtain employment and for egalitarian integration of work, or will gender inequities persist, with employers paying less to predominantly female home-based workers and more money to men maintaining the traditional boundaries between home and work? As work-home boundaries blur, will workers multitask successfully or will they become workaholics?

It is clear that the recent radical changes in the work and educational environments are challenging many of the fundamental tenets of gendered organizations, such as (1) the male model of work, (2) continuous full-time careers based on advancement, and (3) the physical and psychological separation of work and family. The possibility for shifts in gender roles and experiences at work certainly exists but is by no means certain. Women have been in the workplace in significantly large numbers for over 30 years, and they have made considerable gains. Many men have become increasingly involved in family life but not on parity with women. The glass ceiling, especially at the top of the work hierarchy, has remained firmly in place. Work and educational organizations continue to be led by men and structured according to male values. Women continue to take primary responsibility for home and family life and for home and family responsibilities. The evolving global economy will affect American jobs and introduce gender roles from other cultures. The impact of the recent terrorist attacks on the United States and the related world conflicts that are evolving and the potential repercussions for the economic and work climate remain to be seen. Cooper and Lewis note that it is unlikely that these emerging structural changes in the workplace alone can alter embedded gender elements that currently exist, unless the need to challenge gender role inequities is articulated and specifically pursued in the larger sociocultural arena.

The way in which women are pursuing this agenda will be discussed in the next chapter, which deals with the legal environment. I will first explore in this chapter the way in which the current work and educational environments contribute to discriminatory experiences for women.

Work and Educational Environments Experiences for Women

Researchers from a variety of disciplines have constructed a spectrum of theories to explain the current inequity between the sexes in the work and educational environments. Some were designed to explain sex discrimination in general, and others apply specifically to sexual harassment. Many of these etiologic theories overlap, and some lend themselves to psychological interpretation more than others do. In general, these models point to an interaction between (1) factors at the socioenvironmental level that impact on the workplace, such as sex role prescriptions or labor market conditions; (2) factors inherent in the structure of the workplace such as hierarchical and power differentials, interactions between workgroups and employees, and biases at the level of key decision makers; and (3) factors at the individual level, such as motivation, attitudes, personality, and coping strategies. An understanding of the etiologic factors of sexual discrimination can help both clinicians and patients/clients assess the external factors that contribute to the patient/client's situation. This not only provides an opportunity to analyze the problem and develop effective coping strategies but also prevents the likelihood of the victimized person's internalization of guilt, shame, and responsibility for the situation. This section will summarize the most important etiologic models of sexual harassment and gender discrimination. Clinical examples will be given to illustrate each model, which lists conceptual focuses, strengths and weaknesses, and psychological implications for each model. Models of gender discrimination will be described first, followed by models specific to sexual harassment.

Gender Discrimination Models

Model #1: The Individual Deficit Model

This perspective, defined by Nieva views gender discrimination in terms of men and women as individuals. The model focuses on differences in innate biology and early socialization, which presumably lead to fixed results in adulthood. Women are seen as more emotional, less logical, and more motivated by wishes for security and connection than are men. Men are perceived as logical, stable, and more comfortable with high-risk challenges and individual achievements. Women may have difficulty with leadership positions, due to fear of success or tendencies to achieve via indirect and vicarious routes. Women's subordinate status as workers or students is best explained in terms of deficits in motivation, in personality development, and in essential traits, such as a lack of assertiveness and sensitivity to organizational networks and political gains.

Although this model emphasizes female deficits, it can also be utilized to highlight the negative impact of male attitudes and perceptions about female workers or students. This impact is especially significant for women working at higher levels or at nontraditional jobs or educational tracts, where their presence is more unusual and where they are prone to be viewed as deficient by superiors. In addition, male deficits, such as insecurity regarding masculinity and defensiveness regarding healthy competition from women, can also be used to explain women's problems in the workplace.

This model has many significant shortcomings and is not substantiated by the bulk of empirical literature. It exaggerates biological difference and oversimplifies the complex factors leading to discrimination. From a psychological standpoint, it can also lead women to internalize blame and responsibility for situations created by organizational, cultural, and political factors well beyond the scope of their individual culpability and strengths. It is included in this text because it helps to explain the specific cases in which adverse early socialization significantly impacts a woman's employment or academic status. The following case example illustrates this point.

CASE VIGNETTE 5-1

Early Socialization Results in Deficits in Individuals' Work Functioning

Gretchen Young was a 45-year-old middle-management business executive who had worked in a series of public relations companies with moderate success. Although she received regular promotions and salary increases, her work history was punctuated by a series of love affairs with her immediate bosses, all of whom were married and none of whom could offer a gratifying personal relationship. One of her lover-mentors also discouraged her from pursuing her goal of developing her own small company, minimizing her ability and maximizing his displeasure at not having her accessible to him. The blurring of boundaries between her work and her personal relationships also undercut Gretchen's confidence in her work performance. She was uncertain as to whether or not her promotions were the result of her abilities or her sexual relationships with her bosses. Despite an awareness of the disadvantages of her behavior, she continued to respond to sexual overtures in the workplace with no conscious understanding of her motivation. In the context of her therapy, she identified the origins of the patterns in the context of her family of origin. Her father, a successful business executive, very much like herself, functioned well at work but was a closeted alcoholic who physically and verbally abused both Gretchen's mother and brother. They remained his intimidated victims but expressed their own pent-up anger toward Gretchen. Her father spared her his verbal and physical abuse but fondled Gretchen's genitals for a brief period early in her childhood and explained his behavior as "special coddling for a special girl." He constantly expressed his delight in Gretchen's physical attractiveness and "cute behavior." He consistently responded warmly toward her and with apparent favoritism. Gretchen's mother exacerbated the problem by overemphasizing traditional sex roles, especially the importance of attracting men who could provide for her economic security. Gretchen was devastated when her father emotionally abandoned her in the context of her first dating relationship. She ultimately identified her repetitive colluding in the sexualizing of her work relationships with her bosses as an attempt to maintain the only emotional form of gratification that she had experienced as a child. In addition, this replicated the only form of economic and personal security that she had been socialized to achieve.

Model #2: The Structural Institutional Model of Gender Discrimination

In this model, Nieva addresses the limitations that Kanter and others have raised regarding the individual deficit model's tendency to leave the work or educational environment unexamined and unchanged. This model focuses specifically on the impact that the work or educational organization has on individual men and women and the ways in which people reflect their work or educational environment in their individual behaviors. Women's personalities and motivations are seen more as the consequences of work or educational situations than as the causes. If low aspirations exist in women, they are seen as adaptive adjustments to the reality of limited opportunities. Women's difficulties with integrating into traditionally male work or academic environments result from their low numbers, token positions in the organization, and the accompanying unconscious group dynamics that make these women extremely visible and subject to special pressures and stereotyping, yet at the same time excluding them from essential networks of information and alliances. Leadership problems are not the result of women's inappropriate styles but rather are the logical consequences of powerless and dead-end isolated positions to which they are assigned. Women's limitations thus are similar to the legitimacy and entitlement problems experienced by other newcomers and minority groups who do not control the operations of the environments in which they work. The following case vignette illustrates the difficulties of such a token woman attempting to integrate into a traditionally male work environment.

CASE VIGNETTE 5-2

Group Dynamics Impede Progress of Token Women

Mary Doe was a 32-year-old courier service driver and single mother of two who entered treatment with symptoms of anxiety and depression, following an episode in which her union representative had failed to support her in filing a discrimination claim. That same afternoon her tires were slashed at work. She suspected her angry coworkers. Mary 's 4-year experience in the position had been highly unpleasant, but she had remained at the job due to the excellent pay, which was well above that of several other traditional female positions she had considered. The company employed only two women drivers out of 40, and each of the four regional supervisors was male. While on the job, her male colleagues usually talked around her, focusing on subjects related to sports or sexual exploits. Whenever Mary would try to enter a conversation, usually to discuss union matters, the other conversants would stop and walk away. The men nicknamed her "britches," after a dockloader began the habit of nudging her buttocks with a forklift whenever she entered the warehouse. On the few occasions she was called to the office to pick up a parcel she had erroneously delivered, the supervisor would announce the situation over the loudspeaker. Her coworkers would then clap and some would shout, "Way to go, britches!"

After being in the position for over 18 months, Mary applied to be certified to deliver biological specimens, a job that paid a significantly higher salary. Within the next year, she approached her supervisor on three separate occasions regarding her application. Each time she was turned down and told she did not qualify. Finally, she requested qualification information from her union rep and learned that she did indeed meet the prerequisites. When her supervisor learned that Mary had spoken to the union representative, he angrily advised her to get married if she wanted to bring in more money. He began assigning her deliveries in the slum areas of town. She approached her union representative regarding the possibility of filing a discrimination complaint. His response was critical, and he discouraged her from moving forward. He stated that he doubted that she had much of a case. Mary telephoned the other female worker for advice but was cautioned by her female colleague not to be a troublemaker. When she entered work the following morning, she heard several of her co-workers snickering at her. One of them whispered loudly, "Britches is getting too big for her britches." That afternoon she left work to find her tires slashed in the employee parking lot.

Model #3: The Sex Role Model

In this conceptual model of discrimination, Nieva focuses on societal behaviors and attitudes. Cultural definitions of male and female roles are stressed, including but not limited to, the work or academic aspects of life. The focus of this model is the amount of congruence between a woman's exhibited behaviors or attitudes and those prescribed by her sex role ideal or those appropriate to specific female roles exemplified by wife, mother, and sexual object. This model suggests that sex role prescriptions impose upon a wide range of work-related behaviors. Women will select or be pressured into jobs or academic situations that require traits that are seen as congruent with their sex roles or that allow for major commitment to their roles as wives and mothers, even if these jobs or educational situations offer a low level of reward. According to the sex role model, the problems of women workers stem from the inappropriate spillover of sex-related roles into the workplace. Independent of their capabilities or preferences, women are forced to perform or are perceived as performing functions similar to those they perform in their nonwork roles. Current perceptions and assessments, as well as future expectations, derive from traditional female role traits such as nurturer and supporter, even though these traits may be irrelevant or damaging to the performance of their specific work or academic roles. Women's job and academic descriptions involve functions that are typically auxiliary and satisfactions that are typically vicarious. Training and advancement opportunities are prescribed as appropriate for male colleagues only. Women must choose either to stagnate or to deviate from accepted norms and risk sanctions.

For women workers or students who are also wives and mothers, the problems are even more severe. These traditional expectations demand they accommodate their work or academic lives to the demands of their husbands, households, and children. The interrupted patterns and part-time employment or student characteristics of women adapting to these demands carry a multitude of career penalties, such as disproportionately low salaries, limited benefits, and truncated career or educational ladders.

Conversely, men are expected to alter their family responsibilities to suit their work roles so that men who attempt to help their working wives with family responsibilities may face their own sanctions. Women who choose to violate traditional sex role prescriptions of behavior in work or educational settings face entry and acceptance problems. They may be exposed to harassment, hostility, and ostracism. Such groundbreaking women must tolerate internal strain, resulting from role conflicts and the uncertainty and self-doubt that arise from nonsupportive work or academic environments. The following two case vignettes illustrate the multitude of problems exemplified by this model.

CASE VIGNETTE 5-3

Culturally Defined Sex Roles Negatively Impact Nontraditional Couple

Dr. Sandra Hughes was a third-year psychiatry resident, married happily to Dr. Arnold Young, who was a third-year resident in radiology. The couple were enjoying and excelling in their training programs. They had enjoyed a long-standing relationship that had resulted in their desire to begin a family. Sandra was delighted when she learned that she was pregnant. As she and her husband discussed their situation, they decided jointly that Sandra would take a short maternity leave, but Arnold would take a longer child-rearing leave because the nature of his training program compartmentalized rotations, allowing him to be more readily able to schedule a prolonged period of time at home. Both Sandra's and Arnold's department chairs sanctioned their plans. Arnold, who was being groomed by his department chair to join the junior faculty, was even told that he was especially respected for this position. The chair mentioned that he himself felt that he had taken too little time to be with his children.

The pregnancy and the delivery went well, and Sandra returned from her short maternity leave on schedule. Although she continued to do well in the program, she was somewhat dismayed by a variety of experiences with colleagues that negated the lip-service sanction she had received for her plan. On several occasions, colleagues worried out loud regarding her capacity to bond with her child. An administrator commented on her getting home early to make dinner for her husband. She was automatically left out of plans to attend professional meetings. When she spoke with her residency director about this, he apologized and said, "We assumed that you would want more at-home time now." She also was dismayed to learn that she was now assigned a half-time office, the underlying assumption being that she would see fewer outpatients now that she had a child.

Arnold, on the other hand, was having difficulty integrating into the predominantly sfemale mothers' network active in their community. He found that the women were awkward regarding talking to him about the new baby he was caring for and seldom approached him in the park. One month prior to his scheduled return to his residency, Arnold checked in with his department chair, who told him brusquely that his research project had been given to another resident. Three months after Arnold returned to work, his department chair informed him that he would not be selected as a chief resident and that his leave had created great animosity among the residents. Arnold's chief also said that he would not be recommending Arnold for a postgraduate fellow-ship, because the chief had some concerns about Arnold's commitment to the workplace. Angered and dismayed, Arnold changed specialties and ultimately became quite depressed, precipitating anxiety and guilt in his wife and creating significant problems in their sexual relationship and in their adjustment to parenthood.

Model #4: The Intergroup Relationship Model

In the fourth model of discrimination, the intergroup relations model, Nieva focuses on the relationship between men and women as group members. This model expands upon the previously described dynamics associated with tokenism. The premise of this model is that men and women, as members of two fundamentally different groups, will interact according to the dynamic factors that typically develop in relationships between groups. When work and educational groups are formed based on dominant characteristics such as sex, both the differences between groups, as well as similarities within groups, are emphasized and exaggerated, resulting in stereotypes that supersede individual characteristics in actual job or academic performance. For example, all men are assertive and committed to their careers, or all women are nurturing and committed to child rearing and family life. Such stereotyping affects the interactions between members of the two different groups, creating more stress and discomfort when they are placed in an interactive situation. Their stereotyped roles and expectations of each other generate incompatible sets of behavior, resulting in further distancing, polarization, and exacerbation of the existing stereotypes.

Intergroup dynamics also result in the creation of a hierarchy, wherein one group is seen as superior to the other group. Traditionally, males have been viewed as the dominant "in-group" in the workplace and academia. Male characteristics are automatically used to set the norm for "goodness," regardless of what traits might in reality correlate best with performance of a designated work or academic task. Promo tional and career track performance expectations are based on the male life cycle, with no allowances for child rearing. In addition to the assumed superiority of male traits is the assumption that male occupational and academic activities are automatically superior to female occupational and academic activities. This is demonstrated by Touhey's research, which showed that simply changing the composition of an occupation to include more females lowered the desirability and prestige of that occupation.

According to this intergroup model, individuals are treated in strict accordance to the status associated with their characteristic group membership. In work settings, when an individual's educational level or job title may not be immediately evident, that person's sex is always obvious. Women, as members of the lower-status group, may automatically be perceived to have less power, less prestige, and less potential for accomplishment, independent of their actual level of performance. In addition, as members of the subordinate status group, women themselves may

1. Expect less
2. Initiate less
3. Overevaluate higher-status males
4. Denigrate members of their own group
5. Accept the dominant group's distorted definitions of them
6. Attempt to identify with the dominant group members at their own expense or at the expense of their female colleagues

Numerous researchers have correlated women's subordinate sex status with their lesser degrees of control over the resources valued by society, such as money, land, political influence, legal power, and intellectual and occupational resources, as compared to youth, beauty, and child-rearing potential. Although valued resources may differ from society to society, economic power is seen as the key variable in most cultures. Protection of the established system of reward allocation and resources controlled by the male-dominant groups remains a major obstacle for females entering the work-place. Multiple rationalizations, including the individual deficit model of females, are utilized to preserve the status quo. A variation of the intergroup model originates from economic and labor relations theory and focuses on the concept of vulnerable workers. Some aspects of this theory can be applied to academic settings as well. Wilborn identified vulnerable workers through the analysis of three interacting variables. First, a group's level of vulnerability in the workplace depends on the ability of employers to distinguish at low cost between group members and non-group members. Women's gender meets this criterion. Second, a group's level of vulnerability depends on ideas or preoccupations about the group that might cause employers or coworkers to discriminate against the group. Sex role stereotypes and perceptual biases about women's competence meet this criterion. Finally, a group's level of vulnerability depends on structural aspects of the labor market that are disadvantageous to them. Some examples that apply to women are

1. Tax laws that discriminate against secondary earners within families
2. Proportionately low compensation packages for part-time workers
3. The unavailability of child care and elder care

The following example illustrates the issues addressed in the intergroup model.

CASE VIGNETTE 5-4

Stereotype Gender Issues Polarize Male-Female Interactions and Incapacitate a Work Group

The CEO of a small pharmaceutical company, wishing to introduce a new women's health product to the marketplace, appointed a six-person educational advisory panel, consisting of two male physicians, two female physicians, a female nurse, and a female president of a women's health consumer group. This team was to work collaboratively with one female marketing executive, two male marketing executives, and a male pharmacologist from the corporate headquarters. Although one male marketing executive assumed the role of leader of the group without discussion by the others, the team members nonetheless worked well together until it was time to travel to an international conference where they would supervise and coordinate a series of educational lectures to be given by an outside male physician, using educational materials that the group had designed. During the course of his lectures, the outside speaker made several sexist jokes that created some consternation among the advisory committee. The lecturer caused further consternation when at an informal dinner he showed a series of slides with sexist portraits of women. The audience, which was largely male, clearly was not offended by the presentation, but the advisory group was split. A further bone of contention was the issue of an earlier presentation made by the nurse who represented a strong women's health organization. Some members of the conference audience were offended that a nurse should open the presentation. The group was split as to how to handle the situation. All of the women and one of the men found the male presenter's jokes and slide show offensive. This group also felt strongly that it had been appropriate to open the conference with the nurse's presentation, even though some members of the audience had objected. As the discussion progressed, the female marketing executives and one of the female physicians shifted and ultimately took the position that the male physician and presenter was acceptable and that the nurse's presentation should be eliminated at future conferences. Although the objecting members reluctantly acquiesced to continuing the program, the group was not able to agree on either additional curriculum materials or future conference plans. It was ultimately disbanded by the CEO. Although the advisory group was composed of an equal number of men and women and displayed an initial ability to work effectively, it became polarized and incapacitated when stereotype gender issues were introduced at the conference.

Behavioral and Conceptual Models of Sexual Harassment

In keeping with the current widespread publicity and legal activities surrounding the issue, theoretical models explaining the etiology of sexual harassment appear more frequently and in greater numbers in the research literature than do models of gender discrimination. There are, however, parallels between the two sets of models. The conceptual framework for the etiology of sexual harassment depends on the same three levels of factors as those addressed in discrimination, namely:

1. Factors at the macro or environmental level, such as socioeconomic inequities, sex role prescriptions, legal sanctions, and economic and labor market conditions;

2. Factors at the organizational level, such as hierarchical and power differentials, organizational climates, sex ratios, employee composition, and disparate compensation and benefit structures; and
3. Factors at the individual levels, such as motivation, attitudes, personality, communication, leadership styles, and strategies of workplace victims and offenders.

The bulk of the literature on sexual harassment focuses on four explanatory models, three of which were developed by Tangri, Burt, and Johnson and a fourth by Gutek and associates. Based on their review of courtroom cases of sexual harassment,

Tangri defined (1) the natural biological model, (2) the organizational model, and (3) the socioeconomic model. Gutek and associates defined (4) the sex role spillover model, based on their own extensive research. Table 5.1 provides a brief comparative description of each model, including its psychological implications.

Model #1: The Natural Biological Model of Sexual Harassment

The model explains the occurrence of sexual harassment as a personal issue, based on natural sexual interactions between men and women. Sexual harassment is simply an idiosyncratic outcome of the natural expression of men's stronger sex drive and not an intentional effort to harass. This model denies the negative consequences of sexual harassment on women's psychological health and upon their employment or educational status. Tangri et al. note that if this model were adequate in explaining harassment, given recipients should be similar to their male harassers in age, race, and occupational status. They should be unmarried, and their behavior should resemble courtship and should stop once the woman shows disinterest. Harassed women should report feeling flattered by the behavior. Testing of this model with data from the U.S. Merit Protection Board Study found that it was not supported. Saal provides an extensive discussion of why this model does not serve well in explaining the widespread phenomenon of sexual harassment. Included for completeness, however, is one example known to the author of a sexual harassing situation in which the primary motivation appeared to be misguided courtship behavior.

CASE VIGNETTE 5-5

Sexual Harassment Resulting from Misguided Courtship Behavior

Kathy Smith was a 23-year-old graduate student working in a lab with her preceptor, Dr. Jon Boonvell, who had 20 years of research experience. At age 44, Jon was undergoing a painful divorce. Having focused most of his time on lab work, Jon had few social skills and was not reacting well to the isolation he was experiencing since his wife left him. On several occasions while working in the lab, he approached his student protégé and clumsily asked her for a date. Kathy was courteous but firm, tactfully making it clear that she already had a boyfriend. Her preceptor persisted, becoming more and more desperate, pleading with her and offering to buy her a plane ticket to accompany him to an international meeting. He began collecting Kathy's papers and kept a photograph of her in his room. In the evenings, he would write her imaginary letters, which ultimately he began to send. Kathy consulted her dean and was advised to continue her firm denial of his request for dates. Ultimately, her professor appeared at Kathy's apartment one evening, claiming that he did not think he could live if she would not agree to date him. Kathy did not file a harassment complaint, but the administration intervened and assisted the preceptor in obtaining psychiatric treatment.

Model #2: The Organizational Model of Sexual Harassment

This model shifts the focus away from the individual and focuses on the organizational structures and situations in which men and women work and study. This model suggests that sexual harassment results from the opportunity presented by power and authority relationships derived from the hierarchical structure of organizations. It defines the problem as an abuse of power, based on

1. Differential power positions within the organization,
2. Numerical ratios of males to females within those positions,
3. The norms and the social climate of organizational life, and
4. The unavailability of effective formal and informal grievance and resolution procedures.

By focusing on the asymmetrical relations between supervisors, primarily male, and subordinates, primarily female, this model provides a better explanation for the studies by Tangri et al., showing the consistent negative reactions of women who are victimized and the tendency of individuals with greater degrees of personal vulnerability and dependence on their jobs to experience more harassment. The following example illustrates many of the issues delineated in the model:

CASE VIGNETTE 5-6

Sexual Harassment Involving Organizational Power Differentials and Ineffective Grievance Procedures

Susan Stone was a 26-year-old unmarried graduate student at a prestigious Ivy League school. She was honored to be working as a junior editor on an international journal edited by her professor Dr. Jon Smith, who was an international celebrity in this highly specialized area. Recognizing the unique opportunities for networking, as well as the special literary and editing expertise she could accomplish through this work, Susan willingly agreed to work late at the request of her professor. One evening when they were working alone, he approached her from behind and kissed her neck while stroking her hair. Startled, she jumped and firmly asked him to "Stop that." He responded in a highly offended manner, and Susan became concerned that she may have damaged their relationship. Her professor continued to make the same overtures every evening that they worked together alone. Susan attempted to discourage this by finding daytime hours in which to complete her work. Jon then persisted in his advances publicly during the day, prompting a male colleague to state, "I see how you are advancing in the field." Troubled, Susan consulted an administrative dean, who acquainted her with the institution's sexual harassment policy. Susan first tried to speak directly to Jon by solicitously asking him to allow their relationship to remain purely professional and reiterating her respect and gratitude for the opportunity to work on the journal. His response was curt and abrasive, as he reminded her that "There are twenty more where you came from." This prompted her to worry that her job was in jeopardy. She returned to the dean, who assisted her in filing a sexual harassment complaint. The committee investigating the claim found that it had merit but did not feel able to dislodge Jon from his position, given the revenue and prestige his reputation brought to the school. They instead offered Susan a transfer to another supervisor, acknowledging freely that there was no way to transfer her work on the journal. She became depressed and confused with regard to whether or not her actions were appropriate, given that she had lost a valuable opportunity by filing a complaint.

Model #3: Sociocultural Model of Sexual Harassment

The sociocultural model, like the organizational model, focuses on the unequal distribution of power and status between men and women, but the sociocultural model takes the issue one step further. In this model, sexual harassment is seen as only one manifestation of a larger patriarchal system, in which men are the dominant group in society as a whole. Harassment, then, is a specific example of men asserting personal power based on their sex. According to this model, sex would be a better predictor of who harasses and who is victimized than would organizational position. Women would be more likely to be victimized, especially in male-dominated populations in the workplace. Using data from U.S. Merit System Protection Board Study, Tangri et al. reported stronger empirical support for the organizational and sociocultural models, which both view sexual harassment as arising from power and status disparities. Following is a case vignette that exemplifies the sociocultural model.

CASE VIGNETTE 5-7

Sexual Harassment Involving Male Asserting Personal Power Despite Equal Organizational Position

Jenny Boyd was a 32-year-old married mother of two who was returning to the workforce for the first time since her graduation from college, concurrent with her children's return to school. Jenny was especially pleased to have obtained a job as a sales person and distributor for a regional telecommunications firm that permitted her to maintain a flexible and autonomous work schedule. Almost immediately, Jenny noticed a good deal of flirtatious behavior and exchange of sexual jokes between men and women in the central office. She remarked to a coworker, "Gee, I'm a little shocked at what goes on here. I've been an old married woman, so I must be out of step with the time." Her coworker responded "I'm sure you won't be left out." Things nonetheless went well, and Jenny was soon making significant commissions that greatly added to her family's economic stability.

Jenny was especially pleased to be selected to be one of the resource people to attend a 3-day company conference held 100 miles from her home. She found the didactic sessions stimulating but was greatly concerned when one of her coworkers persistently sat next to her and put his arm around her shoulder. When she tried to deter him in a joking manner, he replied, "Honey, you are just too cute. I can't help myself." The coworker seated himself at her dinner table and asked him to join her for a drink after dinner. Jenny made it quite clear that she would be returning to her room to study for the next day's seminar.

When her roommate, Sue, told Jenny that she would be joining some other sales people for a drink, Jenny wished her a good evening and told her she would be turning in early. She was awakened from a deep sleep at approximately 12:30 A.M. Her roommate, Sue, had returned. Jenny heard Sue's voice, along with a male voice. Before she could sit upright and turn on the light, her coworker Tom came into her bed. He slid on top of her and proceeded to push up her nightgown, massaging her body. Completely shocked and startled, she froze but then attempted to push him off. She screamed to her roommate when she realized that she was being raped. Her roommate was in a drunken state in the other bed and did not respond. Tom slid off and exited the room, leaving Jenny humiliated and in shock. She left the conference the following morning but was unable to tell her husband about this experience. Her work performance declined, and she ultimately entered treatment for depression. Four months after the incident, she was able to admit to her therapist that she had been raped and discuss her shame and guilt for not being more active in fending off the attack.

Model #4: The Sex Role Spillover Model of Sexual Harassment

None of the three previous models has received absolute empirical support in the literature. As an alternative, Gutek and Morasch proposed the sex role spillover model. Sex role spillover explains sexual harassment as a carryover of gender-based role expectations of behavior into the work and educational environments. When an occupation is dominated by one sex, the gender roles associated with that dominant sex group become incorporated into the work or academic role expectations of the occupation. Sex role spillover is exacerbated by skewed sex ratios, and it impacts women in two ways: (1) women employed or studying in nontraditional settings under a token status will be treated as role deviants because their sex does not correspond to the sex roles normally associated with their occupation. They are perceived and treated differently from their male colleagues and are more likely to report instances of sexual harassment. In this case, the role spillover is to the individual. (2) Women working or studying in traditionally female areas will experience a different type of sex role spillover, in which their sex role and their work role merge together. These women may be unaware that some of their treatment in the work or educational setting is based on their sex. These types of occupations tend to be devalued and underrewarded because of the sex typing associated with them. In this case, the role spillover is to the occupation as a whole. The sex role spillover model is compatible with the sociocultural model of harassment and gains support from research that demonstrates a greater incidence of sexual and gender harassment of women working in nontraditional areas. The following case example illustrates sex role spillover occurring in a traditional female occupation.

CASE VIGNETTE 5-8

Sex Role Spillover to a Traditional Female Occupation

Karen Cliff was a 25-year-old engaged dental assistant who had been happily employed by a small dental practice for approximately 5 years. Although friends had warned her that dental assistants were underpaid in this practice, Karen had always remained loyal. She appreciated the generous personal bonuses that her boss provided. Karen enjoyed her work, found the office atmosphere friendly, and respected her boss's expertise and professionalism. She was proud of the fact that he taught at a local dental school. She was therefore flattered when he offered her extra pay to work some additional hours to assist him on the weekends in upgrading the practice's sterilization techniques and equipment. The work was to take place over a 3-month period that involved nearly every Saturday. Karen enjoyed the time with her employer and found the work stimulating. An easy social rapport developed between them as they ate out for lunch and occasionally dinner on Saturdays. Her employer teased her that her fiancé might get jealous. In the context of what Karen perceived to be an innocent social relationship, her employer began to discuss his problems with the office and with his marriage, stressing how he appreciated her caring and concerned attitude toward him. He continued to confide important details of both the practice and his personal life to her in their times together. Karen felt confused, not sure whether to be flattered or uncomfortable with his overtures. As the period of overtime work drew to a close, Karen's boss presented her with a bonus envelope at one of their luncheons together. To her shock, he then invited her to a motel with him that evening, stating that he loved her for her kindness and understanding. Karen reminded him that she was engaged, declined the offer, and left work early that afternoon. She immediately spoke with her fiancé about the situation and was dismayed that he became angry with her, accusing her of being seductive toward her boss.

Model #5: The Terpstra and Baker Models

Terpstra and Baker have developed a lesser known but somewhat parallel set of sexual harassment models, defined as follows:

1. Biological
2. Sex role conditioning
3. Intentional-instrumental
4. Organizational

Each of their models focuses on the motivation of the perpetrator. A brief description will be included for completeness. The biological model is identical to the natural biological model previously described. It is based on the notion that men are biologically more aggressive than women and that men have stronger sex drives than women and that these behaviors present themselves in the work and educational settings. The sex role conditioning model is similar to the sex role spillover model previously described and centers on the role of learning or conditioning, noting that men and women, prior to entering work and academic environments, have been exposed to different socialization patterns and have learned behaviors consistent with existing sexual definitions. In these settings men will behave as dominant, aggressive, and forceful and will initiate sexual activity. Women will be submissive, passive, and receptive to the demands of men. Sexual harassment, then, is simply the exhibition of conditioned sex role behaviors. The intentional-instrumental model is similar to the sociocultural model. It focuses on the role of the conscious intentions of harassers, as opposed to the biological conditioning situations described in the previous two models. In this model, sexual harassment provides a means for men to maintain dominance over women in work or educational settings, as well as in society. Sexual harassment serves as an instrumental function for men, who intentionally harass women in order to maintain their own position of economic privilege, power, or high status. The organizational model is similar to the organizational model previously described by Tangei, which emphasizes the power differentials between men and women in work and educational organizations and the abuse of power by men in positions of authority toward women in subordinate positions.

Secondary Models of Sexual Harassment: The Dispute Model, the Role Model, and the Group Relations Model

Three additional models of sexual harassment are worth noting but are limited in scope and empirical support. Lach and Gwartney-Gibbs proposed a workplace dispute model of sexual harassment, that could also apply to academic settings. They propose that sexual harassment is a concrete example of a multitude of workplace disputes and resolution processes that systematically disadvantage women. Their model describes workplace disputes, including sexual harassment, as consisting of origins, processes, and outcomes. Unlike other models that view harassment as a unique and deviant workplace behavior with unique consequences, the workplace dispute model suggests that harassment is only one type of significant dispute in the workplace with gender implications.

Sexual harassment appears to be patterned by gender roles, occupational sex segregation, and social organization of work. Individual, occupational, and organizational level variables influence the origin of sexual harassment. The processes and outcomes of such disputes are best explained on the individual level. Due to their gender roles, women are more likely to experience workplace difficulties over leaves, absenteeism, and scheduling related to family responsibilities. They are also likely to be the passive recipients of sexual attention. Sex role spillover can result in unwanted sexual behavior for women working in both traditional and nontraditional positions. Because women are often socialized to avoid conflict and to doubt their own perceptions, they may attempt to resolve their disputes informally and not pursue formal complaint channels. This trend would be compounded for all women working in the skewed groups who might feel pressured not to voice difficulties to gain acceptance by the dominant group. Because women workers and students are often distributed differently across work and educational organizations, they may also lack access to formal channels of dispute resolution. In addition, they may lack access to informal networks for resolution or for information and support to facilitate pursuing complaints. Lacking appropriate resolution, workplace disputes for women may result in greater job turnover, lower job satisfaction, lower vocational functioning, and psychological sequelae, as compared to those of men, whose problems are heard in a safe setting and resolved. Although very limited in its scope, this model does help explain

1. The widely documented underreporting of sexual harassment experiences by women, and
2. The multiple reports documenting psychological trauma and difficulties with the complaint channels, written by professionals working with women who were involved in the complaint process.

Connecting Theories of Sexual Harassment and Gender Discrimination

The social-psychological or cognitive-behavioral model of gender provides a connecting link between all of the models of harassment and discrimination just reviewed. This model describes how gender is defined, created, and maintained through sociocultural influences in the context of social interactions. It provides a way of understanding how negative perceptual biases regarding women as workers and students creates and perpetrates workplace discrimination at individual, group, organizational, and cultural levels. Haslett, Geis and Carter provide a comprehensive discussion of these phenomena. They outline a self-fulfilling prophecy of gender beliefs and behaviors consisting of two basic elements: (1) a mental element, consisting of knowledge, beliefs, expectations, feelings, attitudes, values, goals, and motivations; and (2) a behavioral component, including actions, words, pictures, body language, and facial expressions. The premise behind the self-fulfilling prophecy is that stereotypic beliefs about men and women cause biased perceptions and discriminatory behaviors, including discriminatory role and status assignments at work and school, and biased perceptions of performance, which then result in behaviors and achievement levels that seem to confirm the initial stereotypic expectations.

Clinical Psychological Implications of Sex Discrimination Theories

This section has outlined the principal models of sexual harassment and gender discrimination with regard to theories of etiology. All of the theories imply a dynamic relationship between individual, interpersonal, organizational, and sociocultural factors. Many of the theories overlap. No one theory fully encompasses the complexity of the phenomena, yet each one contributes a layer of understanding with regard to the many external factors that contribute to the discriminatory experiences based on gender. They provide a compelling and empirically based illustration of how environmental factors operating in the workplace and academia transcend the importance of any individual characteristics of the victimized person in creating discriminatory events. Few clinicians are familiar with these theories, despite their relevance to the psychological treatment of victimized people. Well-intentioned treatment can in fact be harmful to clients/patients if the treating clinician is unfamiliar with the associated environmental factors. The following discussion highlights this relevance with regard to three key treatment issues.

Reduction of Unconscious Internalization of Blame and Responsibility

Theoretical models of discrimination consistently stress the high significance of conscious and unconscious cultural and organizational factors, as compared to the lower significance of individual characteristics, in contributing to discrimination. In addition, both harassment and discrimination models highlight the potential for perceptual fallibility, abuse of power among key decision makers in the work and educational settings, or both. Such theories counteract traditional forces operating in the educational and work environments, as well as in society, that automatically press women to internalize blame and responsibility for inequities. People victimized by harassment who are familiar with conceptual models are less likely to blame themselves for provocative behavior or lack of finesse in managing unwanted sexual attention. Difficulties with tenure, promotion, pay equity, and training opportunities will not be immediately interpreted as personal inadequacies, such as lack of talent, poor performance, insufficient expertise, or poor leadership abilities. More psychological energy may be available to direct toward changing work environments and discriminatory systems, as opposed to blaming oneself and becoming depressed, anxious, and immobilized.

Women who, in the course of their work, encounter discouragement, decreased self-confidence, and lowering of their career aspirations and motivations may consider their reactions in the light of the cycle of powerlessness models suggested by Ragins and Sundstrom. They describe two separate paths for power-one for men and one for women-and they outline the special difficulties encountered by women. Instead of opting out of the workplace, thus decreasing their investment in their work, women may consider strategies based on a more realistic assessment of their situation. They may take into consideration the specific way in which men are socialized and tracked into powerful positions, which enables them to gain access to more powerful coalitions, networks, and mentors, which in turn enhances their confidence and career aspirations, whereas women, on the other hand, are socialized to accept primary responsibility for children and domestic duties and are not expected to pursue or are not tracked into high-power occupations or positions with accompanying positional resources. Women, therefore, do not gain as ready access to coalitions, mentors, or networks that would enable them to use their interpersonal or individual powers to compensate for a lack of positional power. Discouraged from trying to advance, they may turn to more domestic roles for reward and become less motivated, less confident, and less career-oriented. Women familiar with Ragins and Sundstrom's model may be less likely to consider their reactions as permanent and intransigent or intrinsically related to their abilities. They are less likely to develop psychological symptoms and disorders and more likely to seek other strategies in dealing with their reactions, as discussed in the next section.

CASE VIGNETTE 5-9

Internalization of Blame for Discriminatory Experience

Dr. Simone Barns was a 32-year-old female physician, a member of a bimonthly network group for professional women. She had two small children and was happily married to a businessman. Shortly after joining the group, she became pregnant with her third child. Her career had proceeded smoothly to this point. She currently held a staff position at a top-ranking hospital associated with an Ivy League medical school, to which she was also given a faculty appointment. She frequently expressed feelings of satisfaction in mastering her work. The network group especially appreciated her energy, good humor, honest enthusiasm, and pleasure in approaching her work and home life. Her input to group discussion focused on the challenges she encountered in raising her children and fostering her career and the joy that she experienced in meeting these challenges.

Simone's pregnancy proceeded smoothly; she delivered a healthy baby, and then began a 3-month prearranged maternity leave. During her leave, she continued to attend the group regularly, focusing her discussions on the new baby and on the reactions of her older children toward a new sibling. Although she missed her baby, she felt that her new family was settled and she was comfortable with her children's nanny when she returned to work. Shortly after resuming her job, she expressed great pleasure at being back, stating she was increasingly aware of how much she had missed the challenge.

During the next 6 months, she gradually became reticent in the group. When she did participate, she spoke more of her family and less of her job. When asked specifically about her work, she began to express some doubts about her ability, focusing on a variety of specific tasks, ranging from medical student teaching to publication requirements within her department. She responded to the group's supportive comments but clearly lacked enthusiasm. When she failed to take any pleasure in being a recipient of a highly coveted teaching award at her hospital, a group member asked her specifically, "Are you depressed?" Simone responded in the negative but began to miss meetings and was again confronted by a group member asking, "What has happened to you? You used to be our role model." Simone responded by crying and acknowledging that she had begun treatment for depression. She stated that she felt she might need to leave the group because she no longer felt competent and had a sense of letting down her co-members. With support, she was able to continue and she began to explore a series of problems related to her department head's negative comments regarding working mothers, criticism for lack of publications, unpleasant work assignments, and a punitive nightcall schedule, arranged to "pay her back for all the time she missed." Although the group acknowledged that her situation was discriminatory, she quickly became identified as the "needy one," a position associated with some humiliation for her. She felt that she had lost her position of leadership and respect.

The climate changed when one member brought a newspaper article to the group describing gender discrimination as common in professional settings. Although Simone was initially targeted to be the recipient of the article, other members began to identify with the situations described. Over the next month, group members expressed dismay as individuals began to cite specific examples of work experiences that had been humiliating, devaluing, or detrimental to their careers. Following these disclosures, the group was temporarily immobilized but eventually shifted to a stance that acknowledged the reality of discrimination but focused on brainstorming strategies to address problems. In this context Simone become less depressed, and at the end of the second year of group meetings she was able to negotiate a new position that involved a promotion, a salary increase, and a relocation to a more hospitable work environment.

Assistance in Formulation and Enactment of Adaptive Strategies

For people victimized by harassment and discrimination, a critical step in recovery from psychological sequelae is the formulation and enactment of a strategy to deal with this situation.

Reviewing a variety of options, choosing an option that best suits their needs and minimizes their losses, and proceeding with that plan at a pace reasonable for them as individuals is crucial in reestablishing a victimized individual's sense of control and confidence. The shift from a powerless stance associated with depression, anxiety, psychosomatic complaints, and traumatic reactions to a cognitive problem-solving stance is uniformly associated with a reduction in psychiatric symptomatology. Theoretical models of discrimination assist in this process by providing a cognitive explanation for complicated, emotionally laden employment situations. Models enable victimized people to isolate the etiology of their difficulties-a manager's bias, a tracking problem, and so on. They can then formulate effective strategies that focus on the specific problems they are encountering. Models also enable them to identify in advance which work situations will be most favorable to them or to readily locate more positive work environments, if their current situation is untenable.

Correction of Therapist Bias

Genovich-Richards and Bernstein and Lenhart have reported on the lack of information regarding sexual harassment and gender discrimination in the health-care and mental health literature. Clinicians are traditionally trained to focus on intrapsychic factors. Familiarity with conceptual models of discrimination leads to a heightened awareness of the importance of also assessing external sociocultural factors during the evaluation of women with work-related complaints. Beginning in this context allows the therapist to validate the serious reality of the patient's experience and to assist the patient in realistically assessing her situation and in mobilizing effective coping responses. This approach prevents her from internalizing blame and regressing to a devalued, depressed, and helpless state and essentially reexperiencing the work-place trauma within the treatment. Awareness of the complicated cultural and organizational climate in which women work also assists the clinician in appreciating the challenge and the special areas of stress to be addressed. Appreciating in advance the way the conflict between sex roles and work roles can create double binds for women at work can assist the therapist in avoiding two common pitfalls at the onset of employment-related therapy:

1. Devaluing the patient for initial inability to take definitive action in her work situation.
2. Failing to intervene when the patient is taking immediate actions that are impulsive and not in her best interests.

Finally, theoretical knowledge of discrimination can sensitize clinicians regarding the essential importance of work, not only for men but also for women. The value of taking initial work histories on both male and female patients, as well as of eliciting a more detailed work history from patients who present with psychological symptoms but make only vague references to work problems, is considerable.

CASE VIGNETTE 5-10

Exacerbation of Sexual Harassment Problems Secondary to Therapist Bias

Carmen Gonzales was a 28-year-old married mother of three who worked as a clerical supervisor for a shipping company. She was referred to therapy by her internist for a series of psychosomatic complaints that were unresponsive to treatment and that were causing frequent absences from work. In the course of eliciting a history, her therapist found that Carmen had had numerous arguments with her husband regarding her work status. Both Mr. and Mrs. Gonzales grew up in a Hispanic home, where traditional sex roles were emphasized and mothers stayed at home to raise large families. Carmen had consistently worked throughout her marriage because of her family's real economic needs and because of her own firm stance that she liked her job and wanted to work. In pursuing this conflict, the therapist learned that, recently, Carmen had begun to experience guilt regarding her decision to remain employed outside the home despite her husband and family's values. With her therapist's support, Carmen began to explore the possibility of staying at home full time. Six weeks later, she quit her job. She continued to meet with her therapist on a weekly basis for an additional month, during which time she focused on transition issues and noted the subsiding of her somatic complaints. Viewing her problem as resolved, she and her therapist agreed to a mutual termination of treatment. Three months later Carmen was hospitalized for depression. In the course of her inpatient evaluation, her new therapist learned that she had been sexually harassed by a trusted supervisor who was in the midst of a tumultuous divorce. Carmen had felt humiliated by the experience and too embarrassed to discuss it and had felt that her inability to prevent her supervisor from touching her breast had brought shame to her husband and family. Her guilt reactivated her unresolved ambivalence about resisting her spouse's wishes and her family's injunction that she not pursue a job that she enjoyed. Her therapist had pursued this traditional conflict without taking a complete work history. Her treatment inadvertently contributed to the escalation of her problem.

This chapter has summarized the clinically relevant aspects of the current employment and academic environments in which discrimination occurs. Emphasis has been placed on how the nature of this work-place contributes to the etiology of discriminatory events in a manner that transcends the characteristics of the victimized individual, as illustrated by the theoretical empirically based models presented. The clinical relevance of the models is discussed in terms of three key treatment issues. Relevant trends and emerging trends in regard to gender issues in the workplace and academia are also described. It is emphasized, however, that any emerging structural changes in the workplace are unlikely to alter the embedded discriminatory elements that currently exist, unless the need to challenge gender role inequities is articulated and specifically pursued in the larger sociocultural arena.

❑❑❑

6

Consideration of Care and Justice

Introduction

The unfortunate representation and/or understanding of the ethic of care as not only contextualized but also 'particularist' and therefore opposed to, or even incompatible with, a universalist ethic of justice, I shall spend most of this chapter arguing that principles of justice do have an important place in an acceptable ethic of care. Thus I argue, by looking at Gilligan's own writings on the ethic of care as well as her interpreters, that the important distinction between the ethic of care and the ethic of right and justice is one of content rather than form (in a sense to be explained) and that this opens up a detailed enquiry into how considerations of care and justice are related to each other.

(i) Content and form in Gilligan's ethic of care

Since the publication of Gilligan *In a Different Voice*, in which she argued that women tend to speak and deliberate in a 'different moral voice', there has been a lively and controversial debate about the possibility and shape of what she called the 'ethic of care', its relationship to what she called the 'ethic of right and justice', and about whether such an ethic would be specifically feminine as

Noddings, for example, would claimor feminist as other authors have argued. One of the characteristics, and problems, in this debate, however, is that the contrast between the two ethics has been interpreted in very different ways by different participants in the debate. These varying interpretations may be traced back to Gilligan's original argument which used a number of dichotomies and dimensions with which to contrast and thus define the two ethics. It is, unfortunately, not very dear which contrast(s) she meant to be basic, nor is it therefore clear how exactly the two ethics are defined. As a consequence, different dimensions and dichotomies delineating the contrast are focused upon by different contributors to the debate. More specifically, it is useful to distinguish the interventions in this debate by certain moral and political philosophers from the rest by looking at their very specific reception and understanding of it. I shall refer to this specific reception as the *particularism debate* and distinguish it from the *ethic of care debate* which is much broader and which has branched out into many disciplines. In fact, one might argue that Gilligan's book did not just start a debate, but initiated a new research paradigm by opening up new and promising lines of enquiry in the vast interdisciplinary field of gender studies and feminist theory. The particularism debate, by contrast, addressed itself to a very specific problem, namely the question to what extent and how particular moral concerns and commitments could figure in moral theories whose basic structure was universal and impartial. These latter theories are usually referred to as impartialist theories, and the metaethical approach of these theories as impartialism.

This debate started independently in moral philosophy, but at least one of the critics of impartialism, Blum, subsequently used Gilligan and her ethic of care as one good example of such a particularist ethic whose distinct features could not be done justice to by incorporation into an impartialist framework. Other participants in this debate, such as Noddings and Tronto, used Gilligan's ethic of care as a good illustration of the need for a new metaethical approach. Now the reason why I have to mention the particularism debate is because, unfortunately, it seems to have monopolized the ethic of care debate at least in moral philosophy and has thereby marginalized other possible uses that could have been made of Gilligan's findings and insights.

More specifically, it has focused discussion on formal, metaethical aspects at the expense of a discussion of the different *content* an ethic of care might have. In virtue of this focus, care and justice have tended to be posited as incompatible because based on different metaethical frameworks.

Now, as far as the metaethical issue is concerned, I want to remain agnostic at this stage of my argument, mainly because I think that issues arising about the content of an ethic of care and considerations of justice within it are much more straightforward, interesting, and moreover have not been discussed in any detail yet. What I am interested in, therefore, in this chapter, is to explore in detail how considerations of care and justice arise from the practice of care and whether and how they fit together. Before I start on this task in section ii, I would like to take a short look at Gilligan's own characterization of the two ethics over the years in order to substantiate my point that Gilligan's concern is not only, or not even mainly and even not at all in her later work with differences in form between the two ethics, but with differences in content, even if it sometimes looks as if differences in form were quite central to her distinction between the two ethics. This discussion of Gilligan does obviously not serve as an argument for looking at the content of the ethic of care, but it illustrates how a stress on (supposed) formal distinctions between the two ethics can eclipse some of the most interesting points in her work.

The particularism debate does not only distract from questions about the content of the ethic of care and about how confsiderations of justice and care are related to each other, it is also based on a fairly one-sided and to some extent misleading representation of Gilligan's own claims. While it is true, on the one hand, that Gilligan stresses the particularity and contextuality of women's moral judgements and their refusal to cite any principles a stress that has been made much of by both the 'particularists' and the 'impartialists' in the particularism debate she also envisages, on the other hand, the possibility of *generalizing* the care perspective. Thus on the one hand, one finds quotes such as the following:

Claire's judgement is a contextual judgment, bound to the particulars of time and place, contingent always on 'that mother' and 'that unborn child' and thus resisting a categorical formulation.

To her, the possibilities of imagination outstrip the capacity for generalisation.

On the other hand, however, Gilligan refers to care in the highest stage of development as a 'universal injunction' against hurting others, as 'the most adequate guide to the resolution of conflicts in human relationships', and as the 'principle of judgment' that is 'universal in its condemnation of exploitation and hurt'. The question therefore arises how seriously Gilligan meant her assertions of the particularity of her subjects' moral judgements.

Furthermore, and very much in contradiction to the metaethical oppositions of the particularist ethic of care and the impartialist ethic of justice which were asserted by contributors to the particularism debate, Gilligan does not see considerations of justice and care as incompatible or fundamentally opposed. Thus it is worth noting that Gilligan attributes women's transition from the second, self-eclipsing to the third (and highest), selfinclusive stage of the ethic of care at least contingently to the influence of considerations of rights and justice: the ideal of selflessness and selfless care for others which is typical of the second stage is called into question by the concept of rights, by the assumption underlying the idea of justice that self and other are equal. The concept of rights entered into their thinking to challenge a morality of selfsacrifice and self-abnegation. The concept of rights changes women's conceptions of self, allowing them to see themselves as stronger and to consider directly their own needs. Thus changes in women's rights change women's moral judgments, seasoning mercy with justice by enabling women to consider it moral to care not only for others, but for themselves. The issue of inclusion first raised by the feminists in the public domain reverberates through the psychology of women as they begin to notice their own exclusion of themselves.

Gilligan thus seems to have no qualms about asserting that considerations of justice and women's rights can be crucial factors in enabling women's moral development to the highest stage of the ethic of care by including their own needs in their moral deliberation. Considerations of justice and care for Gilligan are therefore not as fundamentally opposed as her particularist interpreters would have it.

Furthermore, and even more importantly, although Gilligan's assertion is contingent and seems to imply for her that women can reach this stage *without* explicitly considering their rights, her assertion of contingency with regard to considerations of moral equality of the self with others is mistaken. It is obviously necessary rather than contingent that women consider themselves as deserving of equal moral concern, respect, or consideration if they are to move from the self-less second to the self-inclusive third stage of the ethic of care: how would they come to include themselves in their considerations of care if not because they consider themselves as equally worthy of such considerations, or because they consider their own needs as much as they do those of others? Now in so far as this type of consideration is a consideration of justice and I will argue below that it is at least one consideration of justice is in fact a necessary condition, logically and psychologically, for reaching the highest stage of the ethic of care as Gilligan conceives it. This is an important point, however, not only because it corrects distortions of Gilligan, but also because, more generally, it shows that considerations of justice are at the very heart of what to any feminist, surely, must be a version of the ethic of care which is preferable to the self-less version. Gilligan's ethic of care in its highest stage has therefore ceased to be a 'pure' ethic of care such as Noddings would have it.

Now one might object to this argument that Gilligan is simply inconsistent. However, while it is true that Gilligan is not interested in philosophical subtleties and is at points annoyingly vague or even contradictory, it is more interesting to interpret this particular point as indicative of an understanding of the relation between the ethic of care and the ethic of justice which is crucially different from that of a full-blown particularist. For the latter, considerations of justice are not compatible with considerations of care because of the metaethical divide between them. For Gilligan, by contrast, justice and care are compatible in one respect, but not in another. Thus if a distinction is made between considerations of care and justice and moralities or ethics of care and justice, it is clear that what may be true at the level of moralities or moral frameworks may not be true at the level of specific considerations or conceptualizations. In fact, Gilligan makes just that distinction in a later paper where she points out that we need to distinguish 'care as understood or construed within a justice framework' that is, considerations of care as they figure within a morality of justice and 'care as a framework or a perspective on moral decision". From this paper on, Gilligan refers to care and justice as different perspectives each of which 'frames the problem in different terms' and which 'denote different ways of organising the basic elements of moral judgment: self, others, and the relationship between them".

The difference between the perspectives is that care and justice appear within very different contexts in the two perspectives or occupy different places in the overall construction of the perspectives:

> *Within a justice construction, care becomes the mercy that tempers justice; or connotes the special obligations or supererogatory duties that arise in personal relationships; or signifies altruism freely chosen; or characterizes a choice to sacrifice the claims of the self. All of these interpretations of care leave the basic assumptions of a justice framework intact: the division between the self and others, and the logic of reciprocity or equal respect.*

Care as a moral framework, by contrast, is grounded in the assumption that self and other are interdependent, an assumption reflected in a view of action as responsive and, therefore, as arising in relationship rather than the view of action as emanating from within the self and, therefore, 'self governed' justice in this context becomes understood as respect for people in their own terms.

While Gilligan's notion of justice from within a care perspective is different from the idea of equal rights that she stresses in her earlier book, and while both representations of considerations of justice as well as her idea of the presumptions of the justice perspective are questionable and severely limited, the distinction itself is crucially important, since it opens the way for a more detailed investigation of how considerations of justice may relate to considerations of care from within an overall perspective of care (or justice), instead of focusing on the formal or metaethical differences between the two moralities. Furthermore, this distinction also clarifies where, for Gilligan, the main difference between the two moralities or perspectives lies. Note that I asserted earlier that it is not clear from Gilligan's book what contrasts between the two ethics are basic for her, and that I remarked that the contributors to the partialism debate focused on the formal or metaethical dimensions of the contrasts. The nearly exclusive focus on formal contrasts might have been avoided, however, by a closer, and ultimately more accurate reading of Gilligan, starting with her very first introduction of the ethic of care at the beginning of her book "The different voice I describe is characterized not by gender but *theme*' and proceeding with attention to the many places where she characterizes the contrast in terms of *content* rather than form. Thus notice, in particular, that the description of 'two different constructions of the moral domain' recurs frequently, and that it does not refer primarily to different formal features, but to substantially different claims about specific moral problems as well as different moral frameworks. Furthermore, a recurring contrast of Gilligan's is the contrast between the two perspectives in terms of their basic premisses, foci, principles or 'injunctions', or ideals:

> *A justice perspective draws attention to problems of inequality and oppression and holds up an ideal of reciprocity and equal respect. A care perspective draws attention to problems of detachment or abandonment and holds up an ideal of attention and response to need. Two moral injunctions not to treat others unfairly and not to turn away from someone in need capture these different concerns.*

The two frameworks thus provide, according to Gilligan, and in more technical parlance, different conceptualizations of the moral realm. Hence Gilligan has been misrepresented in the particularism debate, and with this misrepresentation a detailed enquiry into the relationship between considerations of care and justice was left out, too.

In what follows I shall start to redress the balance. This is all the more important since, while a lot has been said, at least programmatically, by impartialists eager to defend themselves against the particularist critique by spelling out how particular considerations of care are compatible with an impartialist framework or ethic, there has been a comparative lack of argument by theorists of care with regard to how considerations of justice fit into an ethic of care. This is partly due to the very small number of authors who have worked on spelling out an ethic of care, and partly to the metatheoretical construction of the ethic of care as particularist. Thus, as I shall argue in the following section, Noddings blinds herself to the recognition of principles of justice arising from within the practice of care by interpreting her ethic of care as radically contextualized.

In conclusion, much more needs to be said, and in much more detail than has hitherto been provided, about how considerations of justice fit into a perspective of care. The particularism debate has not only misinterpreted Gilligan, but also done a disservice to the development of the ethic of care and the discussion of the role of considerations of justice within it, by focusing on the formal contrast between the ethic of care and the ethic of justice to the virtual exclusion of a detailed discussion of their differing contents.

(ii) Considerations and principles of justice in Noddings's ethic of care

Whilst Noddings is not absolutely opposed to admitting principles in general and therefore should not be opposed to admitting principles of justice in particular into her version of the ethic of care, she accords them a very circumscribed role. There are other points in her discussion, however, where she presents an even stricter view. In what follows, I shall discuss two cases at length where, it seems to me, Noddings dodges the question of considerations of justice where they are at least implicitly at work. The first case will serve as an occasion to derive two principles of justice which are part of an ethic of care, as I shall argue. The second case raises the question of justice with regard to the justice of a carer's burden of care. Both cases thus point up the need for considerations of justice.

Consider, then, the first case: the example of a 'dilemma' for a carer given by Noddings herself in the course of her discussion of the role of principles. Ms Brown has promised to go to a concert with her husband, but her child has fallen ill. So she has to decide whether to stay at home with the child or to accompany her husband. Here is Noddings's description of the carer's difficulty:

> *Sometimes the decision is easy: the child is obviously too ill to leave, or the child is hardly ill at all and happily engaged in some activity. But often the dilemma is real, and we struggle with it. There is fever, and, while there is no real danger, the child keeps asking, 'Mother,* must *you go?' The solution to this sort of conflict cannot be codified. Slogans such as 'Put your husband (child) first!' are quite useless. There are times when he must come first; there are times when he cannot.*

Note, first, that the situation described here is an instance of what is commonly termed the 'circumstances of justice'. What makes it a dilemma for Ms Brown is the fact that there are two mutually exclusive demands on her care and that she cannot satisfy both. Her care, in other words, has become a scarce resource for which two persons compete. In making her decision, she cannot help but make a decision which is either just or unjust since she cannot help her-

circumstances, which are circumstances of justice. Noddings renders her decision as follows:

> *When she decides, if she cares, she decides not by formula, nor by a process of strict 'rational decision making'. There is a turning point.*

She turns away from the abstract formulation of the problem and looks again at the persons for whom she cares. Perhaps her child is still anxious and irritable; she receives his pain clearly. Perhaps her husband is merely annoyed, not hurt; perhaps, at some deeper level, he too wants only support for his best (i.e. caring) self. If she sees this, having received both persons, she decides to stay with the child [Her decision] is right or wrong according to how faithfully it was rooted in caring-that is, in a genuine response to the perceived needs of others.

What Noddings describes in this passage is a typical example of a decision-making process. There are two mutually exclusive alternatives between which she has to choose: meeting the needs of her child or those of her husband. Now any decision-making process of this kind, it would seem, involves two steps. The first step is the collection of as much information as is needed about the current situation, i.e. information about the respective needs for care, and, by inference, about the prospective outcomes. This is the step that Noddings would describe as 'receiving both persons'. But a correct and detailed enough assessment of the needs of both persons does not by itself generate a decision. As a second step, the carer has to compare their needs and decide to respond to one of them, since action can only ensue after one alternative among the two has been chosen as the right, desirable or, as in this case, the just one.

In a situation of conflicting needs and demands on the carer, the carer cannot avoid some harm from occurring, given that the failure to meet needs results in harm. The situation is thus not only conflictual for the carer, but *dilemmatic* because she cannot avoid harm from arising whatever she decides. She can, however, try to minimize the harm by responding to the greater need. In fact, this is what Ms Brown does according to Noddings: her perception of the situation is clearly though not explicitly according to Noddings's description that the child needs her attention and care more than her husband, and this is why she decides to stay with the child. Of course, she would not put her husband always first, nor her child, because what she 'puts first' the way she prioritizes exclusive alternatives is the person who has the greater need. Now this 'principle' of responding to needs in order of their magnitude not only involves the kind of 'calculus' that Noddings denies her carers engage in, but it is also a principle of distributive justice. More specifically it is a principle of *harm minimization*: given that some harm will result from her not meeting one of the demands for care, the best a carer can do is to minimize the harm she cannot prevent from occurring. But the harm minimization principle is also and at the same time a distributive principle of justice which allows the carer to decide whose needs to meet in preference if and when she operates under circumstances of justice.

Such a principle may not be explicitly endorsed by Ms Brown, but as a carer she responds to situations of conflicting needs in correspondence with it. Indeed, as a response pattern, the strategy to minimize harm could probably be observed in any good carer under similar circumstances. Now since no carer can avoid circumstances of justice, i.e. conflicting demands on her care, every carer has to have some sort of strategy of dealing with such situations. Given that caring consists of the meeting of needs, that is, given that caring as an activity is geared towards avoiding harm being incurred by others, a harm minimization principle would seem the most obvious candidate for such a strategy. An ethic of care, in other words, will not be complete unless it contains guidelines for circumstances of justice, and the harm minimization principle is the best and most obvious option. Carers may endorse such a principle explicitly or only tacitly, but it is impossible for them, short of acting uncaringly, not to endorse it at least tacitly, since they cannot help but encounter circumstances of justice. Noddings, then, is mistaken in thinking that an ethic of care does not contain any principles of justice. The first principle of justice in care that I have derived in this section is the harm minimization principle. There is (at least) one more principle of justice that I believe carers endorse and act by: the principle of equality.

Consider the following example. A mother spends the whole afternoon with one of her children, playing and chatting with him because he is ill in bed. Her other child complains that she hasn't played with her. 'It's not fair, the girl says, 'if you play with him but not with me. I'm bored.' What her daughter raises here is an issue of distributive justice: she questions her mother's spending more time with her brother than with her. Now the mother might respond like this:

> *Look, as you know, your brother is ill and he just needs me more at the moment than you do. You won't be too sad if you play by yourself for a while, but your brother would be very sad if I didn't cheer him up right now. I tell you what, though. I can see it's no fun being all by yourself. Why don't you join us for a bit, and we'll play a game that all three of us can play together.*

In this response, although the mother asserts implicitly a version of the harm minimization principle as a justification of her spending more time with the ill boy at the expense of the girl, she bases her 'compromise' solution on what I shall call the principle of *equality in care* (or principle of equality, as a short version): she takes her daughter's need for company into equal consideration with the needs of her son.

The principle of equality is not always compatible with the principle of harm minimization. It might look in the above example as though it is, because meeting the needs of both the daughter and the son surely must reduce harm more than meeting the (admittedly greater) need of one child at the expense of the other child. But assume, further, that the daughter's need is really to have her mother's exclusive attention, as is her brother's. The mother can therefore not satisfy both children's needs. Assume, furthermore, that the need of the daughter is not that great and that of the son very great so that spending exclusive time with the daughter would make the son suffer much more than the daughter suffers not spending any time with her mother (sick children are much needier of love and attention than healthy children). In this case, her compromise solution is not necessarily an optimizing solution (hence does not necessarily minimize harm), since both children suffer some harm not having the exclusive attention of their mother. But it is a solution that satisfies the equality principle since the needs of both children are taken into consideration and to some extent met. The principle of equality thus takes account of and, to the extent that it is acted upon, expresses, the fact that the mother loves both children and that the welfare of both of them matters to her.

As with the harm minimization principle, not acting according to the principle of equality would not be very caring nor very just. If it is part of the concern of a carer to maintain or enhance relationships and care a concern that both Noddings and Gilligan stress then meeting even small needs or doing even small things for those with the lesser need may be important precisely because this is a way of affirming and confirming the existence of a caring relationship, whilst the neglect of lesser needs at the expense of meeting greater needs as an unmitigated harm minimization principle will dictate at least in some situations may be a most uncaring and ultimately destructive thing to do. The aim of maintaining relationships thus arguably imposes the principle of equality as a distributive principle in addition to the principle of harm minimization. Again, upon reflection, this principle can be seen at work in carers' practice, implicitly if not explicitly, and, as with the principle of harm minimization, there is no good reason for not accepting it as part of an ethic of care.

To summarize my argument so far, two principles of justice can be derived from the practice and general framework of values of care, the harm minimization and equality principles. These principles are a necessary part of an ethic of care since a carer will invariably find herself in circumstances of justice and will use such principles to inform her action. Note that my argument is different and, in fact, stronger than any of the arguments about the need for principles of justice in an ethic of care in the literature. Typically, arguments for principles or considerations of justice are made on the basis that an ethic of care has undesirable features or consequences without them, or that there are dangers in the practice of care which need to be held in check by such principles. My contention is that (at least some) principles of justice form in fact an organic part of the practice of care, and therefore the ethic of care. Far from being extraneous impositions, as in the usual arguments a view which continues to imply an opposition between justice and care-considerations of justice arise from within the practice of care itself and therefore are an important part of the ethic of care, properly understood.

I now come to the second case which points up the relevance of considerations of justice for Noddings carers, and which conforms more to the argument that considerations of justice are needed to hold in check dangerous tendencies in the ethic of care (as understood by Noddings): the case of what Noddings calls caring 'deteriorat[ing] to cares and burdens'. As in the first case, Noddings does not seriously consider the possibility that this type of case may call for considerations of justice. I have argued above that the worst case scenario of feeling care as a burden may be an important situation for a carer in that it may make her question whether her burden is just. Noddings, by contrast, discusses such situations in very different terms. Either they are, for her, situations which do not raise questions of justice at all, not even potentially, but situations where the carer herself needs to be cared for, either by herself or by others so as to be able to restore her caring capacity: 'There exists in all caring situations the risk that the one-caring will be overwhelmed by the responsibilities and duties of the task and that, as a result of being burdened, he or she will cease to care for the other and become instead the object of "caring."' Or they are situations which threaten to import mistaken notions of care. Thus Noddings reverts to the strategy of rejecting principles and rules when discussing an example where a man does raise questions of justice with regard to his care burdens:

> What we do depends not upon rules, or at least not wholly on rulesnot upon a prior determination of what is fair or equitable but upon a constellation of conditions that is viewed through both the eyes of the one-caring and the eyes of the cared-for. By and large, we do not say with any conviction that a person cares if that person acts routinely according to some fixed rule.

The implication seems to be, for Noddings, that anybody who would act according to what she sees as principles of justice would at least be questionable as a carer. In this passage very early on in the book, the relevance of considerations of justice with regard to the 'burden' of care is thus swiftly ruled out of court.

Hence Noddings either dismisses considerations of justice with regard to the burden of care, or she does not even consider them in the first place. Instead, she treats situations where carers feel burdened as situations which threaten to undermine the ethical ideal, since a carer who feels burdened will not care as well, will not be as receptive and responsive, as a carer who cares joyously. The response to this situation thus has to be that a carer needs to look after herself in order to restore and maintain herself as a carer. While this is certainly a correct analysis of the situation, the difficulty with it is that it treats the problem as entirely subjective, i.e. related to the carer's capabilities and feelings, instead of at *least equally* as potentially an objective problem: if the carer feels burdened that may be because, in fact, she is burdened too much and probably, or at least possibly, unjustly.

The place where this failure becomes most obvious and most telling is when Noddings discusses domestic work which, for her. carers, is an occasion to 'celebrate the ordinary, human-animal fife that is the source of their ethicality and joy' and is 'filled with opportunities for receptive and creative encounters'. While Noddings does ask herself why it is that many women 'feel overworked and underpaid' doing it, the answer she comes up with is equally telling: women may feel they need recognition for this work which they do not get publicly, nor often privately, but strong women do not need such recognition. Hence women must 'learn how to maintain themselves as ones-caring through a general strengthening of self-image'. What is potentially an occasion for a critical discussion of women's unjust material benefits and burdens the recognition of women feeling overworked and underpaid is thus turned into an exercise of blaming the victim. Women who feel burdened are counselled to strengthen their self-image as carers instead of made to question their situation presumably because by questioning their situation they would put 'principles above persons' and thus fail as carers. It is thus in her idealist treatment of the 'burdens of care' that Noddings fails most appallingly, and that the root of the problem with her version of the ethic of care lies. It is her idealism which blinds her and carers who endorse her ethic of care-to potential objective wrongs, and which makes her version of the ethic of care an oppressive ideology. I do not intend to deal with this case at the required length here, but let me stress that this second case unlike the first, which illustrated the fact that (at least some) considerations of justice in fact were part of the practice of care points up the need for further considerations of justice and the inadequacy of Noddings's idealist version of the ethic of care, in parallel to the free-rider case discussed in the last chapter.

To conclude, then, both cases, the 'carer's dilemma' and the 'carer's burdens', illustrate that considerations of justice are either implicit in an ethic of care or are needed to complement it. While the first case has served as a springboard for the derivation of the two principles of justice hi care, the second case has served to illuminate the dangerous limitation of an idealist, agentcentred version of the ethic of care.

(iii) Principles of justice and metaethical positions

As a way into exploring how Noddings might respond to my argument that considerations of justice form part of and are needed in an ethic of care, and more specifically, to my derivation of the two principles of justice in care, let me note that there is, at least by the look of it, a puzzle about her claims about the role of principles, rules, or calculi. Thus, on the one hand, Noddings does not reject principles completely and agrees that deliberation at a more abstract level might be important for carers. On the other hand, as her treatment of Ms Brown's dilemma as well as that of other cases shows, she does refuse to accept that the decision-making of a carer can be done on the basis of or by reference to principles. She also often contrasts two ethical 'approaches' which she clearly thinks are exclusive in the sense that one cannot endorse both at the same time and that they involve opposite mind sets, as it were: one approach putting 'principle above person', the other, caring one, putting person above principle. Can these two positions be reconciled? They can, if we distinguish between the role of principles in an ethic *tout court* and the role of principles in the process of moral decision-making. Thus notice that Noddings repeatedly points to what she calls the 'turning point' in decision-making which, for her, is a point where a carer moves her attention from the consideration of principles back to the situation in order to 'receive' or ascertain it again. If principles cannot straightforwardly 'dictate' a decision, but play some sort of role in the process of coming to a decision, then it is possible for principles to have a place in an ethic of care, but to have a less prominent place than they have in 'principled' ethics such as Kantianism or utilitarianism. We can then understand the contrast of the two 'approaches' in Noddings as a contrast referring to the process of moral decision-making rather than to the role of principles in an ethic as such, and the existence or non-existence of the 'turning point' back to the situation at hand (which implies a weakening of the role of principles in the process) is what distinguishes the two approaches.

If this is a correct interpretation of Noddings, the puzzle is solved and she is consistent, but she is then not in a position to maintain what I described in the last chapter as her myopia with regard to principles: she could not reject them *tout court* because the rejection of the prominent role of principles refers not to the ethic of care as such, but primarily to the process of decisionmaking. She could therefore not reject my derivation of principles of justice in care on the grounds that they are *principles* of justice either, since it is perfectly legitimate to discuss such principles as long as it is not presumed that decisions about the distribution of care are made simply by subsuming such situations under those principles of justice. Nor, as I have argued in section ii, could she reject them because they are principles of *justice*, because it is obvious that, in circumstances of justice, a carer will engage in considerations of justice either implicitly or explicitly.

There are at least three metaethical positions which have historically been endorsed and which Noddings could endorse in order to spell out more clearly exactly what place she thinks principles do have in an ethic of care, both in the abstract and in the process of decision-making. The first position, endorsed by Ross, understands principles or duties, as 'prima facie'. This means that whilst it is possible to come up with a fist of duties or principles which are clearly valid and evidently true, the world is too complex to provide us with situations which can clearly be subsumed under one of these duties or principles. In fact, there are always several under which any particular situation can be subsumed, and this is why duties can only be 'prima facie': it is up to the moral deliberator in particular situations to weigh the various duties in a way appropriate to the situation at hand. Noddings does endorse Ross's conception of 'prima facie duties' as an illustration of a metaethical position like hers which, according to her, 'admits that (principles) yield no real guidance for moral conduct in concrete situations', but it seems clear to me that Ross's position is too committed to the validity of principles *as such* to be a model that Noddings could endorse.

The second position, held by Aristotle, is more radically doubtful of the possible role of principles. Strict rules and laws from which inferences can be made are simply not adequate to the domain of moral deliberation and action, which is the domain of the particular. Principles can only play a limited role because 'among statements about conduct those which are general apply more widely, but those which are particular are more true, since conduct has to do with individual cases, and our statements must harmonize with the facts in these cases.' Unlike Ross, then, Aristotle questions not only the role of principles in moral decision-making, but also their status and validity as such in any ethic. Principles can only be guide-lines or rules of thumb, rough guides rather than ultimate points of reference, not just in moral deliberation, but *as such*. It follows from this, and illustrates this point, that young people can be excellent mathematicians or geometricians simply by following the rules, as it were but they cannot be good moral deliberators because they lack the experience of the manifold particular situations and decisions that those with practical wisdom have, including the ability to generalize over those situations, and this experience is needed in order to form the disposition to respond to situations in the right way. Moral deliberation, as in Ross, is likened to perception rather than rational deduction (of which it would be a species if principles played a central role), and it is the quasi-perceptual appraisal of the particular situation that yields the decision. Hence it is not the role accorded to principles in moral decision-making which distinguishes Aristotle's position from that of Ross, but their epistemic and ontological status in an ethical system: while Ross likens them to self-evidently true mathematical axioms, Aristotle likens them to much less certain and much less reliable 'rules of thumb'.

Now, surprisingly enough, Noddings does not refer to Aristotle at all, but it seems to me that the tenor of her statements on principles would suggest her endorsing the Aristotelian rather than the Rossian model. Thus note especially her treatment of principles as 'guidelines' and 'economies of a sort' that a carer 'formulates and holds loosely, tentatively' and will be 'wary of'. The point, however, is that even if Noddings is best understood to endorse the more radically 'non-principled' Aristotelian position, she still has no good reason to object to a discussion of principles of justice in care, since even on the Aristotelian model such a discussion is illuminative of good practice. Certainly Aristotle himself had an interest in rules and principles, and especially in justice.

There is a third and even more radical position with regard to the role of principles that Noddings could take. Thus she might reject as inadequate the construction I have given above of the moral deliberation that carers engage in when responding to dilemmas (and other situations calling for a caring response). More specifically, what I suggested in reconstructing the principles of justice was that there are two stages to any process of decision-making the taking in of information about the situation, and the processing of that information to yield a decision and that the working of the principles of justice comes into play in the second stage of this process. Noddings might retort, however, that no distinction can be made between the perception of a situation or the ascertaining of the facts about a situation and the moral evaluation or 'moral processing' of these facts. For a carer, she might say, the process of perception itself yields an interpretation of what is morally salient and there is no second stage at all, hence no further process of deliberation is necessary. To become a good carer thus involves most crucially the formation of a certain sensitivity or perceptivity which, once developed, ushers in reasons for action without there being a need for further deliberation. What is stressed in this reply, then, is the centrality of perception, even more so than in the Aristotelian position. Perception, or, as Noddings would put it, the 'receiving' of others, is so crucial precisely because it is all there is.

Noddings herself has not actually taken this line, but she could do so in order to resist admitting that there are principles of justice. However, even on this model, it is not clear to me that it would be impossible to insist that such morally interpreted perception can be reflected upon and that what would be reflected upon would precisely be the patterns that such perception ushering in action follows. Those patterns could be described as following 'rules of care' or even 'principles of care' allowing for the required degree of flexibility, of course some of which would be principles of justice. Thus short of denying that anything can be said generally about caring as a (good) practice, I do not see how even the third position could ultimately defeat the quest for reflection upon the principles that inform caring as a practice. Thus even if 'generalizations will be approximate at best, and examples will need to be taken with the sort of "and so on" which appeals to the cooperation of a hearer who has cottoned on', that is, even if, when discussing principles, there is an understanding that they are not written in stone, one can nevertheless discuss them.

I conclude, then, that Noddings has no good reasons for rejecting the discussion of principles of justice that arise from within the practice of care, nor that of considerations of justice more generally. What is worth stressing again is that, short of refusing to consider any generalizations about care, there is no position which would provide the metaethical grounds for refusing to discuss principles of justice. I furthermore conclude that there is no need to take a metaethical stand in order to discuss considerations of justice because any metaethical framework except one that is completely non-principled will allow for principles of justice and this 'allowance' is all I need for the purposes of my discussion. I therefore remain neutral about the three metaethical positions that I have discussed in this section, although the second or third seem to me more plausible. What I have been concerned to show in this section is that regardless of what metaethical position short of a complete rejection of principles Noddings might endorse she does not have any arguments for ruling the discussion of principles of justice in care out of court. Since it seems clear that Noddings does not endorse a completely non-principled metaethical framework, I conclude that her objections against principles, rules, and calculi in considerations of distributive justice are mistaken.

(iv) The generalized and the concrete other

In the last section I have pointed to several metaethical positions which fall short of the strictly principled types of ethics such as Kantianism and utilitarianism and which Noddings and ethic of care theorists more generally might endorse. There is an extreme position, however, that I mentioned in my discussion, but did not seriously consider because it was clear that it would not be endorsed by Noddings: the position that general considerations, let alone principles, have no place whatsoever in an ethic of care. I am not sure anybody actually holds this position, despite the programmatic claims that can be found in the literature, so I might be thought to waste my time and the reader's time by building up a strawwoman and then destroying it. I shall nevertheless discuss this position in this section for two reasons: first, because there is a lingering tendency among ethic of care theorists to voice such extreme particularist intuitions and, secondly, because it seems to me well worth going into the reasons for resisting such intuitions.

Benhabib may be seen as referring to such an extreme position in her distinction between two different 'standpoints', that of the 'generalized' and the 'concrete other', which 'delineate both moral perspectives and interactional structures'. While the standpoint of the generalized other implies that 'we abstract from the individuality and concrete identity of the other' and see her as a 'rational being entitled to the same rights and duties we would want to ascribe to ourselves', the standpoint of the concrete other 'requires us to view each and every rational being as an individual with a concrete history, identity and affectiveemotional constitution'. As a consequence, if the standpoint of the generalized other contains, among other considerations, considerations of justice, and if the standpoint of the concrete other is that of care, it might be said that considerations of care and justice are incompatible, since the standpoints themselves are clearly incompatible. Corresponding to this distinction, considerations of justice are general in that they are about people as instantiations of a generalized other, given that considerations of justice refer to principles or general categories, while considerations of care are particular in that they are about people as the individuals they are, that is, about concrete others.

Now to start, I need to mention (in order to set aside) an inconsequential sense in which 'care is particular. As has been insisted by many, care as a practice is particular in that if we care for people we always respond to and care for particular others in particular situations of need. We cannot care for a generalized other because the latter is an abstraction like the 'average person'. There is, therefore, a corresponding sense in which considerations of care are particular, too: they are particular in the sense that they refer to the particular persons we care for. But by the same token, we cannot be just to a generalized other either, since justice or injustice is never done to abstractions but to concrete, real people. Consequently, considerations of justice can be particular in exactly the same sense, i.e. in that they refer to particular persons, even if they refer to particular persons as instantiations of general categories. If one looks at considerations of care and justice in particular situations of moral action and deliberation, therefore, they are particular in the same sense in that their object is particular. This sense, however, is inconsequential, since it does not distinguish considerations of care from considerations of justice.

It might be insisted, though, in response to this, that there is a sense in which considerations of justice are general and in which considerations of care are not. Thus considerations of justice generalize over a vast range of possible situations and people and are about people in so far as they are instantiations of abstract categories such as 'a person in need', 'a holder of rights', 'a beneficiary of distributive principles', or even simply 'a person'. By contrast, considerations of care do not use any general categories, according to this response, and are therefore particular in the much more radical sense that no general categories can be used, nor can generalizations be made in considerations of care. This response thus spells out the extreme position which I mentioned at the beginning of this section. I shall argue in the rest of this section that this response is mistaken about the nature of care as a practice, and therefore about the nature of considerations of care.

Let me concede, first, that the suspicion held by many feminists of general claims, rules, and principles which are also often very abstract is not groundless, given that the history of social and political thought is littered with the usage of general terms in ways which conceal, obfuscate, or deny actually existing differences. Thus the concepts of 'man', 'human being, or 'person' have been used in general claims that obviously abstract from men's experiences, perspectives, and circumstances only and generalize them falsely as those of men and women. What feminists should object to here, however, is not abstraction or generalization as such, but false generalization and unwarranted abstraction. Abstraction is unwarranted whenever it disregards differences which matter or are relevant to the question at hand, but is acceptable when disregarding irrelevant details. Accordingly, generalization is false when characteristics true of a subclass (men) are attributed to the whole class (human beings) without being true of all instances of that class (men and women). More specifically, then, with regard to the conceptualization of care and justice, I must be aware of the possibility of false generalization. As such, however, abstraction and generalization should not be rejected and, indeed, are necessary tools for feminist theory and argument. Furthermore, those who completely reject general and/or abstract claims commit the very sin of generalization that they accuse their adversaries of: they do not examine specific cases of generalizations with regard to their correctness, but reject *all* possible cases as incorrect, a rejection which is not even possible a priori.

Secondly, it seems to me that one of the points that my discussion of the 'carer's dilemma' case in section ii has illustrated is not only that care is a practice that follows certain patterns that can be described by rules or principles, but also that dilemmas force carers to think more explicitly about the rules and principles that they follow implicitly or tacitly in their normal practice. It is precisely when habitual patterns fail to point unambiguously to the right thing to do that a moral agent is forced to reflect on how to reconcile them, and this, in turn, means becoming aware of what they are in the first place. The very fact that a carer normally may not be aware of the rules and principles she follows, but is only aware of focusing her attention on this particular situation or this particular person, can thus not be taken as evidence that carers do not engage in more general considerations, or do not follow rules and principles. Indeed, as I have argued above, it would be morally irresponsible for carers not to reflect on their practice more generally in such dilemmatic situations.

Thirdly, general considerations also form part of considerations of care every time the carer uses the practical knowledge she has as and when it is relevant to the particular situation at hand. Thus any knowledge which informs a carer's response applies to the cared for as an instantiation of a general type. Take the case of a mother taking care of an ill child. If she knows what can and cannot be done about flu i.e. engages in considerations of care about her child as an instantiation of a flu sufferer she will presumably provide better and more adequate care than if she has no idea about how to care for flu sufferers. General considerations about flu, and more generally considerations about various types of need, conditions, or even types of persons, thus do not interfere with, but on the contrary, if sensibly used, improve the actual care provided.

Fourthly, any practice which one can learn and get better at usually has standards of good practice and rules to follow. Care is most certainly such a practice, since it does not come 'naturally' to anybody, although it may come more easily to some than to others. Some of these standards refer to the appropriateness of the practice and to the corresponding dispositions which have to be acquired, such as attentiveness and responsiveness, and these standards will be learnt from those deemed to be good practitioners in our case, good carers. Distributive considerations, however, will have to be part of such standards of good practice, too, given that circumstances of justice will be encountered by any carer, and there is no good reason to think that distributive considerations would be more general or abstract than other considerations of good practice.

Fifthly and lastly, care in the public sphere illustrates more clearly how general considerations enter considerations of care, in that it necessarily involves the more explicit use of general knowledge and standards and is furthermore subject to the requirements of impartiality governing the public sphere. With the rise of the modern welfare state and the corresponding expansion of the caring professions, more and more care takes place in the public sphere mediated by either an exchange relationship between the caring professional and the cared for or by the state which pays the caring professional to care for persons in need. Now one of the main differences between public and private care is that public care fails to meet the conditions which would allow for fully individualized, 'particular' care: it is not motivated by existing particular relationships and an impulse to act on behalf of the other on the basis of this relationship and the emotions appropriate to it, nor can it use the individualized knowledge that persons who know each other typically have of each other. It is nevertheless a response to needs, informed by general knowledge and motivated by a general commitment to care for those in need. Standards of good practice are also much more explicitly part of public care in that they are spelt out in professional codes of practice and the learning of these standards as well as the knowledge required for good care forms part of the professional or vocational training. Lastly, care in the public sphere meets the general requirement of impartiality by which the public sphere functions at the expense of personalized relationships. Accordingly, the principles of justice in care that I introduced above take a much more prominent role in care in the public sphere. Thus care in the public sphere consists of the meeting of needs in people under the constraint of the two principles of justice which I introduced above and in explicit disregard of existing relationships between people. The favouring of 'one's own people' in the public sphere is favouritism or nepotism and as such an instance of malpractice precisely because everybody's needs are to be considered equally (and to some extent met) in the public sphere, while the basic rationale of public health and social services can be understood as that of harm minimization.

Public care can thus be seen as a major challenge to any conception of the ethic of care which insists on the particular nature of care and of considerations of care, whilst it provides support for those interpretations of the ethic of care which do accept the possibility of general considerations and principles as part of the ethic of care. Indeed the fact that the latter kind of interpretation manages to bring out the commonalities between care in the private and the public sphere instead of obfuscating them is a further point in its favour.

I conclude, then, that the extreme position which denies the existence or appropriateness of any general considerations in the practice of care is clearly mistaken. I would like to add, however, a sense in which the insistence on the contextualized and particular nature of care can be accommodated. As I stressed in the last section, the fact that general considerations and principles are endorsed as part of the ethic of care does not imply the endorsement of a strictly principled metaethical position. There are various ways in which the role of general considerations and principles can be weakened without denying them a role altogether. One important factor that I have not mentioned yet is the role moral sensitivity, imagination, and intuition may play in the practice of care. Thus, as is stressed by holders of even the most principled of ethics, principles cannot be applied mechanically: the application of principles requires sensitivity to the features of the particular situation as well as imaginative sympathy. Intuition may come into play in the appropriate ordering of principles for particular situations. It is even possible that principles provide only very rough guidance and that a large part of what makes caring good caring and a moral practice is the acquisition of a 'responsiveness and yielding flexibility, a rightness of tone and a sureness of touch', a capacity to be 'ready for surprise' and 'resourceful at improvisation'. But the affirmation of some or even all of these claims does not imply that general considerations and principles are not also important.

In conclusion, then, the practice of care, while consisting of a concrete activity involving particular individuals interacting with each other, does not exclude and is arguably even defective without general considerations, standards, or principles forming part of considerations of care. The distinction between the standpoint of the generalized and the concrete other hence does not line up with the contrast between general and particular considerations, nor with that between considerations of justice and care. Hence the extreme position with regard to the 'particularity' of considerations of care and the ethic of care is mistaken.

(v) Care and relatedness

Before I can move on to consider the relation between considerations of care and justice in further detail, I have to address a last objection that some die-hard particularists might make to my argument in the last section. They might argue that the very fact that I had to use public care in order to make my point about general considerations as part of the practice of care illustrates that I have misunderstood the nature of care. According to this objection, care undertaken by 'caring' professionals does not qualify as real care: it takes place because the caring professional is paid, either by the person cared for or by the state or some other third party. It is a market or public sector relationship of service. *Real* care, by contrast, takes place between persons who know and care about each other.

I shall introduce the term '*relatedness*' to refer to this kind of personalized relationship between people. Thus by 'related' or 'relatedness' I mean to refer not only, and not even necessarily, to kinship relations, but to the kind of relationship that exists between individual people who have personal knowledge of each other, have a shared history between them, and who feel emotionally close and involved with as well as committed to each other on the basis of and because of their mutual knowledge and shared history. Hence I can be related in this technical sense to people friends, loved ones who are not relatives in the sense of kin, and conversely, the mere fact of people being relatives does not imply relatedness. Now it is this kind of relatedness, the objector might insist, which makes people concrete and real to us, more real than strangers on the street, and it is because we are related to some but not others in this way that we care about them and know how to care for them. Relatedness, according to the objection, is therefore constitutive of care. Public care, then, parades as care, but is not care at all because carer and cared for are not related, and it is therefore a service like many other services provided in the public as opposed to the domestic sphere.

This objection, however, does not strike me as very strong. First, it makes unintelligible why public care is called care in the first place. As I pointed out in the previous section, it is the same as care between related persons except for the lack of relatedness: it meets somebody's needs, it involves the same skins and virtues, the same standards and principles, and the same forms of general knowledge. The crucial question therefore is whether relatedness is as central to care as it is made out to be in the objection. Now it is true that relatedness calls forth feelings of 'caring about', and that in turn, it seems, is what impels people to act on behalf of those they are related to. The absence of relatedness, however, does not necessarily imply the absence of any impulse to act on behalf of others who are (more or less) unknown strangers. It seems to me that attentiveness and willingness to respond with care to those in need the two main requirements in a carer are dispositions which, if they are developed in a person, will make her care *generally*. In other words, caring is a disposition that has no inherent boundaries. Conversely, if there is no such disposition, caring even for those one loves is going to be boring, a chore, or a drag. Thus a crying child may be a stimulus for some to ask her what is wrong while it may cause the reaction of 'brat' in others and may make them want to tell her to shut up, whether parent or unknown stranger. Similarly, somebody's depressed face may be boring to some whilst calling for concern and care in others, whether friend, teacher, or stranger on the bus.

It might be objected that my claim about the generality of the disposition to care is contradicted by the well-known fact that people make very rigid distinctions between 'their own' whom they care for and 'others' who are left to look after themselves. My first response to this is that it may be true, but it does not prove that the disposition to care is not general, nor does it prove that people are 'naturally' selfish or 'naturally' only disposed to care for their own. With regard to the first point, it seems to me that boundaries to people's willingness to care are imposed through belief and value systems extraneous to the practice of care such as racist, classist, religious, nationalist, 'familialist', and other discriminatory attitudes which *prevent* the care disposition from getting activated. To the extent that people have such attitudes they impose boundaries, and to the extent they do impose boundaries they stunt their moral agency and development as carers. Now, as I have pointed out in the last chapter, it may be the case that carers need to draw boundaries if they are to prevent their caring disposition from being exploited, but there is a further question as to which boundaries are justified. Prejudice and parochialism certainly do not provide justifiable boundaries, nor does their existence prove that the disposition to care itself has boundaries.The degree or intensity of relatedness, by contrast, as well as the type of relationship between carer and cared for, may be seen justifiably to influence the amount and type of care given.

In elaboration of the second point it is worth stressing that the question whether care, sympathy, or benevolence are 'natural' or 'artificial' virtues or moral sentiments is very old and far from decided. I cannot answer it in any detail here, but the following considerations may give an indication of how the question relates to my argument. If, on the one hand, the disposition to care is 'natural', there are two possibilities: either it is natural and generalized, or it is natural but restricted. The first alternative is unproblematic for my argument. The second alternative, pressed by sociobiologists as the latest representatives of a long tradition of argument, may be slightly more problematic. Suppose it were true that the disposition to care were naturally restricted—a supposition which, in view of the varied evidence, I find more implausible than alternative, social constructionist interpretations it could nevertheless not be concluded that it is morally justifiable for it to be so restricted, that is, that we do not have a moral obligation to transcend our supposed 'selfish genes'. If, on the other hand, the disposition to care is 'artificial', that is, acquired, it raises important further questions about how it might be acquired by all, and this in turn reflects negatively on the sexual division of labour, given that the disposition to care must then be acquired by engaging in caring. If the disposition to care is artificial, in other words, the question of who cares in a society turns into an important issue not just because it raises questions of justice, but also because it raises questions of the possibility of social co-operation and cohesion, and the omission of such discussion in the past would seem rather unintelligible and irresponsible. Hence the objection does not cause any major problems for my account of care: if the disposition to care were naturally restricted this would not imply that there is no moral obligation to generalize it; if, however, the disposition is acquired, there is no deep problem about how people can acquire it through practice.

My second response to the objection based on people's supposed tendency only to care for 'their own' is that relatedness (in the sense defined above) does not necessarily imply good care, nor does non-relatedness imply bad care. It seems to me that the insistence by some theorists on the particularity of caring relationships is at least partly motivated by the underlying idea that care by and for non-related persons cannot possibly be as good as care by and for related persons. Two obvious points need to be made in response to this. The first point is that care by and for related persons is not necessarily good care. This is illustrated not only by the now pervasive evidence of physical, sexual, and emotional abuse of children, the elderly, and other so-called 'dependants', but also by the fact that not every person who is related to someone in need of care is necessarily their best carer. Thus relatedness may refer to a history of emotionally involved, but mutually or one-sidedly destructive patterns of interaction between two persons. Such interactive patterns do not allow the kind of attentiveness and responsiveness required for good care, and even less pathological patterns of interaction between persons may still involve systematic biases or blindnesses which prevent care from being given at all, or from being the care that is really needed. Cases in point may be not only sado-masochistic types of relationship, but also apparently less extreme cases such as the completely 'self-centred' friend, the 'insensitive' or violent husband, the 'overprotective' mother or the overly strict father, or a mother not responding adequately to her child's abuse because of her complete denial of her own past abuse. All this, of course, should not be taken to imply that abuse does not take place in the public sphere. But it does go a long way towards debunking the sentimental myth that care by and for related persons is necessarily good care or the only 'real' care on offer.

The second point to be made is that care by and for unrelated persons, i.e. public care, is not necessarily bad or worse care than private care. There are good and bad nurses and doctors as there are good and bad parents and friends. Notice in particular the earlier mentioned point that a lot of care if not all care requires skill and knowledge in carers. In so far as professional education involves the acquisition of such skills and knowledge, there is every reason to think that professional carers, in virtue of their training as well as their much more wide-ranging and varied experience, make better carers than 'lay' carers. Their actions and reactions are potentially much more self-conscious and self-reflective than those of 'lay' persons, and it is precisely this informed awareness about their care that may allow them to be better carers. Take the case of a professional counsellor or psychotherapist. Her training will have made her aware of the pitfalls of projection and transference in interaction between individuals and she is therefore in a better position to recognize and work with these emotional phenomena instead of being trapped by them as most untrained people would be. In the same way, indirectly expressed needs or strange symptoms will not be a problem for a nurse because she may recognize the condition underlying the symptoms or the vaguely expressed need for what they are, given her experience with such conditions or needs, while non-professional carers may be at a loss as to what they should do in those kinds of situations. Public care at its best, then, is more informed and hence in this respect better or at least as good as private care.

Lastly, let me venture an explanation of the kind of motivation underlying the definitional restriction of care to care on the basis of relatedness in order to disperse any lingering doubts about the adequacy of my argument. I suspect that the attempt to restrict care in this way stems from the distorted stereotypes we have of private and public care. We hold, on the one hand, an idealized picture of private care by and for those we love, a picture which obstructs the recognition of abuse and bad care as and when it takes place, while we have, on the other hand, a picture of public care which is worse than it need be. More specifically, it seems to me that the reasons why public care is often so bad have nothing to do with the fact that it is care by and for unrelated persons, but relate instead to the chronic underfunding and bureaucratization of the provision of care in the public sector. Thus chronic underfunding perpetuates a condition of scarcity of resources. For a caring professional not to be able to care as she thinks necessary because of a lack of time or other resources must be especially demoralizing, given her commitment to care which implies her wanting to meet needs and avoid harm. Under chronic scarcity of resources a carer must therefore be immensely resilient if her morale is not to be undermined by constant pressure, and it can easily be seen how such circumstances would end up producing burn-out and more generally low morale. They also force carers to use further criteria for the distribution of care which cannot be justified from within the perspective of care. Bureaucratization will be equally undermining of caring commitment and practice by imposing constraints extraneous to, and often conflicting with, the imperatives imposed by care.

In conclusion, public care is not necessarily bad if and to the extent that the causes of its shortcomings are tackled, that is, if and to the extent that the political will is there, the resources are committed to it, and the problem of bureaucratization is resolved. The important point is that these causes do not necessarily derive from the fact that public care takes place between unrelated persons, while there are, by contrast, some causes of bad private care that do derive from the fact that it takes place between related persons. Furthermore, the possibility of abuse is real in both public and private care because its occurrence is based on the dependency and resulting powerlessness of the cared for on the carer rather than either their relatedness or nonrelatedness. Relatedness, therefore, may matter emotionally and subjectively, but it does not necessarily make a difference to the quality of care. Thus one of the points of this section was to show that the appropriate theorization of care is hampered by, and requires the giving up of, various deeply ingrained habits of thought and presuppositions. I conclude, furthermore, that relatedness is not constitutive of care and that there is no good reason to insist on care by and for those related as the only true care. Hence public care is care as much as private care is, even if the constraints in the public sphere may be more severe and may lead to more severe distortions of care than those in the private sphere of care on the basis of relatedness.

(vi) Care and justice in public and private

I have readied the following conclusions at this point in the argument: not only do general considerations and hence considerations of justice form part of the practice and considerations of care between individuals who are related (in the technical sense) at least implicitly, but also care does not exclusively take place between related individuals since a lot of care takes place in the public sphere. I argued, moreover, that public care is not necessarily bad in virtue of being public, and that private care is not necessarily good in virtue of taking place between people who know and care about each other. Considerations of care and justice, then, arise in both private and public care. In my argument so far, then, I have stressed the similarity of care in both public and private. In this section, by contrast, I shall explore the differences between care in the two spheres as well as look at how these reflect on the relationship of considerations of care and justice in the two spheres.

The difference between care in the private and public spheres, it seems to me, is best characterized in terms of the presence or absence of relatedness as the ground of care. Thus whilst care in the private sphere is the outcome of a specific pattern of interactions between two individuals based on relatedness, care in the public sphere is an instance of an established function, taking place because both carer and cared for are filling preconceived roles (i.e. the carer is a caring professional, the cared for is somebody in need with either the money to pay for or the entitlement, *qua* citizen, to the care provided by the caring professional *qua* state employee). Jones's fourfold distinction between private and public roles is useful in elucidating the differences between care in public and private:

1. Private roles emerge in 'face-to-face, one-to-one relationships' while public roles are fixed in advance and to some extent standardized. Private role holders are hence unique and irreplaceable while public role holders are replaceable as long as they meet the requirements of the role.
2. Private roles have a unique set of expectations attached to them which evolve and change with changes in the relationship, while expectations linked to public roles are standardized and determined by the function of the role rather than by the personalities of the role holders.
3. Private roles have a symbolic quality in that they express the particular relationship which has developed between the role holders and in that the actions of the role holders express their attitudes towards each other, while public roles are not supposed to express any particular relationship at all. Public roles, if anything, are expressions of the impartiality of the public sphere and require impartial behaviour from their holders.
4. Private roles are 'organic patterns' which grow and whose 'end is the substance of this pattern rather than aggregation of components combined into this role only because they subserve some external goal' while public roles are clearly

and unchangeably defined on the basis of the function they are supposed to fulfil.

Not all of these points of distinction can be applied straightforwardly to the distinction between private and public care, but in elucidating how they do apply the differences as well as the similarities between the two forms of care can be explored further.

Note, to begin with, that there is one major point of difference underlying these various points: what shapes private roles and thus private care is the existence of individualized relationships between people over time, or, in other words, relatedness, while public roles and public care are shaped by the requirement of impartiality, i.e. the non-influence of relatedness (3), and explicit goals (4) which in turn determine the standardized role expectations (2) and the replaceability of role holders (1). Now the reason why Jones's points of distinction cannot be applied straightforwardly is the following: if relatedness is the underlying factor of the distinction in the sense that it implies all the points of distinction that Jones makes between public and private care it implies the endorsement of the claim that relatedness is constitutive of private care. Thus note that the four points of distinction can be understood to follow from such a claim: relatedness can be understood to imply the irreplaceability of private carers (1), the unique set of expectations in private care (2), the symbolic and expressive character of such care (3), as well as the unique organic and evolving pattern of care given and received by people (4). Accordingly, private care would be a completely individualized practice and essentially the kind of particularized activity that particularists ultimately had in mind.

I therefore need to clarify quite how Jones's points of distinction apply to private and public care. While there does not seem to be a problem with regard to the application of the points to public care, there is a problem with the characterization of private care. First of all, and with regard to his fourth point, while private care does form part of an overall pattern of interaction between related individuals which is unique and always open to change and evolution without obvious aim, care itself certainly is not without goal: in fact it has the same goal as public care, namely the meeting of needs. Hence in so far as private care consists of the meeting of needs and has this as its aim, it is in this respect closer to a public than to a private role. It also follows, and this is the basis for my claims about good and bad care in the last section, that it can be evaluated according to how well it meets this aim. Secondly, and with respect to the first and second points, private care is not irreplaceable, nor are the expectations of those cared for unique in all respects. Thus whilst it is true that relatedness makes people irreplaceable to each other, and it is also true that private care is given mainly on the basis of relatedness, it is not true that private carers are irreplaceable. If an infant is not fed by her mother, she can be fed by her father, by a babysitter, or by a nurse, and her need for food will be met. None of these instances of care are exactly the same because they are also expressive of the different relationships between the infant and the carer because in so far as the way care is given is expressive of relatedness it is unique but one instance can be replaced by any other as long as they meet the need in the infant. Moreover, and again in so far as care is expressive of relatedness as well as reliant on different degrees of knowledge of the cared for, the infant would be right in expecting slightly different care from these different carers. But what she can equally expect from all of them is that she be cared for. Private care, then, is entirely private only with regard to Jones's third point, that is, its symbolic and expressive character, but is less than private according to the other criteria. The one point, therefore, that remains and that reliably distinguishes private from public care, is the expression or non-expression of relatedness as that which determines patterns of caring between persons: private carers care (mostly) *because* they are related and their care is expressive of their relatedness, whilst public carers care because that is the role or function they have and their care must not be influenced by relatedness. Relatedness, therefore, remains the basic factor which is operative in the distinction between private and public care.

Furthermore, and even more importantly, relatedness does not only underlie and explain the actual differences between private and public care, it also provides a criterion for distinguishing their morality. While relatedness justifiably determines interaction and care in the private sphere, it must not make a difference in the public sphere and therefore in public care. Thus a private carer usually cares the more, the more closely or intimately she is related to the cared for. The care she gives, how much of it, and what kind, not only expresses the fact and the quality of her relatedness to the cared for, i.e. has a symbolic quality, but it also reflects the morality of the private sphere in that she is justified in caring for this particular person and not others precisely because she is related to the cared for but not to others. A public carer, by contrast, must not allow relatedness to interfere with her care. A doctor in the public health service cannot allow her mother to jump the long waiting fist for hip replacement operations, even if this seems an unbearable restriction, since to do so would be an obvious case of malpractice. Nor must a nurse be seen to provide more and better care for some patients only, except when different needs require different levels of intensity of care. Carers in the public sphere are thus, *qua* participants in the public sphere, subject to the requirement of impartiality, and one of the implications of this requirement is that they must not let relatedness influence their actions: what is appropriate and morally justifiable in private care, namely the favouring of those one is related to, becomes favouritism or nepotism in public care.

I conclude from this that the principles of justice have more force in public care in virtue of its being part of the public sphere than they do in private care. Take the following situation to illustrate the point. I have to choose between responding to a stranger on the street who has to be taken to the hospital and responding to my closest friend who has come to talk a very difficult problem over with me. If I decide to talk to my friend, I do so against the harm minimization principle which would have made me take the stranger to the hospital the stranger's need being somewhat greater than, but as urgent as, that of my friend. While hoping that somebody else will take care of the stranger, I would thus allow relatedness to qualify and ultimately override the harm minimization principle. Is such a decision justifiable? It is in so far as relatedness implies a certain commitment and obligation to the persons one is related to, that is, in so far as relatedness has moral force, too. My contention is that it does have moral force and that, in virtue of that moral force, considerations of care based on relatedness can come into conflict with considerations of justice in a way that is characteristic of private care but impossible in public care.

One might object to this that my decision is not morally justifiable at all because it is obvious that I should act according to the requirement of justice. This objection, however, misses the point that I have been trying to make about private care, that is, that relatedness does make a moral difference in private care and that, therefore, the taking into account of relatedness is morally justifiable or even required. If relatedness does matter, however, the situation is a moral dilemma rather than a simple case: the choice of either alternative is equally justifiable and equally unsatisfactory. The characterization of this situation as a simple case thus misses the moral character and force of relatedness. Hence what this example illustrates is how relatedness matters morally in private care in ways which are inadmissible in public care. It furthermore illustrates that considerations of care based on relatedness can conflict with considerations of justice in private care in a way that is specific to private care because generated by the morality specific to it. Public care, by contrast, in virtue of being constrained by the impartiality governing the public sphere, does not generate the same conflicts and thus brings out more clearly the two principles of justice, 'undisturbed' by relatedness, that I introduced earlier.

Distribution of care in the public sphere should thus follow both the harm minimization principle and the principle of equality in that both principles express as well as satisfy the requirements of impartiality in the public sphere: the harm minimization principle implies that, in the calculus of harms, everybody's need is to count for one and nobody's need for more than one, whilst the principle of equality requires that everybody's needs be taken into equal consideration and to some extent be met. Distribution of care in the private sphere, by contrast, follows patterns of relatedness and therefore the two principles of justice in a rather weak fashion: the principles of justice are satisfied if compatible with considerations of care based on relatedness. The principles of justice are compatible with such considerations, however, only in cases where relatedness is equally strong or weak between the carer and the prospective beneficiaries of care. Thus in cases of equal relatedness, the two principles of justice serve as tiebreakers (as illustrated by the example of the mother finding the compromise solution of spending time with both her sick child and her healthy child), while they are qualified in all other cases exhibiting circumstances of justice by differences in relatedness (as illustrated by the example of my deciding to stay with the less needy friend at the expense of the more needy stranger).

It might be thought that I am contradicting my earlier claims about the role of principles of justice in care in this section since I seem to be taking back much of what I claimed earlier. Note, however, that when I derived the two principles of justice in section ii I did not make any claims about their status or force. In fact, I could not have done so because I had to choose specific cases (cases of equal relatedness) in order to be able to point at the force of these principles. The minimal claim I made, therefore, was that these principles form part of the considerations a carer engages in under circumstances of justice. I had to await the discussion of care and justice in public and private in this section before I could provide a more detailed analysis of the differential status and force of principles of justice. What I argue in this section, therefore, is consistent with what I have claimed before.

In conclusion, the main difference between private and public care is the extent to which relatedness matters both actually and morally. This difference, in turn, has implications about the force that considerations of justice and, more specifically, the two principles of justice which I have introduced above, have within considerations of care. As an outcome of the impartiality constraint on care in the public sphere, and as an expression of this constraint, the two principles of justice override relatedness in the public sphere. In private care, however, the two principles are qualified by relatedness and have full force only in the special case of equal relatedness between the carer and those in need of care.

(vii) Considerations of care and justice reconsidered

I have spent most of this chapter arguing against various versions of particularist objections to the prospect of conceiving of considerations of justice as part of considerations of care and an ethic of care. This focus was forced, first, by the unfortunate association of the ethic of care with particularism that has been typical of the ethic of care debate as well as, more particularly, of course, of the particularism debate. It was forced, secondly, by the corresponding association of justice with impartialism and what I have called strictly principled types of ethics. While these associations can to some extent be traced back to Gilligan, they certainly took on a life of their own in the particularism debate by focusing the discussion on a metaethical level which then made considerations of justice and care seem incompatible because of their association with incompatible metaethical positions. This focus moreover prevented a detailed discussion of how considerations of care and justice are related at the level of the content of the two ethics. More specifically, it also prevented an enquiry into how considerations of justice could form part of an ethic of care. I have thus also tried, in this chapter, to redress this balance by deriving the two principles of justice in care and by looking at their differential force in private and public care. In this section, I shall draw the different threads of the argument together and draw some conclusions with regard to the 'ethic of care vs. ethic of right and justice' debate.

Note, then, that I have systematically avoided giving any answers to the question which metaethical model an ethic of care does or should follow. I have done so mainly because the most important task seemed to me to make the case for considerations of justice as part of an ethic of care at a less abstract level. I have therefore discussed the question of how considerations of justice relate to considerations of care by looking at examples taken from the practice of care instead of discussing, at the metatheoretical level, what the relation between the two ethics in question was. On the basis of this more concrete discussion, I have argued, first, that considerations of justice had to be part of any responsible practice of care, and therefore of an ethic of care based on this practice, and, secondly, that there are various metaethical models that an ethic of care inclusive of principles of justice could adopt. The metaethical question the particularism debate is therefore at least to some extent independent of the question of how considerations of care and justice are related. It is not, however, completely independent. Thus it seems to me unlikely that an ethic of care theorist would endorse a strictly principled type of metaethical model such as those endorsed by Kantians, utilitarians, or contractarians simply because the ethic of care is too closely linked to a practice and hence fits more easily into a virtue-based metaethical model such as Aristotle's than into a strictly principled one. Regardless of what conclusions about metaethical models one might want to draw, however and I leave those to other ethic of care theorists what should be of interest to the metaethical debate is that the outcome of my substantive discussion in this chapter may be used in evaluation of such metaethical models. Thus my derivation of the two principles of justice in care has allowed me to draw quite a detailed picture of the place these principles have in an ethic of care: how they are related to other considerations and how these relations are differentiated by the public/private divide. On the basis of this picture, it is now possible to return to the metaethical discussion and evaluate some of the metaethical positions with regard to whether or not they can accommodate such a differentiated picture. I shall thus use the outcome of my substantive discussion to throw a critical light on the particularism debate. In fact, there are two opposite positions in the particularism debate that can be ruled out on the basis of my discussion. These are the positions:

1. Considerations of care have strict lexical priority; i.e. whenever in conflict, considerations of care override considerations of justice.
2. Considerations of justice have strict lexical priority; i.e. whenever in conflict, considerations of justice override considerations of care.

The two positions are not formulated as metaethical positions, but on the basis of the conclusions they draw with regard to the relationship between considerations of justice and care. They coincide, however, with two opposed metaethical positions in the particularism debate in so far as these metaethical positions were and they usually were interpreted as implying the more concrete claims which I have used to characterize these positions.

Position 1, of course, is that of Noddings and of what I have described as the 'pure' or 'Noddings-type' carer in the last chapter. It is an explication of the particularist interpretation of the ethic of care. This position is illustrated by Noddings's barricades example: if considerations of justice and care pun in different directions, care overrides justice, and hence the carer will not fight against her bigoted relatives in the name of justice. Note also, and in a similar vein, the 'carer's burdens' case where considerations of justice are dismissed with the argument that anybody who follows principles or rules too strictly is suspect as a good carer. Position 2 is an explication of what I have called a strictly principled type of ethic or any impartialist theorist, most strikingly illustrated by an example of Brian Barry's intended to explicate the priority of impartial justice. If your son is wanted for an offence and he is hiding in your home you must not deny his presence should the police knock at your door. Justice thus overrides care, according to Barry, and it overrides care whenever they may be thought to be in conflict.

Given the results of my discussion in the last section, it is obvious that both positions are implausible because they are too simplistic in their structure to accommodate the differential relations between considerations of care and justice in private and public care that I have argued obtain between them. Thus Noddings is not only unable to acknowledge the role of principles of justice in the practice of care, but she also clearly models her ethic on private rather than public care. She therefore comes up with a framework that cannot make sense of the different morality in the public sphere, nor of the different moral constraints on public care. She thus also bars the possibility of expanding the ethic of care beyond the confines of the private sphere into a public and/or political morality.

Barry, on the other hand, models his position on a contractarian public morality which is unable to account for the moral force of particular considerations of care based on relatedness that I have argued is specific to the morality of private care. Nor is he therefore able to appreciate the moral dilemmas that carers encounter in their practice, such as in the example above which, to an ethic of care theorist, would be clearly dilemmatic whilst it looks like a straightforward case to Barry. Barry thus illustrates very strikingly the chill of a strict insistence on, or superordination of, justice and impartiality, which is well captured in the old saying *fiat iustitia pereat mundus*. It is that chill that has turned feminists and some moral theorists against impartialism. This, however, should not have been taken to imply that particularism was the answer, especially not a particularism without considerations of justice.

In so far, then, as these two positions can be taken to reflect much of the 'ethic of care vs. ethic of right and justice' debate in its stress on formal contrasts care being understood as particularist and justice as impartialist it would seem obvious that the discussion could not advance much. Much of the argument between the different positions was geared to show the implausibility of one position and then conclude that, therefore, the other position must be correct. If, however, both positions are implausible and flawed, the correctness of one cannot be concluded from the implausibility of the other. What both sides of the debate thus overlook is the possibility and plausibility of a more complex alternative, consisting of the position that neither considerations of care nor those of justice take lexical priority and that the picture is more complex than either of the opposite positions would have us believe. I have started to develop such a position in the last section by pointing at the differential role of considerations of care and justice in private and public care: while justice overrides relatedness and hence considerations of care based on relatedness in the public sphere, relatedness and hence considerations of care based on relatedness qualify considerations of justice in the private sphere. The main flaw of the two opposite positions thus lies in their oversimplicity which, in turn, is linked to their endorsement of the metaethical contrasts with which the whole debate has been riddled.

❑❑❑

7

Psychobiosocial Perspective to Understand Cognitive Sex Differences

Introduction

We have dissected the body of knowledge that pertains to the immensely complex system we are trying to understand. But medical science could not proceed unless the students can comprehend the way the pieces work together and can see the connectiveness and interrelatedness of all of the systems. Similarly, we need to put the biological and psychosocial theories and research together because, in reality, they are as connected as the mind and brain.

Myopia USA

Biological and psychosocial hypotheses provide two frameworks for studying sex differences in cognitive abilities. But this division, like any other scheme for dissecting the multiple determinants of human development, is artificial because these two types of influences are inextricably entwined we all are biological organisms that develop within a cultural environment. In North American society, for example, males receive more spatial toys as children and more rewards and encouragement for engaging in spatial activities like playing with building toys, joining various ball teams, and traveling on their own. They also have the male chromosome configuration, a preponderance of male hormones, and other biological indexes that define them as male. At birth, they are classified by the shape of their genitals and, on average, are somewhat more active and physically aggressive than females. Because biological sex and psychosocial environment are confounded, it is impossible to ascertain the independent contribution of any of these variables. All of the methods that have been discussed, such as examining medical anomalies, correlating twin data, and providing specific educational experiences to selected groups of participants can suggest only an approximation of the relative importance of each of the variables under investigation. Another technique for approximating the relative contributions of biological and psychosocial variables is to look to other cultures.

The underlying rationale of cross-cultural research in this area is that all females, everywhere in the world, share a similar biology, as do all males. Although there are obvious differences among people in their skin color, hair texture and curl, eye shape, and so on, the biology of femaleness and maleness is the same everywhere. Except for medical anomalies, members of each sex have the same chromosome configuration for determining sex, internal reproductive organs, gonads (sex glands), genitals, and sex hormone balance. In addition, cognitive abilities are universal in that everyone must learn, use information, make decisions, represent and communicate meaning, navigate through space, reason with quantities, create, decide, solve problems, and so on. In a seminal book, Cole and Scribner concluded, "We are unlikely to find cultural differences in basic component cognitive processes" However, societal and environmental milieus differ from culture to culture. Consider, for example, the implications of cognitive sex differences research conducted in a society in which sex roles are very different from those in Western cultures. Suppose that some hypothetical society existed in which sex role stereotypes were the reverse of those in North America, such that girls were encouraged to succeed in mathematics and science areas and boys were encouraged to be nurturant and to engage in more quiet activities like reading and sewing. If we were to find the same cognitive sex differences that we typically find in North American studies, then we would have strong support for the importance of sex-related biological variables in the determination of cognitive abilities. Conversely, if we were to find the reverse or a different pattern of cognitive sex differences, or no differences at all, then the psychosocial variables would have received a strong endorsement. Thus, one of the major advantages of cross-cultural research is that it allows the possibility of, at least partly, unraveling biological and psychosocial contributions to cognitive sex differences.

Unfortunately, high-quality cross-cultural research that has used comparable measures in a wide variety of cultures is rare. More than 30 years ago, Fairweather used the term *myopia USA* to describe the relative paucity of cross-cultural data designed to investigate the origins of cognitive sex differences. Although there is much more cross-cultural research available now than when Fairweather coined the phrase "myopia USA," much of it is still conducted in industrialized societies that share many similarities with North America and Europe. There are several reasons why researchers have been so nearsighted in their search for answers to sex differences and other psychological questions. One of the primary reasons for the paucity of research is that cross-cultural data are difficult and expensive to collect. Unlike anthropologists, who tend to examine cross-cultural issues, few psychologists have the necessary connections in other countries to arrange for data collection.

They also lack the requisite language skills to converse with foreign participants and foreign researchers. Subtle differences among languages and nuances that are lost in literal translation can render a research instrument that is valid in one culture invalid or even ludicrous when administered in another culture. There are also numerous experimental controls that are necessary in cross-cultural research. For example, much of the early research designed to compare Mexican youth with U.S. youth used poor Mexicans and middle-class Americans as participants. Not surprisingly, large cultural differences emerged; however, these so-called cultural differences were really created by differences in socioeconomic status.

Politics of Cross-Cultural Investigations

The majority of knowledge about cognitive sex differences comes from research conducted with participants in Western industrialized nations by researchers living in those nations. Very little sex differences research is conducted in Majority (sometimes called Third) World countries. Sex differences research is simply not a priority in underdeveloped countries struggling to provide enough food for their citizens and fighting for economic and political survival.

There are also political ramifications to research of this sort because beliefs about the roles that men and women should and do play in any society are always embedded in a historical, religious, and political context. For example, the "emancipation of women" was one of the tenets of communism as defined by Marx and Engels. The Russian newspaper, *Pravda,* interpreted the failure of Americans to pass the Equal Rights Amendment as tantamount to endorsing sex discrimination. In fact, there are large numbers of women in the scientific community in Russia and the other countries of the former Soviet Union. Detractors are quick to point out, however, that Russia cannot claim to be a sex-egalitarian society because there are still very few women in positions of power in the government or in the newly created countries. In fact, sexism is so blatant in many of the newly formed countries that emerged from the breakup of the Soviet Union that employment advertisements, even for professional positions like accountants or business managers, often specify that a young, attractive woman with "good legs" is desired. Whatever your political persuasion, the fact that a high proportion of engineers and scientists in the Soviet Union are women shows that if women are encouraged by society, they can demonstrate the ability to succeed in what has been construed by Western society as "traditional men's fields."

Cross-cultural research is complicated by the possibility that although biological indicators of sex are nonvariant, other concomitant variables could vary by sex between ethnic and racial groups. For example, it is likely that different ethnic groups mature at somewhat different rates. (Differences in the average age at puberty could be due to genetically programmed ethnic differences and/or environmental variables such as nutrition, sanitation, and working conditions.) If maturation rate were an important determinant of cognitive sex differences, as some researchers believe, then between-group sex differences could be due to maturation rate differences and not sex per se.

Unfortunately, the hypothetical example of a culture that differs from our own only in terms of its sex roles has never been found. In early research, world-renown anthropologist Margaret Mead studied societies with radically different sex roles for women and men. Her findings, based on data from three different cultures, used to be routinely included in classes on the psychology of sex differences, but soon after her death, her research was questioned by another noted anthropologist who believes that she misinterpreted the cultures she visited. (His actual criticism of Mead was much stronger he implied that she was "duped" or perhaps even falsified or exaggerated her findings.) Freeman also believes that the finding of societies with radically different sex role stereotypes was too coincidental to be real. Unfortunately, these allegations were made after Mead's death, so she was unable to respond to them. Thus, we are left with no strong data comparing societies with fundamental differences in their sex role stereotypes. It seems that cross-cultural research, like all of the other research that has been reviewed, cannot provide us with "the definitive answer" about the etiology of cognitive sex differences, although it can provide support for or against any particular hypothesis.

Outcomes of Cross Cultural Research

Williams and Best reported the results of an extensive cross-cultural project whose objective was "to identify the beliefs commonly held in many cultures about the psychological characteristics associated with men and women and to examine these sex-trait stereotypes for evidence of cross-national similarities and differences". They examined the sex role stereotypic beliefs of adults and children in 39 different countries selected from 6 different areas of the world (Africa, Asia, Europe, North America, South America, and Oceania). They found a surprisingly high degree of similarity in sex role stereotypes. Williams and Best coined the term *pancultural generality* to describe the finding that instrumental or goal-oriented traits tend to be associated with being male and expressive or interpersonal traits tend to be associated with being female in all of the cultures they studied.

Western Industrialized Nations. Perhaps not surprisingly, when we look at other countries with sex roles similar to those in the United States, we find congruence between their patterns of sex-differentiated cognitive abilities and the ones discussed in this book. A London newspaper, for example, reported on the low level of participation by girls in science and technology courses. There are more than four times as many boys as girls studying college preparatory physics in high school in England. Research on schools in England has shown the same sex-differentiated pattern of classroom interactions that was revealed by Sadker and Sadker in their research on U.S. schools conducted in four states and the Washington, DC area. Like their U.S. counterparts, English boys are asked more questions by teachers; receive most of the teachers' attention and; according to the report in *The London Times*, "monopolise science laboratory equipment, consistently depriving girls of practical experience." It seems inevitable that classroom experiences reflect societal biases about what is appropriate behavior for girls and boys, although I note here that some psychologists have criticized this conclusion because it does not control for other variables such as how often the children volunteer answers.

One country that offers the possibility of assessing societal influences on sex-related cognitive differences is Sweden. Sweden has a government policy that institutionalized sexual equality, including a parental leave policy for fathers as well as for mothers. In a comparison of sex role stereotypes between children, adolescents, and adults in the United States and Sweden, Intons-Peterson found that there is less sex role stereotyping in Sweden. Have Sweden's more egalitarian attitudes manifested themselves by changing the sex-differentiated pattern of cognitive abilities? Stage examined this question by investigating sex differences on the Swedish Scholastic Aptitude Test. This test has been used to select candidates for higher education in Sweden since 1977. Although it has a similar name to the SAT that is produced in New Jersey by the Educational Testing Service, it is a different test. The Swedish test provides six subscores: Vocabulary; Quantitative Reasoning; Reading Comprehension; Interpretation of Diagrams, Tables, and Maps; General Knowledge; and Study Ability. Stage reported that the largest sex differences favoring males are found on the subtests of Quantitative Reasoning and Interpretation of Diagrams, Tables, and Maps. Females have a slight advantage on the Vocabulary subtest, with no differences on the other subtests. This pattern of results is highly reminiscent of the one found with the SAT in the United States.

Although results from the Swedish Scholastic Aptitude Test suggest that sex role stereotypes may not play a substantial role in establishing and/or maintaining cognitive sex differences, critics will point out that it is not a fair test of the hypothesis. Swedish society is more egalitarian only in its sex role stereotypes than is North American culture, but the stereotypes that exist in Sweden are similar to the ones with which most North Americans are familiar. A strong test of the contribution of sex role stereotypes to cognition requires that we examine societies that are much more different from our own.

The Israeli kibbutz is another culture that was founded on a basis of social and sexual equality (all property is jointly owned), and sex differences are "less pronounced" for children raised in the kibbutz than for Israeli children raised in the traditional family setting. But, as in Sweden, the sex role stereotyping is a matter of degree, not of kind. In Israel, every male is a future soldier, and there is greater emphasis on scholastic success for boys than for girls (in keeping with Jewish tradition). Safir examined cognitive sex differences in Israeli youth and concluded that when they are found, they tend to favor males on all cognitive measures. In general, the patterns of cognitive sex differences found in Israel parallel those reported for the United States and other industrialized countries, despite the cultural differences and expectations that kibbutzim and other communal living arrangements would have resulted in reduced differences in sex-related cognitive outcomes.

A study of the cognitive achievement of White children and their parents in South Africa (Afrikaans) mirrors the Swedish and Israeli results. Both mothers and fathers reported that they regarded mathematics as more important for their sons than for their daughters. Correspondingly, more White South African males persist in advanced mathematics courses in high school, more males are identified at the highest levels of mathematics achievement (the Math Olympiad), and males score significantly higher on tests of spatial abilities.

You are probably wondering about Black South Africans does the same pattern occur? I could not find any research on cognitive sex differences among the Black majority of South Africa. This is not surprising because such research would not tell us much. Black children in South Africa continue to receive less education than the White children, and they receive it in seriously overcrowded, substandard schools. Any sex differences would be lost amid the massive other influences on academic achievement crushing poverty, discrimination, disease, and poor nutrition.

The countries that were formed from the breakup of the Soviet Union provide an interesting backdrop for contrasting the effects of socialization on the way cognitive abilities develop. In the early part of this century, a large number of American immigrants came from the countries that comprised the former Soviet Union. During the years following World War II, U.S. women were pressured to leave their war jobs, marry, and have children. The situation in the Soviet Union was very different. World War II claimed the lives of a substantial number of young males in the Soviet Union. Whereas large numbers of U.S. males returned home after the war, the Soviet Union was left with an entire generation of males that had been decimated by war. In 1994, I was fortunate to receive a Fulbright Award to teach courses in the psychology of sex differences and similarities and critical thinking at Russia's premier university, Moscow State University, and to study cognitive sex differences in post-Soviet Russia, so this is one region of the world where I have been personally involved in cross-cultural research.

The relative absence of old men in Russia is particularly striking. According to an official Russian guide, in the years immediately after the war, the proportion of males in the population was approximately 35%. Thus, many women never married because of the demographics of postwar Russia. Postwar Russia was left in rubble, and the reconstruction effort still continues. For this reason, women assumed many of the physically demanding jobs that were traditionally men's jobs, such as plastering and building construction and reconstruction. Women also assumed the majority of the jobs in medicine. Unfortunately, the assumption of work in traditional men's fields by women did not lead to sexual equality. The status of physicians in Russia and the other countries formed from the former Soviet Union is much lower than in Western nations. And, as mentioned earlier, women are still underrepresented in high-paying professions and government positions. The role that women and men will play in the future as Russia attempts to recover from severe economic hardship is unknown, but it seems that Russia will need to rely on its cadre of educated women to make the economic recovery it so badly needs.

In general, cross-cultural studies find that although there are differences among cultures, the relative skills and abilities of males and females within each culture are fairly similar. Consider, for example, a study that compared female and male performance on two tests of spatial ability mental rotation and space relations. The performances of comparable samples of adults from Canada and Japan were compared on these two tests. As you may recall from earlier chapters, the mental rotation test typically yields very large effect sizes, that is, large differences between females and males, with the advantage on this test shown for males. The space relations test tends to yield medium effect sizes when the sexes are compared. The size of an effect is usually given in terms of standard deviation units. In this comparison, both the Japanese and Canadian samples showed large sex differences for the mental rotation test ($d = 1.36$ in Japan and $d = 1.19$ in Canada) and medium sex differences for the space relations test ($d = 0.31$ in Japan and $d = 0.46$ in Canada). It is interesting to also note that, overall, the Japanese performed much better than the Canadians on both tests, so culture was an important variable, but within each culture, the relative performance of females and males was almost identical. Thus, both culture and one's sex are important determinants of performance on spatial tests.

More Isolated Majority World Ethnic Groups. Although we live in a large world, you would never know it by perusing the literature on cognitive sex differences. It is only by looking at a variety of cultures that we can understand how psychosocial factors interact with the biology of femaleness and maleness to create each of us as unique humans. One study that is frequently cited as an exception to the usual shortsightedness is a study by Berry that compared Canadian Eskimos from the Baffin Islands with the Temne tribe in Africa on a variety of spatial tasks. Overall, the Eskimos outperformed the Temne on every spatial test. Most interesting from the perspective of the sex differences literature, there were no differences between females and males in the Eskimo sample; whereas among the Temne, the males scored higher on the spatial abilities tests than the females. One interpretation of these data is that for the Eskimos, the males and females tend to lead similar lives. For both sexes, traveling from home and hunting are important and frequent activities, and both of these activities should help to develop spatial skills. Among the Temne, traveling far from home is largely a male prerogative, and the sexes tend to be more segregated in their daily activities. Although these results seem to favor environmental explanations of differences in spatial abilities, proponents of the biological position would be quick to point out that there may be genetic differences among isolated groups, which have a restricted gene pool.

Another early study that is of particular interest in examining the nature-nurture controversy compared two different New Zealand ethnic groups, the Maori and Pakeha, on eight different cognitive tasks. Brooks found that male children in one ethnic group performed better on two different spatial tests, whereas female children in the other ethnic group performed better on the same two spatial tests. Brooks concluded that cultural differences through different patterns of socialization develop unique ability patterns for each sex. With respect to verbal abilities, the Pakeha seemed to have a clear-cut advantage. Brooks concluded from this finding that verbal ability is the most sensitive to cultural influences of the cognitive abilities. It is interesting to note that this is the same conclusion that was reported in previous chapters on the basis of correlational research with twin and nontwin siblings.

Other reports from more isolated tribal groups are not easily interpreted. For example, it is difficult to know what to conclude from reports that in rural Kenya, girls score higher academically in Grades 1, 2, and 3 and boys score higher academically in Grades 6, 7, and 8, with no differences during the transition years of 4th and 5th grades, or the report that among the Mizo children in India, males get more items correct on the Embedded Figures Test. The lives of females and males differ in every world society, with many of the psychosocial differences occurring at the same time that biological differences become most pronounced. Even if we were to find a worldwide cross-cultural advantage for males on some tests of spatial abilities, we still would not know whether females would score as high or higher if they were exposed to male life experiences.

The Devalued Female. One truth that seems to hold up across cultures is the relative devaluation of what is female. In a newspaper article on helping couples select the sex of a child they are about to conceive, a physician in this field warned, "If we had 1,000 women coming to us in the next year, and all were going to have their first baby, and if all could easily select the sex, there's a substantial chance that we'd have 800 boys". This is a frightening thought as we quickly approach a time when sex selection techniques will be widely and easily available. The excess number of males in many countries of the world was documented in the first chapter of this book. It is important to return to this theme again at the end of this book because we need to consider the state of females and males throughout the world when we consider cognitive performance. The cognitive focus of this book needs to be interpreted within a larger framework of sex differences and similarities because cognition is only one of many variables that varies as a function of one's sex.

Equal participation in education by males and females is still a widespread myth. In 1979, women became the majority on college campuses in the United States, with the enrollment gap between women and men increasing almost every year since then (Many college campuses are 60% to 70% female. But what these data fail to note is that the large female enrollment is still found primarily in education, nursing, and other helping professions, which have less prestige and lower pay than the male-dominated fields. These data also change radically when we examine other cultures. For example, one of the first proclamations when the religious-based government in Afghanistan assumed power in 1997 was that females would not be allowed to attend school. Women were also forbidden to work, thereby leaving begging as the only way single women of any age could obtain enough money for food and other necessities. Perhaps even more shocking to Western readers, and largely ignored by the Western press, is the fact that girls as young as 12 can be and are bought as slaves in Sudan and other countries for as little as $50. When a worldwide perspective is assumed, it becomes clear that whether someone is male or female remains a major determinant in many aspects of one's life.

Changing Data, Changing Minds

Please try this important experiment:

Take a few minutes and reflect on the theories and research results presented in the hundreds of pages in this book. Think about your beliefs when you first picked up this book and compare them with what you now believe to be true. Have your beliefs changed in any way? If so, how? What information was most influential in changing your beliefs? If you have not changed what you believe to be true about sex differences in cognitive abilities, think about the reason for the lack of change. Did you fairly evaluate the information? Did you maintain both the open mind and the amiable skepticism of a scientific thinker?

If you are like most people, then you are already thinking that you're not like most people. In other words, most people like to think that only "other people" are average, but we are unique and not like the average others. But, like it or not, as you read the chapters in this book, you probably examined the evidence for and against each hypothesis with a bias for information that supported your own preferred views of what, where, why, and how the sexes differ and are the same with respect to cognitive abilities. This tendency is not surprising, because the preference for information that supports what we believe to be true helps us maintain a consistent set of beliefs and a fairly constant worldview. The data concerning cognitive sex differences have been accumulating at a rapid rate, and there are not only new data (e.g., new cross-cultural studies like the one conducted by Silverman) but also new kinds of data (e.g., brain imaging techniques that show areas of brain activity while normal people engage in different types of cognitive tasks) that provide support for new conclusions about cognitive sex differences. Shouldn't you rethink your beliefs about cognitive sex differences on the basis of this new information?

Confirmation Bias

The tendency to look for and use information that confirms what we believe to be true is a powerful and pervasive effect. It operates in a wide range of settings, and few of us are even aware of the many times that our own thinking is influenced by this bias. Confirmation bias is the predilection to seek and utilize information that supports or confirms one's hypotheses or premises while ignoring or discounting disconfirming evidence. It involves building a case to justify a conclusion that has already been made. When we reason, we evaluate evidence to reach a conclusion. In contrast, when we rationalize, we begin with a conclusion and then look for evidence that will support it. In building your own conclusions about cognitive sex differences, did you use reason or rationalization?

Consistency is the Hobgoblin of Closed Minds

Attitudes about controversial topics like cognitive sex differences are highly resistant to change because these attitudes are embedded in a system of values (e.g., suppose you believe that all people should have the same abilities), a social identity (as a female or a male), and other related beliefs (e.g., all the girls you know are good in mathematics). This web of beliefs creates a kind of barrier that makes new information that runs counter to the beliefs very difficult to assimilate. The unwillingness to consider new information is the hallmark of a "closed mind." Given all of the information you now know about the topic of cognitive sex differences, have you changed your thinking about this topic in any way? If not, was it because you closed your mind to information that did not conform to your prior beliefs?

Note that in this attempt to get you, the reader, to reflect on what and how you think about the controversial topics presented in this book, I have not tried to tell you how to think. Instead, I have presented the information in the fairest way that I can and have asked that you consider the strength and consistency of the evidence and theories that were presented and that you remain open to new information and ideas while also using the rules of critical thinking and scientific understanding as a guide. This is a difficult task.

Any reader who picked up this book in the hope of finding easy answers is certainly frustrated by now. At one moment the data seem to favor one conclusion, yet on reflection or the accumulation of contradictory data, each theory seems inade quate, subject to alternative explanations, or completely wrong. This state of affairs is not unique to cognitive sex differences. It seems to be the norm in all areas of psychology and in the other sciences that are trying to understand the what, when, where, why, and how of complex phenomena. In the search for understanding why the sexes differ in some abilities, we have amassed a considerable quantity of information, although we still have many questions without answers and answers for which we haven't yet formulated the questions.

One thing that we clearly know is that there is no simple or single answer for the many questions about cognitive sex differences. The answers we have are as complex as the questions we are asking. This will come as a disappointment to some readers who want a simple answer that can explain how and why females and males differ on cognitive abilities. The disappointment is not surprising because even sophisticated scientists who work in this area want a simple answer. I recently sat in a small auditorium with approximately 100 department chairs from graduate programs in psychology. Claude Steele, a distinguished psychologist from Stanford University, described his research on "stereotype threat" to this group. I hope that you can recall that his research showed that the fear that one might confirm negative stereotypes associated with one's group (e.g., female or male) actually lowered performance on difficult exams. This is exciting and powerful research, and the audience responded enthusiastically, so enthusiastically that several were quick to proclaim that Steele's research proved that biological factors are not important in determining performance on difficult tests. Similarly, I also attended a meeting of biological psychologists where Doreen Kimura, a respected psychologist from the University of Western Ontario in Canada, presented research that showed the cyclical nature of performance on several cognitive tests as a function of the proportion of testosterone and estrogen in one's blood. This is also an exciting and powerful finding about the role of hormones in cognitive performance for normal adult women. In this audience of biological psychologists, many were quick to conclude that biological variables are clearly the most important determinants of male and female cognitive abilities. I hope that you can see that both explanations are, in part, true and that the need to declare either nature or nurture as the winner" is a false dichotomy.

With some reflection, it should not be surprising that there is no single correct answer to complex questions. There is a lore among college professors that freshmen enter college wanting to know the correct answer to life's difficult questions. As freshmen turn into sophomores, juniors, and then seniors, the search for the right answer also changes. As students mature, they come to understand that not only do we not know the right answer, but we may not even be asking the right questions. This state of affairs is not particular to psychology because all of the difficult questions in the other sciences chemistry, biology, and physics, for exampie-are intricate and multifaceted. The ability to accept uncertainty and ambiguity is a sign of cognitive development because questions about complex phenomena do not have simple answers.

The kinds of answers that we can accept will depend on what we want to know and, correspondingly, the questions we ask. There are different levels of analysis for different sorts of questions. We know that there are average differences for males and females on some types of tests, for some types of abilities, and for different portions of the abilities distribution. There are numerous differences in brain activity for males and females for some tasks, but the link between the brain indexes and performance are still indirect and weak. Females perform better, on average, than males on some measures, with the reverse being true for other measures. Learning histories are always important (at least within educable ranges of intelligence), but learning is a biological and social phenomenon, and although everyone can (probably) improve on any cognitive task; some people will improve more quickly than others. There are multiple research questions whose answers depend on the age and developmental phase of the participants, the type of data collected, and the level of analysis (e.g., brain recordings, self-reports, test performance, beliefs about group and individual abilities).

It remains the task of future research to come up with creative new ways of finding and answering questions that may be as old as the human race. The number of questions posed by researchers is increasing as rapidly as new data are being collected. If the maturity of a field is measured by the number of unanswered and unasked questions, then cognitive sex differences is maturing well as an area of inquiry.

Psychobiosocial Perspective

The nature-nurture dichotomy has created a framework that has guided much of the research on cognitive sex differences. As noted in numerous places throughout this book, there are problems inherent in this dichotomy. A dichotomy requires an "either/or" answer or, at best, a "more or less" type answer. Instead, we need to change the framework in which we are thinking. This framework was created, in part, by our data analytic techniques. If you are familiar with the data analytic technique known as analysis of variance, then you already know that psychologists think of the effects on what we are measuring as being explained by independent variables and their interaction. Thus, it is common to think of environmental and biological influences as acting independently and their joint effect as an interaction. With a psychobiosocial perspective, we cannot partition variables into those that are environmental and those that are biological because all humans are biological organisms developing in an environment. Thus, biology and environment cannot be conceptualized as independent effects. The psychobiosocial perspective eliminates the nature-nurture dichotomy because within this framework, there are no variables that are distinctly biological or environmental.

In psychobiosocial models, cause and effect are circular, and we cannot tell where biology ends and environment begins. Consider, for example, the findings that portions of the human brain that are unrelated to reproduction are sexually dimorphic. Although this may seem like biological evidence of cognitive sex differences, recall that both the structural and functional differences in the anatomy and physiology of the brain could result from different environmental experiences and cause individuals to select different experiences from their environment or to alter the environment to which they are exposed. Original research by Greenough et al. showed that intellectually enriching environments caused neural growth in the brain and created new connections among neurons in the brain. More recently, Ungerleider used brain imaging techniques to show changes in cortical representations that occurred after specific experiences. What people learn influences brain structures such as dendritic connections and cell size; brain architectures, in turn, support selected skills and abilities, which may lead people to seek additional similar experiences, thus completing the circle of variables.

Similarly, the prenatal and postnatal hormones that are critical in brain and other nervous system development also respond to internal and external stimuli and the genetic messengers that direct development. Although this may seem like a clearly biological process, people respond to environmental experiences with changes in hormone levels. Individuals will then alter their environment in a variety of ways or example, they may decide to flee from a fearful situation or to engage in an aggressive response. Environments are not experienced randomly. To some extent, we make selections from our environment, and we alter our environment in ways that correspond to biological states. Any model of the multiple, sequentially interacting variables that cause and effect changes in hormone levels, brain structures and organization, the environments we select, and those that are correlated with our genetic predispositions must recognize the way psychological, biological, and social variables operate reciprocally on each other. Nature-nurture is a false dichotomy; they are as inseparable as conjoined twins who share a common heart.

Although laws of parsimony require researchers to accept the simplest explanation of a phenomenon, there is little likelihood that we will be able to respond to the many questions regarding cognitive sex differences with a simple answer. Like most researchers, I find beauty and elegance in simple answers single explanation for all of the differences. However, I do not believe that cognitive abilities are simply determined, nor do I believe that a single answer like "It's all in the hormones" or "It's all because of mothers' attitudes" will ever emerge as the origin of all sex differences in cognitive abilities.

The most important component of any psychobiosocial model is the reciprocal and simultaneous effects that biology, psychology, and socialization have on each other. A developmental psychobiosocial model has been proposed by Petersen. Petersen's model takes into account the relative contributions of hormonal influences, family, peers, and broader society throughout the life span. Petersen's model is depicted in. As you can see in hormones have the greatest impact during the prenatal and perinatal periods and through adolescence and middle age. By contrast, family influences are greatest during childhood. Peers and broader society assume a proportionally greater importance late in childhood and have a fairly constant influence into old age. Although the relative importance of these types of variables fluctuates throughout the life span, they all operate simultaneously and exert mutual effects on each other.

Nature Needs Nurture

In a review article on sex differences in the rhesus monkey, Wallen concluded that "nature needs nurture". His conclusions fit well with the psychobiosocial perspective assumed here. Wallen noted that male rhesus monkeys exhibited more "rough and tumble play" than females, but when the monkeys were raised without their mothers, the males were more aggressive than normally raised males, and the females were more submissive than normally raised females. By comparison, when prenatal androgen was suppressed in male monkeys who were reared in their normal family groups, they did not appear different from control males on any of the sex-typed measures. Wallen concluded from these and other studies that the expression of a host of sex-typed behaviors is biologically possible, but the ones that actually emerge and the extent to which they emerge are shaped by the social environment. Development is always in a context, and it is the totality of variables, both inside and outside the body, that determines what develops.

Into the Future

Unfortunately, there are no crystal balls to tell us about the changing nature of cognitive sex differences. No one believes that conclusions based on today's cognitive sex differences literature will remain unchanged even a few years from now. But where the changes will be and when they will occur are, of course, unknown. Predictions about future research results are always risky and sometimes humorous when viewed with the benefit of hindsight; yet, I believe that we will find that the magnitude of all of the sex differences will diminish as we learn new ways to teach and learn, because all of cognitive abilities can improve with appropriate experiences. Future technology may, however, create new sex differences. We know, for example, that many more males than females are pursuing careers in computer-related fields and males are scoring substantially higher than females on advanced placement tests in computer science and physics. The nature of the skills required for success in computer-related occupations varies with different jobs. Some computer jobs, like documentation analyst or writer, require high verbal ability. Others, like programming in "low-level languages," require mathematical ability, and still others, like computer graphic designer, require spatial ability. It would seem that almost everyone could find a niche in a computer field. Yet, computer science majors are predominantly male. If a major field of study becomes predominantly male or female, it seems likely that the skills stressed in that academic area will soon show sex differences.

Two anthropologists published very different texts on the future of women and men. In one book, Helen Fisher sees a better world because of the feminizing of corporate America a world where personal relationships are strengthened, greater compassion is found, and enhanced interpersonal skills enrich the gathering and processing of information. According to Fisher, these benefits will accrue from the increased participation of women in all aspects of the workplace. By contrast, Lionel Tiger sees the decline of males because women can now control contraception, a state of affairs that has allowed women to exclude men from the family unit. For Tiger, "the sex war is real"; for Fisher, "women are more interested in balancing work and family, so they much more regularly do not strive for the top". Fisher adds that men are, on average, better at mechanical and engineering skills, an advantage that will continue to be critically important in the coming decades. Thus, Fisher believes that men will continue as leaders of most of the world's large, traditional, and hierarchically organized corporations and governments. These books provide two very different views of how the future will unfold because of the changing roles and differing abilities of men and women. Predicting the future is risky business. Maybe one of them will be right, maybe neither.

Suppression of Knowledge Poses the Greatest Danger

It is not surprising that I return in the last chapter to themes that I introduced in the beginning of this book. It is critically important to a free society and to science to be able to investigate questions that may have unpopular answers. Research into the many questions about sex differences in cognitive abilities is fraught with political minefields and emotional rhetoric from every comer of the political spectrum. Flynn, a New Zealand philosopher and political scientist, recently wrote about the many moral and ethical dilemmas associated with studies of group differences. He eloquently explained how his own beliefs about social justice were tested along with his commitment to the highest scientific ideals as he pursued questions about race differences in intelligence. It is inspiring reading for anyone who is thinking about research on a controversial topic. But it is not just scientists and philosophers who need to struggle with conflicting values. I believe that all educated citizens have an obligation to support honest research on any scientific topic, especially ones that are controversial. Informed citizens also have obligations that extend into the way the data are being interpreted and used, the way numbers are translated into conclusions, and the way conclusions from social science research are used to determine public policies. Of course, I am talking about you, the reader. Despite the risks of misusing research data for political purposes social correctness or biological politics the greatest risk is in the failure to seek answers for the most controversial questions. It is these questions that are most in need of honest inquiry. The greatest danger lies in censorship, even self-censorship, not in the open scientific study of controversial issues.

Education for the 21st Century

Today's young people are tomorrow's citizens, and the future is in their hands. How can we best prepare them for life in the 21st century and ensure that every individual develops her or his unique abilities to their fullest? Here are some suggestions for educators, parents, and other concerned citizens:

1. Separate the fact that there are average differences between males and females in some cognitive abilities from the tendency to evaluate these differences as "better" or "worse." This is an important distinction regardless of the nature of the group. Do not permit the misuse of data for the advancement of biological politics, political correctness, or any other ideology. The truth about sex differences in cognitive abilities depends on the nature of the cognitive task, the range of ability that is tested, the age and education of the participants, and numerous other modifying and context variables. There are intellectual areas in which females excel and others in which males excel; these data do not support the notion of a smarter sex, nor do they mean that the differences are immutable.
2. The research summarized here is based on group averages, and no one is average. These results cannot be applied to any

individual because there is a great deal of overlap in all of the distributions of abilities. For example, even though boys outnumber girls among those who are in the most gifted abilities range on standardized tests of mathematical achievement, there are many girls in this elite group. Similarly, boys excel in some tests of language usage, even though there are many more verbal tasks that show an average advantage for girls. We cannot afford to write off anyone or allow group membership to limit talent development.

3. Recent research has shown that beliefs about group differences exert powerful effects on thoughts and behaviors that occur without conscious awareness. These results highlight the importance of understanding stereotypes and offer a pessimistic outlook for the ease with which prejudice can be attenuated. For this reason, all of the stakeholders in education need to examine school texts for possible bias and speak to teachers and counselors about the nature of their group-based messages. We cannot pretend that children will select options that are best suited for their individual abilities and interests if we do not give them real choices.
4. The hormone-like chemicals that are polluting our environment are having negative effects on the animals that live in and near the polluted areas. Alterations to the hormone-sensitive reproductive organs of those animals provide reason to believe that these chemicals can affect the hormone-sensitive regions of the brain that support human cognitive functioning. No one can predict the long-term consequences of dumping chemicals, particularly pesticides, that mimic the actions of sex hormones. It is possible that they will alter the intelligence of humans who are exposed to them, a hypothesis that remains untested.
5. Support research on human cognition. We may be close to genuine breakthroughs in cognitive aging. New reports show that estrogen therapy can delay or reduce the occurrence of Alzheimer's disease in elderly women. Although the research on the effects of testosterone replacement therapy is decades behind that of estrogen replacement, both offer the possibility of great hope to an aging society.

6. Boys mature later than girls. Be sure that flexible criteria are used when making assignments to low-ability groups in the primary grades, especially in reading. Some of the boys will catch up with their peers, if they are not allowed to fall too far behind.
7. We have remedial instruction for reading and mathematics, but spatial reasoning, a skill that might benefit more girls, is virtually never taught in school. There is ample evidence that training with spatial tasks leads to improved achievement on spatial tests. Researchers and others need to provide all children with opportunities to develop spatial reasoning skills.
8. Most of the standardized tests that are used for admissions to college, graduate and professional schools, programs for gifted youth, and scholarships underpredict female performance and overpredict male performance. Be sure that multiple measures of ability and achievement are used in these decisions, especially course grades and tests of writing, which tend to favor females.
9. There are no cognitive reasons to support sex-segregated education. The fact that girls get better grades in every subject shows that they are learning at least as well as boys. For those concerned with increasing the number of females in science and math, the problem lies in convincing more females that "math counts" and to make academic and career choices that are "math-wise."
10. Interpret research findings with an amiable skepticism, and examine conclusions to determine if they are data-based. Conclusions about a topic as complex as cognitive sex differences will rest on the cumulative results of many studies. Although each person has social-political preferences for particular types of explanations, it is also necessary to strive to maintain an open-minded fairness when assessing a variety of theoretical and empirical findings, including the conclusions presented in this book. Explain the many pitfalls of this sort of research whenever you hear simple statements like "It's all in the hormones," or "It's all in the mother's attitude" are being made.
11. Remember that the brain remains plastic throughout life, which means that it is altered in response to experiences even

into very old age. Work to keep old age a time of useful activity. This is one benefit that you personally can reap when you enter your own old age.

Sex Differences

It seems safe to assume that most Americans and American allies would agree that the U.S. Air Force should have highly qualified officers. To ensure that this is so, prospective officers take a test that measures their verbal, quantitative, and spatial ability. In general, results obtained with this test agree with the sex differences literature in these areas, with females scoring higher on verbal ability and males scoring higher on quantitative and spatial ability. Because spatial ability seems particularly important for air force officers, who often need to rely on aerial landmarks and spatial coordinates, it is likely that many women are disqualified on the basis of this test. In fact, 98% of all student aviators are male.

In an examination of the question of whether females can, on average, become as qualified for air force officer duties as men, McCloy and Koonce trained women and men on standard simulated flight maneuvers. They found that men were faster on learning the flight tasks than the women were. But, as they pointed out, is this the right question? The more important question concerns the level of ability after training. Were women as good as men? The dependent measure in this study was the number of trials to criterion. In other words, the women required more training trials than the men did to learn a particular task. Perhaps the most important point is that the women apparently were as good as the men when they completed the training. These results are in accord with the general finding that spatial skills are trainable. If we rely on tests of abilities to decide who may enter training programs, we will miss able candidates who can learn to perform as well as their peers who scored higher on these tests prior to instruction.

We do not know why the women in McCloy and Koonce experiment required more trials to learn the same flight maneuvers as the men. It could be due to biological or psychosocial reasons, or both, or some other yet undiscovered difference between the sexes. Although the etiology of cognitive sex differences is very important from a theoretical perspective, it is irrelevant in most applied settings. With appropriate training, the sex differences in this study disappeared. We also do not know if the women who received this training will be able to transfer their new spatial ability to other novel spatial tasks as quickly as the men can. In other words, if they are faced with a new and different spatial task, will they now perform it as quickly as their male counterparts? This remains another important question for future research.

The example of the air force officers applies in other settings as well. Every teacher knows that some students will take longer to learn certain concepts than others. If one student takes a half hour to complete a homework assignment and another student takes 45 minutes, the difference is unimportant in most contexts. The important fact is that both students now know and understand something that they did not know before and, after training, both are able to perform tasks that require the use of the newly acquired knowledge.

It is important to keep in mind a point that has been reiterated throughout this book. The experimental results that have been reviewed concern average differences obtained from groups of men and women, and no one is average. The data reviewed in this text are largely irrelevant when making decisions about individuals. They should never be used to justify or predict anyone's success or failure. There is considerable between-sex overlap with respect to these abilities.

The literature on sex differences has been proliferating in recent years because the questions are of profound human interest. A firestorm of interest is ignited every time the media carries headlines like those associated with Harris' report that parents' behaviors have little effect on the psychological outcomes of their children or Shayowitz et al.'s study showing that when women take hormone replacement therapy they show different patterns of brain activation than when they take a placebo. Both of these reports made front-page news in the country's largest newspapers and were the subject of television and radio news programs. I hope that every reader of this text will understand the complexities, limitations, and implications of research of this sort. The next time you read or hear about research findings on cognitive sex differences, you have all the rights and obligations of informed consumers. This knowledge should empower you.

❐❐❐

8

Women's International Human Rights Law

Introduction

International human rights law has not yet been applied effectively to redress the disadvantages and injustices experienced by women by reason only of their being women. In this sense, respect for human rights fails to be "universal." The reasons for this general failure to enforce women's human rights are complex and vary from country to country. They include lack of understanding of the systemic nature of the subordination of women, failure to recognize the need to characterize the subordination of women as a human rights violation, and lack of state practice to condemn discrimination against women. Moreover, there has been an unwillingness by traditional human rights groups to focus on violations of women's rights, and a lack of understanding by women's groups of the potential of international human rights law to vindicate women's rights.

This chapter reports a consultation of lawyers from Africa, the Americas, Asia, Australia, and Europe held at the Faculty of Law, University of Toronto, in August 1992. The participants brought legal theory and practice to bear on the relationship between international human rights and women's rights in order to develop legal strategies to promote and protect women's international human rights. This chapter is *a* report of that consultation, but by no means *the* report. There are as many reports as participants, but the real impact of the event will appear only when the findings of the consultation are brought to bear on the prevention, investigation, and punishment of violations of women's human rights.

The intention is to offer some idea of the multiple perspectives that emerged on the consultation themes:

1. to review the progress of women's rights and identify challenges and prospects;
2. to recharacterize internationally protected human rights to accommodate women's experiences of injustice;
3. to guarantee specific human rights of women; and
4. to make international human rights law more effective for women.

Progress, Challenges and Prospects

Hilary Charlesworth, of the Faculty of Law, University of Adelaide, opened the consultation by raising a fundamental question:

> *Do legal rights really offer anything to women? Women's disadvantages are often based on structural injustice and winning a case in court will not change this.*

Her answer was that, "Because women in most societies are starting in such a disadvantaged position, rights discourse offers a significant vocabulary to formulate political and social grievances which is recognized by the powerful."

Celina Romany, of the City University of New York Law School, answered the question differently. She said that rights could be far more powerful if women were not limited by the ways in which men talk about rights, and encouraged women to make "rights talk" their own. She explained that rights are defined by who talks about them, the language that is used, and the process of talking about them. She recommended that women, their language and their ways of talking about their experiences of injustice need to make a far greater contribution to the development of international human rights law. Participants agreed that many more women, and women from many diverse backgrounds, should talk about the kind of content that should be added to women's rights. Andrew Byrnes, of the Faculty of Law, University of Hong Kong, proposed that we need to make "a concerted effort to expand the range of participants in that dialogue, and to wrest some of the power of defining and speaking from narrow androcentric models to address issues of central concern to women."

Other participants questioned the validity of the rights discourse. Adetoun Ilumoka, a legal practitioner from Lagos, Nigeria, said that the rights discourse in Africa is not meaningful, explaining that the severity of socioeconomic problems faced by women in countries undergoing structural adjustment may require a basic needs strategy rather than a rights strategy. Radhika Coomaraswamy, of the International Centre for Ethnic Studies in Colombo, Sri Lanka, said that in Asia the rights discourse is weak, in part because it privileges free, independent women, whereas Asian women tend to be attached to their communities, castes, or ethnic groups.The consultation adopted the working presumption that there should be a relationship between international human rights and women's rights. However, no one lost sight of the limitations of a rights strategy and the fact that its effectiveness would vary from culture to culture. Participants stressed the importance of expanding understanding of the context of women's subordination, especially where oppression is exacerbated by poverty or ethnic status, and agreed that the means chosen to combat discrimination will need to be varied according to its particular contexts. Asma Halim, a legal practitioner from Khartoum, Sudan, observed that, while the nature of subordination and thus the means to combat it may vary, "we must not lose sight of the fact that we are subordinated *because we are women*" and that the goal of eliminating all forms of subordination of women remains universal.

Whose Rights?

In determining whether recharacterization might be effective to protect women's rights internationally, Charlesworth raised a second fundamental question that pervaded discussions at the consultation: Can women's rights be universal? Put another way, is the idea of women's international human rights, premised as it is on the fact that women worldwide suffer from patriarchy, misconceived? Is the pervasive devaluation of women's lives enough to link women in the effort to add a gender dimension to international human rights? Charlesworth sketched three feminist approaches that might serve to recharacterize rights in order to make them more universally applicable by better accommodating women's pervasive experiences of injustice:

- Liberal feminism attempts to realize the equal treatment guaranteed by existing law, and thereby discounts intrinsic differences between men and women. A problem with this approach is that it fails to understand the structural imbalance of power between men and women and the systemic nature of discrimination.
- The goal of cultural feminism is to celebrate the differences between masculine and feminine ways of reasoning. This approach may lead to marginalization of women's rights because presenting them as different from men's needs may induce the response that they are less worthy of resources.
- The purpose of radical feminism is to transform the masculine world where inequality is based on systemic domination and subordination of women by men. This approach is problematic strategically when it requires revolutionary change in a conservative community that is ready at most for evolutionary change.

Participants agreed that these approaches or a mix of them might be useful in recharacterizing international human rights law to be more responsive to the degradation of women. However, they cautioned that feminist recharacterization of law in one type of society cannot be imported wholesale either into other types of societies or into the international human rights system.

The distinction between the public and private sectors of society offers an example of the insights and pitfalls of applying Western feminist theories to other social and legal systems. The distinction, long a target of feminist critiques in Western liberal societies for masking women's oppression, may manifest itself to different effects in other societies, and may illuminate areas of otherwise unobserved subordination. Charlesworth explained that "what is public in one society may well be private in another," but that, whether a matter is considered public or private, it is the women's domain that is consistently devalued.

The public/private distinctions can be perceived in at least two ways. In the first the public sector, where legal and political order exist, is contrasted with the private sector of home and family, to which regulation is deemed inappropriate. Charlesworth noted that this distinction is gendered because women operate in the private sector, where abuses such as domestic violence and degradation are invisible and unregulated by the law. The second is similar to public and private ownership. The public sector is constituted by the state and its agencies, and the private sector is composed of the vast array of nonstate activities.

Manfred Nowak, of the *Ludwig Boltzmann Institut für Menschenrechte* and the Federal Academy of Public Administration, Vienna, Austria, thought the second distinction is more important to international human rights law because it corresponds to the classical theory of state responsibility for human rights violations. It is the state that has to provide effective protection and remedies against human rights violations. International law of state responsibility requires governments to respect, ensure, and protect women's international human rights; when they fail to do so, sanctions can be enforced. International law doctrine now goes beyond the classical state duty not to interfere with individual human rights, to hold states accountable for not acting positively to ensure rights. Moreover, Nowak explained, international law now obligates states to use due diligence to prevent, investigate, and punish systemic and egregious human rights violations between private actors. Nowak acknowledged that state responsibility for individual abusers applies only at one step removed from their direct wrongdoing, but argued that this limitation follows from the general nature of international law, not from any gender bias.

Charlesworth responded to this argument by wondering whether, had women been more influential in the development of international law, they would have constructed it more readily to reach violations of human dignity that dominate women's lives, such as domestic violence.

Legitimize Rights in Different Cultures

A third fundamental question discussed throughout the consultation was How can universal human rights be legitimized in radically different societies without succumbing to either homogenizing universalism or the paralysis of cultural relativism?

Coomaraswamy analyzed the barriers to "indigenizing" rights in South Asia. She emphasized the need to avoid the "Orientalist trap" of dividing the world into bipolar categories. Those in the West must guard against the idea that the West is progressive on women's rights and the East is barbaric and backward. Those in the East must be equally cautious not to subscribe to the reverse notion that accepts the East/West distinction, but believes that the East is superior, more communal, and less self-centered with no place for an "adversarial" concept of rights. She cited the coexistence of the two traditions in South Asia to illustrate the dangers of oversimplification.

Coomaraswamy started from the presumption that, for human rights to be effective, they have to become a respected part of the culture and traditions of a given society. In South Asia, the institution of law is generally viewed with deep suspicion and often hatred because it is seen as the central instrument employed by colonizing powers to replace indigenous cultural, religious, and social traditions with the mechanisms of the modern Western nation state.

When the law of women's human rights is associated with an impersonal and homogenizing Western state, the rights are discredited. Coomaraswamy proposed that the future of human rights in South Asia does not lie with the state but with the confluence of the interests of the state and movements in civil society. She cautioned that "unless human rights values take root in civil society and unless civil institutions and non-governmental organizations (NGOs) take up the cause, then women's rights as human rights will have no resonance in the social institutions concerned."

She cited the case of Roop Kanwar, a university student who was burned alive on her husband's funeral pyre in Deorala, Rajasthan, as an example of the dissonance between women's rights and ethnic identity, explaining that Urban centered women's groups as well as groups of women from all over India were horrified and organized a march in Rajasthan. The Rajasthanis retaliated by filling the streets with thousands of their own ethnic group: the right to commit sati, they claimed, was part of their ethnic culture. After months of delay, the police finally arrested Roop Kanwar's father-in-law and five other members of the family for abetment to suicide. Three months later, the Indian Parliament passed a tough law banning sati, even though an old law already existed, as a sign of central government intolerance of these ethnic practices. In reflecting on the outcome of the case, she observed that though the feminist movement had scored a legal victory, the case exemplified the terrible gulf between human rights and women's rights activists, on the one hand, and those who see the status of women as an integral part of their ethnic identity, on the other. What is the point of all these laws if the people do not believe that putting an eighteen-year-old woman on a funeral pyre and denying her life is not a violation of the most basic fundamental right the right to life? What is the point of all the Constitutional protection if "ethnic identity" is an acceptable justification for reducing the status of women according to diverse cultural practice?

Coomaraswamy pointed out that, in contrast to (ethnic practices that deny women their basic human rights, some social movements and traditional ideologies have been used to enhance women's status. She suggested that rights discourse will have more resonance, and therefore more effectiveness, to the extent to which it can "plug into many of the dynamic social movements taking place in South Asia." According to Coomaraswamy, Asian women activists argue that "legal strategies to emancipate women need to allow women to touch base with their traditional sources of empowerment."

Abdullahi An-Na'im, a Sudanese lawyer and director of Africa Watch, underscored the importance of cultural legitimacy of international human rights. He explained that if the question of the cultural legitimacy of international standards is not taken seriously, "it is some times raised with the intention of undermining international human rights law, or of justifying its violation". It is not enough, he said, to rely on international law obligations to bring national laws, including religious and customary laws, into compliance with international human rights principles. International law, he explained, "is fully consistent with...state sovereignty...since it simply seeks to ensure that states effectively fulfill legal obligations that they have already assumed under international law".

An-Na'im suggested that one must go beyond this formalistic understanding of international legal obligations in order to seek a deeper consensus and sustainable commitment to women's international human rights. He argued that unless international human rights have sufficient legitimacy within particular cultures and traditions, their implementation will be thwarted, particularly at the domestic level, but also at the regional and international levels. Without such legitimacy, it will be nearly impossible to improve the status of women through the law or other agents of social change.

He suggested stimulating "internal discourse" and "cross cultural dialogue" on the issue of women's legal status and rights. "Internal discourse" among different sectors of society that hold different views on women's status can validate national achievements that improve women's status. Such discourse can explore avenues to challenge and discredit discriminatory practices in ways that are relevant to, and understood and accepted by, the population in question. "Cross-cultural dialogue" between groups that want to improve the status of women in different cultures can enhance the ability of internal actors to understand and address the nature of women's subordination in their own contexts. He cautioned that cross-cultural dialogue should not press internal actors into understanding and addressing challenges in terms of the experiences of other societies. He explained that "the combination of the processes of internal discourse and cross-cultural dialogue will, it is hoped, deepen and broaden universal cultural consensus on the concept and normative content" of women's international right to be free from all forms of discrimination.

Some participants questioned the effectiveness of An- Na'im's approach because religions and cultures are often sources of women's oppression. As a result, they thought "going secular" the only option. His response was that in some countries women do not have the secular option because their sole frames of reference or discourse are religious. As evidence of the possibility of religious or cultural reformation, he pointed to the emergence of women's rights organizations within religious frameworks, such as Women Living Under Muslim Laws and Catholics for a Free Choice.

Making International Human Rights Law Gender Conscious

International human rights and the legal instruments that protect them were developed primarily by men in a male-oriented world.

They have not been interpreted in a gender-sensitive way that is responsive to women's experiences of injustice. Critical recharacterization of international human rights is needed in order that women's distinctive human rights will not be marginal, and implementation of such rights becomes part of the central agenda of human rights work.

Treaty interpretation is not exclusively limited to treaty terms. A text may also be interpreted in a way that advances its goals in contemporaneous circumstances, even if they were not imaginable when the treaty was drafted. Moreover, interpretations of human rights treaties by human rights committees and by international, regional, and national courts shall take into account "subsequent practice in the application of the treaty which establishes the agreement of the parties regarding its interpretation." As a result, women can develop the content of treaties on human rights through the "subsequent practice" that adds a gender dimension to those rights.

Human rights may be divided into nondiscrimination rights; civil and political rights; and economic, social, and cultural rights. Developing the "subsequent practice" through recharacterization of all three kinds of rights to accommodate the particular nature of women's vulnerabilities to fundamental injustice is required if international human rights law is to be effectively applied to women.

Recharacterizing Nondiscrimination Rights

The legal obligation to eliminate all forms of discrimination against women is a fundamental tenet of international human rights law. Sex is a prohibited ground of discrimination in the Universal Declaration of Human Rights, the International Covenant on Civil and Political Rights (the Political Covenant), the International Covenant on Economic, Social, and Cultural Rights (the Economic Covenant), and the three regional human rights conventions, namely, the European Convention for the Protection of Human Rights and Fundamental Freedoms (the European Convention), the American Convention on Human Rights (the American Convention), and the African Charter on Human and Peoples" Rights (the African Charter).

The Convention on the Elimination of All Forms of Discrimination against Women (the Women's Convention) develops the legal norm on nondiscrimination from a women's perspective. This Convention moves from a sex-neutral norm that requires equal treatment of men and women, usually measured by how men are treated, to recognize that the particular nature of discrimination against women merits a legal response. The Women's Convention progresses beyond the earlier human rights conventions by addressing the pervasive and systemic nature of discrimination against women, and identifies the need to confront the social causes of women's inequality by addressing "all forms" of discrimination that women suffer. This Convention is thereby able to address the particular nature of women's disadvantages.

One approach to clarifying what constitutes discrimination against women in international human rights law is through the development of General Comments or General Recommendations by the committees established under the different human rights conventions. For example, the Human Rights Committee, established to monitor state compliance with the Political Covenant, has issued General Comment 18 on nondiscrimination based upon the "similarity and difference" model of discrimination. The General Comment states that "not every differentiation of treatment will constitute discrimination, if the criteria for such differentiation are reasonable and objective and if the aim is to achieve a purpose which is legitimate under the Covenant."

Kathleen Mahoney, of the Faculty of Law, University of Calgary, criticized the "similarity and difference" model of discrimination based on the liberal theory of feminism discussed by Charlesworth. It uses a male standard of equality and renders women copies of their male counterparts. Under this model, women are forced to argue either that they are the same as men and should be treated the same, or that they are different but should be treated as if they were the same, or that they are different and should be accorded special treatment. The model does not allow for any questioning about the ways in which laws, cultures, or religious traditions have constructed and maintained the disadvantage of women, or the extent to which the institutions are male-defined and built on male conceptions of challenges and harms.

The understanding of discrimination against women evolves with insights, perspective, and empirical information on how women are subordinated by different legal, social, and religious traditions.

Standards for determining such discrimination must be developed accordingly. As Mahoney explained, Systemic discrimination or inequality of condition, the most damaging form of discrimination, cannot be addressed via the rule-based sameness of treatment approach. Indeed, the use of this model virtually makes systemic disadvantage invisible. By structuring equality around the male comparator, the assumption is made that equality exists and that from time to time, individuals will be discriminated against. The persistent disadvantage women suffer across the board because of societal biases is obscured. The question then becomes, can [international human rights law] support and deliver substantive equality? Mahoney answered that it can, if a test of discrimination is adopted that is based on powerlessness, exclusion, and disadvantage rather than on sameness and difference. A test adopted by the Supreme Court of Canada, for instance, determines discrimination in terms of disadvantage. If a member of a persistently disadvantaged group can show that a law, policy, or behavior continues or worsens that disadvantage, then that law, policy or behavior is discriminatory. She explained that no comparator, male or otherwise, is required. Adoption of the test of "disadvantage," as opposed to the test of "similarity and difference," requires judges to look at women as they are located in the real world in order to determine whether any systemic abuse and deprivation of power that women experience is due to their place in the sexual hierarchy.

Decisions of international and regional human rights tribunals have used the "similarity and difference" test for discrimination, not the "disadvantage" model that can capture the systemic nature of discrimination against women. The "disadvantage" model of discrimination is more consistent with the object and purpose of the Women's Convention in prohibiting all forms of discrimination against women. The Human Rights Committee, established under the Political Covenant, might be encouraged to adopt the "disadvantage" model, replacing General Comment 18 to help clarify what constitutes discrimination against women. The Committee has reflected on, and further developed, other General Comments. The Committee on the Elimination of Discrimination Against Women (CEDAW), established under the Women's Convention, might also be encouraged to develop a General Recommendation that clarifies its intention to use the "disadvantage" test to determine what constitutes discrimination against women.

Recharacterizing Civil and Political Rights

Participants explored ways to recharacterize civil and political rights for women because, as Charlesworth explained, the primacy traditionally given to civil and political rights by western international lawyers and philosophers is directed toward protection from men within public life and their relationship with government.

Recharacterization of civil and political rights needs to be done in a variety of ways. For example, the right to life is traditionally referred to as the obligation of states to observe due process of law before capital punishment is imposed. But this interpretation ignores the historic reality of women that persists in many regions of the world. Currently, at least 500,000 women die avoidably each year of pregnancy related causes, such as lack of access to basic obstetric care.

Cecilia Medina, of the Faculty of Law, University of Diego Portales, Santiago, Chile, who is also a researcher at the Netherlands Institute of Human Rights, argued that women's rights to liberty and security are severely constrained by their lack of access to contraceptives. For example, in El Salvador lack of available means of contraception causes women to have about twice the number of children they want.

Rhonda Copelon, of the City University of New York Law School, explored ways to recharacterize the prohibition of torture and inhuman and degrading treatment to accommodate gender-based violence. She argued that gender-based violence is comparable to torture, and that its prohibition ought to be, like prohibition of torture, a principle of *jus cogens*:

My thesis is that, when stripped of privatization, sexism, and sentimentalism, gender-based violence which is brutal, systemic and structural must be seen as no less grave than other forms of inhumane and subordinating violence, the prohibition of which has been recognized as *jus cogens*, or peremptory norms, by the international community. I focus on the *jus cogens* not to exclude other formulations of gender-based violence, but because, as a normative matter, it embraces the most heinous offenses, precludes exception and binds universally. My argument is not that gender-based violence has attained the status of *jus cogens*, but rather that it should; and that with a revised process, it could.

Nowak pointed out that if violence against women can be characterized as torture, then states would have universal jurisdiction to prosecute perpetrators of violence against women. Copelon's approach is also designed to have the shock effect of making international lawyers think about why gender-specific violations are absent from the *jus cogens* discourse, the symbolic inner sanctum of international legal rules.

Recharacterizing Economic, Social, and Cultural Rights

Participants, particularly from Africa, were concerned about how structural adjustment programs (SAPs) of the World Bank and the Interna- are negatively affecting the economic, social, and cultural rights of women. Women, they noted, suffer in a unique and often invisible way. Florence Butegwa, of Women in Law and Development, based in Harare, Zimbabwe, and Akua Kuenyehia, of the Faculty of Law, University of Ghana, described the double injury sustained by women in their countries due to the demands of structural adjustment; injury suffered as citizens of the South and injury suffered as women. Their stories are echoed in the literature on women and structural development.The findings of this literature show that:

a. The total burden of women's work has increased under recessionary conditions. Structural adjustment programs have reduced social expenditures, rather than increasing them to offset these pressures.
b. Employment creation is weak under SAPs, especially for women.
c. SAPs have done little to address institutional gender inequality in the formal and informal sectors of national economies.
d. In agriculture, the concentration of resources on export crops, which has characterized development and worked to women's disadvantage in the past, has been intensified under SAPs.
e. In both agriculture and industry, women have operated relatively small enterprises and have experienced discrimination because of the bias against smaller scale operations manifest in SAPs.

A consensus emerged at the Consultation that human rights have to be rethought to accommodate women's experience of disproportionate disadvantage under structural adjustment programs.

The first step to rethinking human rights with reference to structural adjustment is to recognize the double injury it causes women. Once recognized, this injury can be addressed in a number of fora in the international system. An additional approach is to confront the financial institutions themselves. As international actors, the World Bank and the IMF are bound by international law, including human rights norms and, therefore, are legally obligated to ensure that women share equally with men in the benefits of their loans.

Guaranteeing Specific Human Rights of Women

Bert Lockwood, of the University of Cincinnati College of Law, examined how the Court of Appeal of Botswana in *Attorney General v. Unity Dow* applied international human rights principles to the nationality problem. The decision held unconstitutional the provision of the Botswana Citizenship Act of 1984, whereby a female citizen of Botswana who is married to a foreigner cannot convey citizenship to her children born in wedlock in Botswana, although a male citizen married to a foreigner can convey such citizenship. The Court of Appeal decided that this provision of the Citizenship Act infringed Unity Dow's fundamental rights and freedoms, her liberty of movement, and her right to nondiscrimination. The Chief Judge, noting the obligations of Botswana as a signatory to the Universal Declaration of Human Rights and the Declaration on the Elimination of Discrimination Against Women, and as a state party to the African Charter, observed that Botswana is a member of the community of civilised States which has undertaken to abide by certain standards of conduct, and, unless it is impossible to do otherwise, it would be wrong for its Courts to interpret its legislation in a manner which conflicts with the international obligations that Botswana has undertaken.

Lockwood explained that women's disability with regard to citizenship is a problem in many countries, underscored by the fact that Article 9 on nationality is one of the most highly reserved articles of the Women's Convention. Women's legal inability to bestow their nationality on their children born of foreign husbands often leaves legitimate children stateless or unable to benefit from attributes of citizenship such as education, health care, and employment. He hoped that this decision might have a positive impact on draft legislation to amend such discriminatory nationality laws, such as is now pending in Egypt and Tunisia. The decision might also have persuasive authority for cases now pending in Bangladesh and in Pakistan, according to Sara Hossain, a legal practitioner from Dhaka, Bangladesh and Rashida Patel, of the Legal Aid Centre in Karachi, Pakistan. It was pointed out that CEDAW, perhaps together with the Children's Committee established under the Convention on the Rights of the Child, might be encouraged to develop a General Recommendation on women's ability to convey nationality to their children, and that it be made an issue during the 1994 International Year of the Family.

Discriminatory Personal Law

In some regions of the world, personal law governs legal relations in all matters regarding marriage, divorce, maintenance, child custody and guardianship, and inheritance, on the basis of religious identity. Christina Cerna, currently on secondment from the Organization of American States to the UN Human Rights Centre in Geneva, was concerned that the persistence of discriminatory personal laws "undermines the universality of international prohibition of discrimination against women."

Kirti Singh, a legal practitioner from New Delhi, explained that the Indian government retains personal law that discriminates against women for reasons of political expediency. The government does not want to interfere with personal matters in the ethnic (usually minority) communities. A case in point is the much discussed *Shah Bano* decision of the Supreme Court of India. A Muslim man who had divorced his wife of thirty years was ordered to pay monthly maintenance pursuant to a criminal law provision on the prevention of destitution. He objected, arguing that the Muslim personal law requiring him only to return her dowry, which he had done, should prevail over the secular criminal law. His argument was unsuccessful in the Supreme Court of India, but the case triggered a reaction that led to the passage of legislation that overturned the

Supreme Court judgment. Singh pointed out that the government, despite the protest of women's groups of all ethnic communities, thought it could not afford to alienate the fundamentalist Muslim community, and so "sealed the fate of millions of Muslim women in India."

Halim addressed the potential for using the Political Covenant and the African Charter to challenge discriminatory aspects of the Sudanese Personal Law for Muslims Act. She said that this act rendered the meaning of equality "valueless." For example, it prevents women from contracting their own marriages, gives men unfettered rights to divorce while requiring women to prove in court some sort of specified harm, and prevents women from leaving their homes without the permission of their husbands or guardians. Even if a divorce is granted, a woman may "be returned" to her former husband without her consent within three months of divorce. She explained that interpretations of the Act consistent with modern realities of women's lives are harshly resisted, even though interpretations of other areas of Islamic law reflecting modernization of men's lives are readily accepted. She pointed out that "women are prisoners of the old interpretations of the Qur'an and sunna."

Halim further explained that the challenges of applying the sexual nondiscrimination provisions of the Political Covenant and the African Charter are formidable:

Muslim women are being told that patriarchy is not what is hindering them, but international law as part of western ideas is the real obstacle to women. Women should be liberated from western ideas that are subjecting them to the double burden of domestic and public work. It is argued that there is no need for women to take up the task of liberation. Men will do it for them through the smooth "Islamic" process, if it is kept outside the ambit of secular international law. Coomaraswamy explained that personal law is usually maintained as part of the politics of communalism, and within that context Shah Bano, and women like her, have no rights. "All men are created equal, but women are bound by the position relegated to them by the different systems of personal law, laws which govern the most important area of their lives, the family."[31] She pointed out that personal law is the most impervious to change in favor of women's rights:

Here women are divided by community and among themselves about whether a rights discourse is relevant or necessary. Unless we begin to examine law's approach to the family and the private space in greater detail and understand the dynamics more fully with regard to ideological constructions which resist legal change, we will not be able to bring rights home to the family. The task is daunting but necessary. Without equity in the family, there will not be equity in society. The law should protect and privilege that kind of family and not any other.

Customary Property Law

Butegwa addressed the use of the African Charter to redress the disabilities that women face with respect to property under African customary law. In law and in fact, women are denied access to real and personal property, whether it be by discriminatory inheritance, divorce, or customary law. If one dies without a will, which is generally the case in many African countries, the customary law of one's clan is applied to determine who inherits assets. She explained that the customary law heir is normally the deceased's eldest son, which denies women not only the fruits of the land but also the incidents of land tenure such as its availability as collateral security for bank loans. Upon divorce, women's claims to matrimonial property are often rejected.

Butegwa said that the African Charter obligates states parties "to ensure that whatever cultural values and practices are permitted by domestic law must comply with the human rights principle of freedom from discrimination on the basis of sex." She recommended that the issue of women's property rights be addressed carefully and pragmatically at the national, regional, and international levels.

At the national level, she said, most governments are not taking the necessary legislative steps to change laws, practices, and customs with regard to women's property rights. Consequently, states parties are failing in their obligations under the Charter to reform sex discrimina tory laws. She observed, moreover, that women's groups working to reform discriminatory laws and practices are dismissed by some governments "as misguided elite women aping Western concepts. This situation is compounded by a general lack of awareness among women of the law and the lack of opportunities for them to meet and discuss their legal status and map out strategies." She pointed out that women's rights discourse must go on at the national level because, until women understand the fact that "some customs are illegal under the laws of the country," the discourse might backfire and little headway on any women's issues will be possible.

With regard to the African Commission on Human and Peoples' Rights, established under the African Charter, Butegwa put it directly: we have "to wake up the Commission." However, she explained that NGOs, women's groups, and the legal profession have "only a cursory knowledge of the African Charter, the Commission, and their relevance and potential in the promotion of women's human rights. It is not surprising, therefore, that the majority has not sought to include the Charter and the Commission in the legal rights awareness programs currently being implemented." As a result, strategies relating to the Charter and the Commission, including improving state reporting on compliance or noncompliance with the Charter's obligations with regard to women, and submitting communications on violations of women's property rights, will be advanced only through considerable effort.

At the international level, Butegwa thought that support is needed from women's rights groups in developed countries to change bilateral and multilateral loan policies. Such women's groups need to lobby their governments to change their aid policies and. the loan and grant policies of international institutions such as the World Bank and, for example, the x, to encourage change in recipient state's laws that discriminate against women's property rights. Donor governments and multilateral funders need to ensure that women have equal access with men to the benefits of their loans. This equity can be very difficult to achieve where women have no land to use as collateral security for loans provided by such institutions as IFAD through recipient governments. CEDAW, perhaps with input from the Food and Agricultural Organization, might want to develop a General Recommendation on women and property. This could set out guidelines for reporting states to specify how they have overcome the general disabilities under their customary law for women to own, inherit, or otherwise acquire land.

Reproductive Rights

Maria Isabel Plata, of Profamilia, Bogota, Colombia, explained how women's groups in Colombia used the Women's Convention to promote equality and reproductive health, observing that "the moment we used an international treaty, the government saw that our claims were legitimate and began to take us seriously." The Colombian womens movement lobbied for incorporation of the principles of the Women's Convention into the 1991 Constitution. In particular, the provision of the Women's Convention on the right to decide freely and responsibly the number of one's children is now part of the new Constitution.

Plata explained that the Ministry of Public Health has interpreted the Women's Convention and the 1991 Colombian Constitution to establish a gender perspective in their health policies that considers "the social discrimination of women as an element which contributes to the ill-health of women." A new ministerial resolution orders all health institutions to ensure women the right to decide on all issues that affect their health, their life, and their sexuality, and guarantees rights "to information and orientation to allow the exercise of free, gratifying, responsible sexuality which can not be tied to maternity." The new policy requires provision of a full range of reproductive health services, including infertility services, safe and effective contraception, integrated treatment for incomplete abortion, and treatment for menopausal women. The policy emphasizes the need for special attention to high risk women, such as adolescents and victims of violence.

Plata considered that this new Colombian initiative might provide ideas to other countries that are making serious efforts to comply with the Women's Convention. She recommended that CEDAW consider issuing a General Recommendation clarifying that the terms "women's health" and "family planning programs" encompass the concepts of "reproductive and sexual health" as used in the new Colombian women's health policy. She urged that CEDAW develop this Recommendation as soon as possible, in part to legitimize the Colombian interpretation of the health provisions of the Women's Convention. Moreover, such a Recommendation would explain that in order to comply with the Convention, states need to develop comprehensive reproductive health services that "empower women and not use women as means to limit population growth, save the environment and speed development." She stressed that it is important for CEDAW to issue such a Recommendation before the 1994 Population Conference, because of her concern that the Conference will be an occasion at which international thinking on population may revert to the solely demographic mentality of the 1960s, when women's well-being was sometimes neglected.

Violence Against Women

Joan Fitzpatrick, of the University of Washington School of Law, Seattle, explored a range of strategies to combat all forms of violence against women. Forms of violence include domestic violence (murder, rape, and battery) by husbands or other male partners, genital mutilation, gender-based violence by police and security forces (including torture of detained women), gender-based violence against women during armed conflict, gender-based violence against women refugees and asylum seekers, violence associated with prostitution and pornography, violence in the workplace, including sexual harassment, forced pregnancy, forced abortion, and forced sterilization.

Copelon explained that domestic violence against women is systemic and structural, a mechanism of the patriarchal control of women that is built on male superiority and female inferiority, sex-stereotyped roles and expectations, and the economic, social, and political predominance of men and dependency of women. While the legal and cultural embodiments of patriarchal thinking vary among different cultures, there is an astounding convergence of cultures in regard to the basic tenets of patriarchy and the legitimacy, if not necessity, of violence as a mechanism of enforcing that system.

No issue raises the inherent limitation of the gender-neutral approach to equality more acutely than does domestic violence against women. Fitzpatrick pointed out that a "special treatment" approach is needed, as opposed to formal equality, to recognize that women exist in concrete contexts. The need for a multiplicity of approaches has been suggested in the CEDAW Recommendation 19 on Violence Against Women, the Draft Declaration on the Elimination of Violence Against Women, the European Parliament Resolution on Violence Against Women, and the draft Inter-American Convention on the Prevention, Punishment, and Eradication of Violence Against Women, as well as the UN Crime Prevention and Criminal Justice Branch 1993 *Resource Manual on Strategies for Confronting Domestic Violence*. Fitzpatrick stressed that victims of domestic violence exist under pressures that are not felt by other crime victims. Battered women often lack the economic, social, and emotional means to leave their batterers. Not employed outside the home, they have no financial resources on which to fall back. They have been socialized to define themselves primarily through their relationships with men, and cannot face leaving these relationships. This points to the need for "special treatment" in such forms, for instance, as battered women's shelters.

Participants struggled with the question whether domestic violence is better characterized as a violation of the civil and political right to liberty and security, or as a violation of the nondiscrimination right to equal resources for crime control. The former characterization may do more in the long term to integrate women's experiences of injustice into the concepts of international human rights law, but the latter may enjoy greater short-term success precisely because it poses less of a fundamental challenge to patriarchal systems.

Participants stressed the importance of strategies that would enhance international standards of prohibition of violence against women, such as the CEDAW General Recommendation 19, and means that would facilitate the enforcement of standards, such as the Communication procedures before the Commission on the Status of Women and the individual complaint procedure before the Committee Against Torture, established under the Convention Against Torture and Other Cruel, Inhuman, or Degrading Treatment or Punishment. They also explored strategies that would bring the issue of violence against women into the mainstream of human rights work, such as the international effort to put the issue on the agenda of the 1993 International Conference on Human Rights, to be held in Vienna.

Working With What We Have: Making International Human Rights Law More Effective for Women

The international law of state responsibility makes a state legally accountable for breaches of international obligations that are attributable or imputable to the state. In other words, only a state and its agents can commit a human rights violation. Nonstate actors are not generally accountable under international human rights law, but the state may sometimes be held responsible for related human rights violations. Modern development of international human rights law through state adherence to multilateral human rights conventions has enhanced prospects of state accountability, and women may be able to turn these developments to their advantage.

Kenneth Roth, of the U.S.based Human Rights Watch, explored the feasibility of applying different theories of state accountability developed in other areas of international human rights law to violations of women's human rights. The international human rights movement has used three distinct theories of government accountability: government agency, government complicity through failure to act, and government responsibility for the unequal application of the law. Roth argued that the same theories of government accountability invoked for state complicity in various forms of violence by nonstate actors, should be applied to domestic violence against women.

Comparing the first and second theories, Roth stressed the limits of the theory of government complicity. Whereas the theory of government agency treats an act of private violence as the act of a government agent and therefore requires that such violence be ended outright, the theory of government complicity requires simply that the state not condone private violence. Where a state is doing the bare minimum in combating domestic violence to escape charges of complicity, an unequal application theory allows insistence on greater diligence as a matter of international human rights law. The demand can be made that a state's efforts to combat domestic violence be at least on a par with its efforts to fight comparable forms of violent crime.

As regards the third theory, Roth argued that the nondiscrimination provisions of the Political Covenant can also be used to require that the same level of state resources used to enforce criminal laws against private acts of violence be devoted to crimes against women. That is, crimes against women, under the nondiscrimination theory of accountability, need to receive at least as thorough an investigation and as vigorous a prosecution as crimes against men. Roth explained that "lesser attention constitutes not only a violation of the antidiscrimination provisions of the Covenant but also evidence of the complicity needed to make out a substantive violation."

Some participants thought the nondiscrimination theory of state responsibility a useful first step. The non-enforcement of laws to protect women's rights was consistently discussed as a reason for women's continued subordination. The nondiscrimination theory of accountability might be applied to require governments to stop neglecting their duties with respect to women and actually implement laws to protect women's rights. The theory might also require the domestic criminal justice system and the international human rights system to at least explore the relative lack of enforcement of criminal laws against those who victimize women, for instance through wife-beating.

Participants questioned whether this approach would be sufficient to combat violence against women. It was pointed out that the approach has all the shortcomings of the "similarity and difference" model of discrimination. Halim questioned whether it would be sufficient in the Sudan to require enforcement of a rarely applied law criminalizing female circumcision. Butegwa observed that comparing this form of violence to other forms of criminal violence committed against other social groups might obscure the systemic nature of violence against women. It was generally thought that further work is needed on theories of state responsibility to hold the state accountable for failures of prevention, investigation, and punishment of violations of women's rights.

International Protection

Byrnes explained that the methods of international protection of women's human rights range from recourse to limited international judicial or quasi-judicial processes to the application of broader means of furthering state parties' accountability, such as through reporting requirements. He noted that the application of human rights norms to national laws and practices alleged to violate women's rights has to be approached in a variety of ways. Any one method may be fragile and inadequate, but there are cumulative ways in which, in Romany's words, "women can make rights their own." Available approaches will be examined below from the perspective of different protective bodies that derive their authority from separate human rights treaties or from the UN Charter.

(a) Treaty-based bodies

Byrnes explained that all major human rights treaties provide for a system of reporting. States parties are required to make regular reports to the responsible supervisory bodies on the steps they have taken to implement their obligations and the difficulties they have experienced in doing so. Reports are examined by the relevant treaty bodies in the presence of representatives of the states concerned. All committees receive information informally from NGOs, which they may use in their questioning. The examination process, he points out, can provide an occasion for exerting pressure on states. For members of a supervisory body to be strongly critical of a state or express the view that the state has not discharged its obligations under the treaty, can put pressure on a government, particularly if the proceedings receive international or national publicity.

All human rights treaty bodies, Byrnes explained, have the power to make General Comments or General Recommendations. These detailed comments can be particularly useful for elaborating the specific content of broadly worded treaty guarantees, and may be helpful in domestic, political, or even judicial contexts. But he cautioned that, with the exception of CEDAW, gender plays a relatively minor role in the General Comments of most committees. Nonetheless, they are grateful for, and in need of, expert input from NGOs, and thus this process is available for advancement of women's rights.

Byrnes pointed out that national NGOs, which might be able to exploit the reporting procedure, may know little about it, the appropriate format for submission of material, and how most effectively to lobby members of a committee or to generate publicity. Every government needs to be encouraged to publish treaty reports in the local language, to share them as a matter of course with the relevant NGOs, and even to debate them in the national parliament.

The Human Rights Committee, established under the Political Covenant, has an individual complaint procedure. This procedure is available to individuals in nearly seventy countries that have ratified the Optional Protocol to the Political Covenant. Under this procedure, the Human Rights Committee has decided a case on a woman's right to enjoy her own culture. and a few sexual nondiscrimination cases. From a women's perspective, the jurisprudence developed by this Committee is limited by the adoption of the "similarity and difference" test of discrimination.

The Human Rights Committee is willing to scrutinize allegations of discrimination in violation of rights recognized by, for example, the Economic Covenant and the Women's Convention. This enables women in those countries to bring complaints about violations of their rights of equal entitlement protected by the Economic Covenant and, for example, the Women's Convention, provided that those countries are parties to the latter-mentioned conventions.

The Committee on the Elimination of Discrimination Against Women (CEDAW) monitors states parties' compliance with the Women's Convention. Norma Forde, of the Faculty of Law of the Univernsity of the West Indies, Barbados, and a member of CEDAW, noted that the work of CEDAW is far more effective when its members have recourse to sources of information in addition to data contained in reports of states parties. Accordingly, she explained, CEDAW has requested the Division for the Advancement of Women at the UN Secretariat in New York to compile statistics garnered from official UN sources relevant to members' reports. CEDAW has also requested UN specialized agencies to provide it with relevant information and encourages NGOs to send them information particularly on major problems facing women in the reporting countries.

The Committee on the Elimination of Racial Discrimination, established under the International Convention for the Elimination of All Forms of Racial Discrimination (the Race Convention), provides an important forum for raising issues of discrimination against women belonging to racial minorities.

Participants were concerned that women of minority communities are subject to discrimination and violence as members of their communities, and additional discrimination and violence as women. Moreover, in Hossain's words "they are further condemned to carry the brunt of resistance to change by conforming to the discriminatory traditions and customs practiced by their community."

The Committee on Economic, Social, and Cultural Rights (the Economic Committee) monitors states parties' compliance with the Economic Covenant. It has developed some innovative working methods to enhance its normative functions. They include formally receiving written submissions from NGOs, holding annual "general discussions" on certain rights contained in the Economic Covenant and involving "recognized experts" to provide oral testimony during these discussions. These methods provide significant opportunities to develop a feminist content to economic, social, and cultural rights.

Important research shows how economic development has exacerbated women's marginalization, despite programmatic initiatives to integrate women into development. The Economic Committee might invite "recognized experts" during the annual "general discussions," in order to explain why some of these programs have not been successful in improving women's actual status, and what implications these insights might have for the effective application of economic, social, and cultural rights. Discussions with these experts might result in a General Comment on how states parties might more effectively ensure that women enjoy rights protected by the Economic Covenant.

(b) Charter-based bodies

The UN Commission on the Status of Women has the authority to review communications sent to it by individuals and organizations in order to identify those that appear to reveal "a consistent pattern of reliably attested injustice and discriminatory practices against women." The Commission is authorized under this procedure to examine communications as a source of information only for purposes of identifying general trends and patterns of violations against women. The Commission can make general recommendations to ECOSOC on the action it may wish to take on trends and patterns, but it is not authorized to take any other action. Byrnes suggested that the Commission should be encouraged to improve this procedure for the purposes of identifying specific situations in which individuals need redress, or inequitable country situations, and conducting thorough studies of them.

The Commission on the Status of Women has contributed to the 1993 International Human Rights Conference, the 1993 International Year for the World's Indigenous People, the 1994 Population and Development Conference, the 1994 International Year of the Family and, for example, the UN Decade of International Law 1990-99. The Commission is planning the 1995 Women's Conference to be held in Beijing, China. It might be encouraged to appoint Working Groups or Special Rapporteurs on such cross-over themes as women's rights and indigenous rights, the impact of structural adjustment on the exercise of women's rights, and ensuring women's rights in the family and in family planning programs. The Working Groups or the Special Rapporteurs could report during these international conferences and years.

The Sub-Commission on the Prevention of Discrimination and Protection of Minorities (the Sub-Commission) has used Working Groups and Special Rapporteurs to address alleged human rights violations where women are particularly vulnerable. The Sub-Commission's Working Group on Contemporary Forms of Slavery has developed a Plan of Action for governments on child prostitution and child pornography and a Plan for the Prevention of Traffic in Persons and the Exploitation of the Prostitution of Others. The Sub-Commission has created a Special Rapporteur on Traditional Practices Affecting the Health of Women and Children.

The Sub-Commission is also considering the role and equal participation of women in development as a sub-issue of the New International Economic Order and the promotion of human rights, and is considering the prevention of discrimination and protection of women as a sub-issue of the program on Promotion, Protection, and Restoration of Human Rights at National, Regional, and International Levels.

The Resolution 1503 procedure requires that the communications before the Sub-Commission reveal a consistent pattern of gross violations of human rights. However, Byrnes concluded that this procedure has made little contribution to addressing issues of sex discrimination or violations of human rights that have a significant gender dimension.

Regional Protection

Regional human rights conventions have been applied only sparingly to violations of women's human rights. There have been five cases concerning the violation of women's human rights before the European Court of Human Rights, and one case before the Inter-American Court of Human Rights. In addition, the European Commission of Human Rights, the Inter-American Commission of Human Rights, and the Court of Justice of the European Communities, established under the Treaty of Rome, have all considered complaints concerning women's legal status. And yet there are many ways at regional levels beyond specifically judicial approaches to enhance the norm of the prohibition of all forms of discrimination against women. Advocacy at the regional level provides opportunities that do not necessarily exist at the international level. Geographic proximity, cultural similarity, and economic interdependence can all facilitate the development and application of human rights standards. Regional systems can provide opportunities to establish legitimacy of women's human rights within the cultures of the region.

According to Anja-Riitta Ketokoski, of the Finnish Ministry for Foreign Affairs and a member of the Committee for the Equality between Women and Men of the Council of Europe, there are many legal and extra-legal ways in which a European heritage is evolving for "parity democracy in decision making." She advised women to concentrate their efforts on the institutions in which they can most meaningfully participate. In the European human rights system, for instance, Ketokoski characterized the Conference on Security and Cooperation in Europe and the European Economic Community as less womanfriendly than the Council of Europe and the Nordic Council of Ministers, where recipes for the protection and promotion of women's rights are exchanged and refined regularly.

Chaloka Beyani, a Zambian research fellow at Wolfson College, Oxford, stressed the importance of using the sexual equality provisions of the African Charter, because most national constitutions in Africa do not include sex as a prohibited ground of discrimination. He explained that the African Charter requires the elimination of all forms of discrimination against women, as stipulated in international declarations and conventions, including the Women's Convention.

He observed that the African Charter obliges the African Commission to draw inspiration from the international law of human rights and international human rights instruments, which enables it to establish a collaborative relationship with CEDAW. Collaboration is appropriate, since some African states are parties to both the African Charter and the Women's Convention. Furthermore, collaboration would facilitate the African Commission in undertaking an investigation into ways and means of protecting women's rights in Africa, which Beyani considered a top priority for the African Commission.

Medina agreed with Beyani that it is important to broaden the basis of comparison. She explained that the Inter-American Commission on Human Rights and the Inter-American Court of Human Rights have the authority to monitor the conduct of states with regard not only to the American Convention but also to all other obligations in the field of human rights, including the Women's Convention. She observed that the Inter-American Commission on Human Rights might be assisted in its task of protecting and promoting the human rights of women if it had working ties with the Inter-American Commission on Women.The Commission on Women has the power to consult the InterAmerican Court on matters concerning the application of human rights treaties to women. The Commission could seek an Advisory Opinion from the Court on the permissibility of reservations to the Women's Convention filed by countries that are members of the Organization of American States. She cautioned, however, that a prerequisite of effective use of the inter-American system for the protection of human rights of women is education and training of women's groups, judges, and lawyers.

Domestic Protection

Domestic protection of women's human rights is usually the first line of defense for women. As Anne Bayefsky, of the Faculty of Law, University of Ottawa, explained, the international machinery for the protection of human rights is subsidiary to the national machinery. A general rule in international law is that domestic remedies (where they exist) have to be exhausted before international or regional tribunals will take up a case. This rule requires the state to afford a prior opportunity to redress alleged violations by its own means and within the framework of its domestic legal system. Bayefsky noted that there are alternative general theories about the relationship between municipal law and international law, and one has to look to municipal law to determine which theory is embraced by each country:

1. The adoption theory states that international law is part of domestic law automatically, that is without an act of incorporation, except where it conflicts with statutory law, or well-established rules of the Common Law.

2. The transformation theory states that international law is only part of domestic law when it has been incorporated into domestic law.

When human rights treaties are directly adopted into internal law, they may be invoked before and enforced by municipal courts and administrative authorities. Domestic protection of women's rights can be strengthened in states that favor the latter theory by the transformation of international human rights treaties, either in whole or in part, through legislation or presidential decrees.

Hossain explored the possibility of using the Women's Convention to challenge discriminatory aspects of personal laws and further to define the content of the right to sexual nondiscrimination in domestic law. She explained that personal laws "sanction discrimination against women through practices such as polygamy, limited rights to divorce, guardianship and custody." Use of the sexual nondiscrimination provision of the Bangladesh Constitution to challenge discriminatory aspects of personal laws is limited by the fact that the constitutional guarantee extends only to the state and public spheres.

Hossain argued that the Women's Convention requires Bangladesh, as a state party, to eliminate all forms of discrimination against women *by any person* and to ensure equality with respect to *marriage and family* relations. She contended that Bangladeshi reservations to the Women's Convention are impermissible as they are incompatible with the object and purpose of the Convention. Bangladesh is therefore obligated to implement the entire Convention without delay. She considered that it is imperative to insist upon the incorporation of universally accepted norms of nondiscrimination in every sphere, which prioritize the rights of the individual above those of the traditionally defined community. State sanction of such norms would assist in the process of their legitimization, critical in a situation where traditional and customary notions of women's roles hold sway. Popular legitimization of these principles would provide leverage not only for substantive internal reform of each community's laws but perhaps also for eventual overhaul of the system.

Common Denominators

Participants at the Consultation focused on the goal of achieving women's equal human rights, and the role that international law could play in achieving this end. They identified certain basic strategies that should be developed in order to equip activists inspired by the ideal of making women's equality a reality. Participants agreed on their common destination, but also concurred that different pathways towards it would have to be followed because they were setting out from different origins. The Consultation was seen as providing ideas for reform that could move from different origins towards the common destination.

Prerequisites to reform included improved education and training in human rights law and processes, provision of legal services for women's empowerment, development of capacities to research facts and publicize findings, and promotion of the feminist presence on human rights committees, courts, and commissions.

Mona Rishmawi, of the International Commission of Jurists in Ge- Ge-, thought that training for judges and personnel providing legal services for women was extremely important. She explained that international law in general and international human rights law in particular is usually foreign to judges. Training is important to show judges how this body of law can be used domestically and to make this law more accessible to them. She also recommended legal services and social counseling for women because, without it, women who are economically dependent on their husbands will not have the means to bring cases.

With training on women's international human rights for judges and legal aid for women, Plata suggested it might be possible to file individual communications from several countries of a region with the regional human rights commission, such as the Inter-American Commission on Human Rights on a particular form of women's subordination, such as the nonenforcement of criminal laws against perpetrators of domestic violence.

Most committees, courts, and commissions are composed of men, a fact that may significantly reduce the chances of success of novel claims about the systemic nature of women's subordination. The feminist presence on domestic, regional, and international human rights tribunals has to be increased to ensure that women's concerns are addressed.

One of the themes that emerged from the consultation was that effective application of women's international human rights depends on both vertical and horizontal interactions. Vertical interaction involves both working down and working up. Working down refers to the process that Byrnes called "bringing the international back home," meaning increasing the use of women's international human rights at the domestic level in legal and political contexts. Working up means introducing legal developments favorable to women, such as the *Andrews* decision, and the diversity of women's experiences within different cultures, into international human rights law.

Horizontal interaction refers to the exchange of experiences among regional human rights systems and among national courts or systems of the same region. For example, Beyani believed that the experience gained in the inter-American system is particularly useful for application of the African Charter. Lockwood spoke of the importance of NGOs filing *amicus curiae* briefs in cases that might have important implications for women fighting similar causes in other countries, as was done by the Cincinnati-based Urban Morgan Institute in *Unity Dow*. States do not have to wait for laws and practices to be challenged, or for human rights tribunals to consider alleged violations of rights, before moving to protect women. They can begin by changing their laws and policies that are similar to those of other countries that have been successfully challenged under human rights conventions to which they are party.

Many recommendations made during the consultation depend for effectiveness on the political will of the state. It must be kept in mind that relationships between women and the state vary from country to country, and are evolving. Ketokoski described the Nordic states as increasingly allied with women, whereas Coomaraswamy explained that Asian women are alienated from the state. Brigitte Mabandla, of the Community Law Centre of the University of the Western Cape, South Africa, spoke of the importance of mobilizing women to ensure that their interests are protected by the new South African Constitution. Karen Knop, of the Faculty of Law, University of Toronto, discussed the different approaches that women might take to the institution of the state, including reconstituting state sovereignty so as to enable women to participate directly in the evolution of international law on issues directly and indirectly affecting them.

The consultation showed that among lawyers there must be better interaction in the work of theoreticians and practitioners. Academic lawyers working on the integration of women's human rights into the universal human rights movement must be aware of how theoretical concepts depend for effectiveness on applicability according to the rules of practice and needs of documentation of human rights committees, courts, and commissions. Legal practitioners must recognize that their work will be enriched by awareness of feminist analysis, and the relation of practical goals to the transcending evolution of the human rights movement.

The nature and extent of violations of women's international human rights continue to be cruel and pervasive. In many countries, violations remain not simply unremedied, but unnoticed as discriminatory or as an affront to human dignity. This widespread failure to honor international obligations poses a challenge to the credibility, universality, and justice of international human rights law.

A slightly different version of this chapter also appears in; *Thatched Patio* 5(4): 29-63. I am grateful to the participants whose insights reflected in their papers and consultation contributions have made this report possible, to Karen Knop for her extensive help in the preparation of this report and to Julia McNally and Valerie Oosterveld for their note taking during the consultation and subsequent research assistance.

❑❑❑

9

Role and Function of Women's International Human Rights

Introduction

Human rights law challenges the traditional scope of international law. It gives individuals and groups, otherwise without access to the international legal system, the possibility of making international legal claims and thus expands the state-centered discourse of international law. International human rights law is a product of the post World War II order. The United Nations Charter recognized in principle the centrality of the importance of the protection of human rights, and a great range of both general and specific international instruments have since given definition and texture to this commitment.

The development of human rights law is often, if controversially, described in terms of "generations": the "first" generation of rights covers civil and political rights, still regarded by many Western commentators as the paradigm against which all newer claims of rights must be measured (indeed some assert that civil and political rights are the only possible form of international human rights); the "second" generation of rights means economic, social, and cultural rights; and the "third," most recently defined, generation encompasses group or peoples' rights. The generational metaphor is controversial because it implies a hierarchy in the development of human rights within the United Nations system. Western states, once the dominant players in the international community, have typically regarded civil and political rights as the most crucial for international protection. Socialist and developing states have usually been the strongest supporters of economic, social, and cultural rights. And group or peoples rights have been the particular concern of many of the developing nations which have more recently joined the international community. From a woman's perspective, however, the definition and development of the three generations of rights have much in common: they are built on typically male life experiences and in their current form do not respond to the most pressing risks women face.

While there have been lively debates about the relationship between the generations of rights and the best methods of implementing human rights law, there has been a general reluctance to question the basis or value of the international human rights system itself. Analyses of the foundations and scope of international human rights law frequently lapse into heroic or mystical language: it is almost as if this branch of international law were both too valuable and too fragile to sustain critique. The development of women's international human rights challenges this reluctance to examine the basis of human rights law.

How is the term "women's international human rights" to be understood? At one level it can be taken to refer simply to those international instruments that deal specifically with women.[5] Most of them are elaborations of the norm of formal nondiscrimination, providing that, in particular or general contexts, women should be treated the same as men. While this development in international law has been valuable, it has not been adequate to address the subordination of women worldwide. Apart from the limited promise of formal equality, discussed below, the creation of a specialized branch of human rights law has allowed its marginalization: "mainstream" human rights bodies have tended to ignore the application of human rights norms to women. Moreover, the structure and institutions of women's international human rights law are more fragile than their apparently more generally applicable counterparts: international instruments dealing with women have weaker implementation obligations and procedures; the institutions designed to draft and monitor them are under-resourced and their roles often circumscribed compared to other human rights bodies; the widespread practice of states in making reservations to fundamental provisions in the instruments is apparently tolerated; as is the failure of states generally to fulfill their obligations under the instruments.

My concern here is to argue for the development of a notion of women's international human rights law in a more general sense. How can women be taken seriously across the entire spectrum of human rights? Some might respond that the very notion of human rights implies universal application and that the term "women's human rights" is a distracting redundancy. But the development of international human rights law generally has been partial and androcentric, privileging a masculine worldview. Non-governmental organizations have recently begun to document abuse of women that falls within the traditional scope of human rights law. But the very structure of this law has been built on the silence of women. The fundamental problem women face worldwide is not discriminatory treatment compared with men, although this is a manifestation of the larger problem. Women are in an inferior position because they have no real power in either the public or private worlds, and international human rights law, like most economic, social, cultural, and legal constructs, reinforces this powerlessness. As Noreen Burrows writes: "For most women, what it is to be human is to work long hours in agriculture or the home, to receive little or no remuneration, and to be faced with political and legal processes which ignore their contribution to society and accord no recognition of their particular needs." A more fundamental treatment of the skewed nature of the international human rights system would redefine the boundaries of the traditional human rights canon, rather than tinkering with the limited existing model of nondiscrimination.

Before developing this argument, I want to consider two important objections to my project. The first is that the pursuit of rights is a flawed feminist strategy, the second that developing a generally applicable women's international human rights law depends on a monolithic, essentialized view of women that cannot take into account the great differences among women worldwide.

Feminist Critiques of Rights

A number of feminist scholars have argued, in the context of national laws, that campaigns for women's legal rights are at best a waste of energy and at worst positively detrimental to women. The critique, developed also by the Critical Legal Studies movement, has several aspects. One is the claim that statements of rights are indeterminate and thus highly manipulable both in a technical and a more basic sense. Recourse to the language of rights may give a rhetorical flourish to an argument, but provides only an ephemeral polemic advantage, often obscuring the need for political and social change. To assert a legal right, some Critical scholars argue, is to mischaracterize our social experience and to assume the inevitability of social antagonism by affirming that social power rests in the state and not in the people who compose it. The individualism promoted by traditional understandings of rights limits their possibilities by ignoring "the relational nature of social life." Talk of rights is said to make contingent social structures seem permanent and to undermine the possibility of their radical transformation: the only consistent function of rights has been to protect the most privileged groups in society.

Feminists have argued that, while the formulation of equal rights may be useful as a first step toward the improvement of the position of women, a continuing focus on the acquisition of rights may not be beneficial: women's experiences and concerns are not easily translated into the narrow, individualistic language of rights; rights discourse overly simplifies complex power relations and their promise may be thwarted by structural inequalities of power; the balancing of "competing" rights by decision-making bodies often reduces women's power; and particular rights, such as the right to freedom of religion or the protection of the family, can in fact justify the oppression of women. Feminists have examined the interpretation of rights apparently designed to benefit women by national tribunals and pointed to their typically androcentric construction.

Feminist critiques of rights are remarkably rare in the literature on international women's rights. Most commentators assume that the quest for rights for women is an important and useful strategy internationally. But is this task worth the energy that must be expended on it? Are we simply creating new sites for the subtle oppression of women?

While the acquisition of rights is by no means the only solution for the worldwide domination of women by men, it is an important tactic in the international arena. Because women in most societies operate from such a disadvantaged position, rights discourse offers a recognized vocabulary to frame political and social wrongs. Martha Minow has described the problems in denying rights discourse to traditionally dominated groups: "I worry about criticizing rights and legal language just when they have become available to people who had previously lacked access to them. I worry about those who have, telling those who do not, 'you do not need it, you should not want it.' " So, too, Patricia Williams has pointed out that, for African Americans, talk of rights has been a constant source of hope: " 'Rights' feels so new in the mouths of most black people. It is still so deliciously empowering to say. It is a sign for and a gift of selfhood that is very hard to contemplate restructuring at this point in history. It is the magic wand of visibility and invisibility, of inclusion and exclusion, of power and no power." The empowering function of rights discourse for women, particularly in the international sphere where we are still almost completely invisible, is a crucial aspect of its value.

Rights discourse also offers a focus for international feminism which can translate into action if responses to women's claims are inadequate. It affirms "a community dedicated to invigorating words with a power to restrain, so that even the powerless can appeal to those words." In discussing the experience of African Americans with the United States constitutional guarantees of rights, Patricia Williams remarks that "the problem with rights discourse is not that the discourse is itself constricting but that it exists in a constricted referential universe." This observation is particularly apt with respect to women's international human rights law, which operates within the narrow referential universe of the international legal order. The need to develop a feminist rights discourse so that it acknowledges gendered disparities of power, rather than assuming all people are equal in relation to all rights, is crucial. The challenge is then to invest a rights vocabulary with meanings that undermine the current skewed distribution of economic, social, and political power. In non-western societies this task may be particularly complex. For example, as Radhika Coomaraswamy points out, in the South Asian region "rights discourse is a weak discourse," particularly in the context of women and family relations.

First and Third World Feminisms

A conceptual problem for all feminist analysis is that of essentialism: assuming that all women have similar attributes and experiences and ignoring the impact of other variables such as race, class, wealth, and sexual preference on the position of women. This issue is particularly acute in international law, which, by definition, is concerned with transnational standards, applicable in a vast range of circumstances. Is it ever possible to speak meaningfully of women's voices in an international framework? Some feminists of color and from developing nations have questioned attempts to universalize a particular understanding of feminism, charging white, western feminists with inappropriately assuming that their concerns are shared worldwide. "Have we got a theory for you!" the title of such a critique of western feminists sums up the concern of a new, feminist brand of colonialism. But patriarchy and the devaluing of women, although manifested differently within different societies, are almost universal. As Peggy Antrobus, Director of Women and Development at the University of the West Indies, told the 1991 Women and Environment consultation in Florida, although we are divided by race, class, culture and geography, our hope lies in our commonalities. All women's unremunerated household work is exploited, we all have conflicts in our multiple roles, our sexuality is exploited by men, media and the economy, we struggle for survival and dignity, and, rich or poor, we are vulnerable to violence. We share our "otherness," our exclusion from decision making at all levels.

Since the very basis of feminist theory is the experience of women, there will inevitably be tension between universal theories and local experience in any feminist account of international law. Differences of class, race, and nationality will lead to differing power relationships among women. But while no monolithic "women's point of view" can be assumed, it is also important to acknowledge commonalities across cultures.

Women and International Human Rights Law

Why has the androcentric nature of human rights law only recently begun to be analyzed? One reason must be simply that, as in all areas of international law, women have been almost entirely excluded from the important human rights fora where standards are defined, monitored, and implemented. Only recently have non-governmental organizations in the human rights area begun to acknowledge the particular disadvantages faced by women. There have been, then, few effective channels to carry women's voices, interests, and concerns into the mainstream human rights law-making arena, and women have remained in a sidelined, specialized international sphere. Another reason may be that the comparatively radical, and vulnerable, nature of human rights law within the international legal order has protected it from internal critique. Those concerned with the protection of human rights in general may well be reluctant to challenge the form of human rights law at a fundamental level, fearing that such a critique may be used to reduce the hard-fought-for advances in the area. A third reason may be the retarded impact that feminist theories have had on the study of legal systems generally, and international law in particular.

Feminist scholars have noted distinct, if overlapping, phases in the study of the relationship between women and western national legal systems generally. And there are parallels in the attempt to take women seriously in the international human rights system. An initial stage of feminist critique of law is often associated with "liberal" feminism. It identifies sexual equality with equal treatment, rejecting any notion that the law should tolerate or recognize intrinsic differences between women and men. The strategy adopted by liberal feminists is to require the law to fulfill the liberal claims for its objectivity and principled basis. They have worked for reform of the law, dismantling legal barriers to women being treated like men in the public sphere. The assumption is that the disadvantages suffered by women can be compartmentalized and redressed by a simple requirement of equal treatment. This approach adopts the vocabulary, epistemology, and political theory of the law as it currently operates.

Such an approach characterizes much of the existing women's international human rights law. The rationale of, for example, the United Nations Convention on the Political Rights of Women of 1953, the United Nations Convention on the Nationality of Married Women of 1957, the UNESCO Convention on Discrimination in Education of 1960, and the norm of nondiscrimination contained in both the Human Rights Covenants is to place women in the same position as men in the public sphere. The activities of the Commission on the Status of Women generally have also been informed by such an approach. Thus the international prohibition on sex discrimination promises equality to women who attempt to conform to a male model, and offers little to those who do not. The problem with such an approach, as Nicola Lacey has observed in the context of national discrimination laws, is that it is "inadequate to criticize and transform a world in which the distribution of goods is structured along gender lines." It assumes "a world of autonomous individuals starting a race or making free choices [which] has no cutting edge against the fact that men and women are simply running different races." The language of "equal rights" and "equal opportunities" tacitly reinforces the basic organization of society. The promise of equality as "sameness" as men only gives women access to a world already constituted.

The comparatively broad definition of discrimination contained in the UN Convention on the Elimination of All Forms of Discrimination Against Women, which covers both equality of opportunity (formal equality) and equality of outcome (de facto equality), is nevertheless based on the same limited approach. The measure of equality in Article 1 is still a male one. And the discrimination it prohibits is confined to accepted human rights and fundamental freedoms. If these rights and freedoms can be shown to be defined in a gendered way, access to them will be unlikely to promote any real form of equality. The Convention's sanction of affirmative action programs in Article 4 similarly assumes that these measures will be temporary techniques to allow women eventually to perform exactly like men. The male-centered view of equality is tacitly reinforced by the Convention's focus on public life, the economy, the law, education, and its very limited recognition that oppression within the private sphere, that of the domestic and family worlds, contributes to women's inequality. The 1992 General Recommendation of the Committee on the Elimination of Discrimination Against Women, describing gender-based violence as a form of discrimination against women, underlines the significance of the private sphere as a site for the oppression of women.

The discrimination approach of the Women's Convention was translated directly, and Noreen Burrows suggests, too hurriedly, from the 1966 Convention on the Elimination of All Forms of Racial Discrimination . Little attention seems to have been given to whether this was an appropriate model, given the problems women face worldwide. Indeed, one of the obstacles faced by women in the area of international law is the general consensus at the state level that oppression on the basis of race is considerably more serious than oppression on the basis of gender. This perhaps explains why the Women's Convention contains much weaker implementation mechanisms than the Race Convention.

Another strand in legal feminism is the counterpart of approaches in other disciplines that have described, for example, a feminist theology or a women's literature. The essence of this approach, sometimes termed "cultural feminism," is the identification of a distinctive "woman's voice" in the legal context and a reevaluation of the contribution it can make to legal doctrine. The work of the child psychologist Carol Gilligan has had a particular influence in the development of this form of feminist jurisprudence. Gilligan notes the disparity between women's experience and the representation of human development contained in the psychological literature. The usual interpretation of this phenomenon was that it indicated problems in women's psychological development. Gilligan turns this analysis on its head by arguing that the failure of women to fit existing models of human growth suggested a limitation in the notion of the human condition. The hypothesis drawn from Gilligan's research by feminist legal scholars in the context of national legal systems is that, just as traditional psychological theories have privileged a male perspective and marginalized women's voices, so, too, law privileges a male view of the universe. Many feminists have pointed out that law is part of the structure of male domination. Its hierarchical organization, its adversarial format, and its aim of the abstract resolution of competing rights make the law an intensely patriarchal institution. Law represents a very limited aspect of human experience. The language and imagery of the law underscore its maleness: it lays claim to rationality, objectivity, and abstraction, characteristics traditionally associated with men, and is defined in contrast to emotion, subjectivity, and contextualized thinking, the province of women.

Celebrating the differences between feminine and masculine modes of reasoning in legal systems is not without problems. But the value of cultural feminist approaches is that they highlight the almost comprehensive exclusion of women's experiences from the development of the law, and challenge its claim of neutrality and objectivity. There is a parallel in the approach of cultural feminists to national legal systems and that of scholars and activists in the area of international human rights law who attempted to develop a category of specific women's rights.

Noreen Burrows, for example, sees the definition of women's rights as the means to move beyond the limitations of the nondiscrimination focus on women's international human rights law. She identifies rights associated with reproductive choice and childbirth as central to the category of international women's rights. Other potential women's rights include the right to a minimum wage for work within the home or in subsistence farming, and the right to literacy: all rights that address particular disadvantages women face. This approach would allow the international vocabulary of rights to be employed in the private sphere, and thus responds more accurately to the reality of most women's lives than does the liberal feminist strategy of prohibiting discrimination in the public sphere. A possible disadvantage is that the formulation of women-specific rights could lead to their marginalization within the human rights system. Laura Reanda has described the strategic dilemma with respect to international legal structures and women well: the price of the creation of separate institutional mechanisms and special measures dealing with women within the United Nations system has typically been the creation of a "women's ghetto," given less power, fewer resources, and a lower priority than "mainstream" human rights bodies. On the other hand, the attempt to improve the position of women through more generally applicable measures has allowed women's concerns to be submerged by what are regarded as more "global" issues.

A third strategy to redress the subordinate position of women developed in feminist jurisprudence is to understand it as the product of domination of women by men: inequality as sexual in nature. Catharine MacKinnon has been the most consistent exponent of this approach. She argues that the common failing of theories associating equality with equal treatment or with different treatment is that they implicitly accept a male yardstick: women are either the same as or different from a male norm. MacKinnon views social relations between women and men as organized so "that men may dominate and women must submit." The law, she says, keeps women "out and down" by preserving a hierarchical system based on gender. MacKing non describes an alternative legal analysis of inequality for which the central question always is "whether the policy or practice in question integrally contributes to the maintenance of an underclass or a deprived position because of gender status." The law should support freedom from systematic subordination because of sex rather than freedom to be treated without regard to sex.

MacKinnon's approach is not always easily applied because many of the relationships of subordination sanctioned by the law are so deeply engrained that they appear quite natural. It involves looking "for that which we have been trained not to see...[identifying] the invisible." If the issue of inequality is redescribed as one of domination and subordination, sex discrimination laws simply promising equal treatment appear of limited utility. Catharine MacKinnon has worked rather for an expansion of the ambit of the law to cover traditionally legally unrecognized harms of particular concern to women such as sexual harassment and pornography. She argues that the feminist project in law is to legitimize the real injuries women suffer in order to make them unacceptable. In this way gender relations can be, slowly, transformed. Using MacKinnon's analysis, other feminist lawyers have described discrimination in institutions, such as the workplace, where practices are more compatible with culturally defined male life patterns than female ones. Christine Littleton, for example, has proposed defining the goal of equality as "acceptance" so that institutions could be required to react to gender differences by restructuring to fit women and their life patterns.

How might the "radical" strand in feminist jurisprudence be translated into the context of international human rights law? It suggests the value of transforming the masculine world of rights, masquerading as "human," by extending it to include protection against all forms of subordination on the basis of gender. We need to identify policies and practices that contribute to women's inferior position in different societies and insist that the structure of human rights law offer protection against them.

Do the three strands of feminist jurisprudence sketched here share the problem of conceding too much authority to law, whether national or international? They may encourage a reconsideration of the values informing the law, but nevertheless all accord it considerable power, preserving its place in the hierarchy of male structures. Carol Smart and others have also questioned whether the construction of Grand Feminist Theory really is useful in achieving equality between the sexes, arguing that such endeavors do not capture the contextualized and partial nature of our knowledge. Moreover, if we get the legal theory correct, will legal practice follow? The best-intentioned laws can be thwarted in practice if their interpreters do not appreciate why and how the prohibited behavior contributes to the subordination of women. Smart argues that we should avoid general, abstract theories and focus instead on the realities of women's lives, studying the inconsistencies and contradictions in legal regulation: the law does not operate in a monolithic way to oppress women and advantage men. She supports action at the micro-political level rather than the slippery path of legal reform. It is better, Smart has said, to be a feminist journalist than a feminist lawyer.

The international struggle against the oppression of women must use all the approaches outlined above because inequality has both overt and subtle forms. The model of nondiscrimination can change the formal language of power and offer particular individuals limited remedies against inequality. Attempting to balance the thoroughly gendered nature of the international human rights system by defining a category of women's rights can alter a monolithic conception of inequality. And understanding the relations of power and subordination endorsed by the law can suggest methods of reform that will not fall into the same trap. At the same time, it is necessary to remain realistic and somewhat skeptical about the importance of any law, national or international, in achieving social change.

Transforming "Men's" Rights Law

A truly human rights law will only be possible when the limitations of the current international system are understood. I want now to explain and develop the claim made earlier that what is presently referred to as international human rights law is thoroughly gendered, using examples from each "generation" of rights. Despite their apparently different philosophical bases, the three generations are remarkably similar from a woman's perspective.

It is worth noting to begin with that, with the exception of the Convention on the Rights of the Child, all "general" human rights instruments refer only to men. The importance of language in constructing and reinforcing the subordination of women has been much analyzed by feminist scholars, and the consistently masculine vocabulary of human rights law operates at both a direct and subtle level to exclude women. More basically, all international human rights law rests on and reinforces a distinction between public and private worlds, and this distinction operates to muffle, and often completely silence, the voices of women.

Analysis of the distinction between public and private spheres has been a recurring theme in feminist scholarship. The dichotomy is central to liberalism the dominant political, and legal, philosophy of the west. It assumes a public sphere of rationality, order, and political authority in which political and legal activity take place, and a private, "subjective" sphere in which regulation is not appropriate. Domestic, family life is typically regarded as the center of the private world. A passage from the 1957 British Government's Wolfenden Committee's Report on Homosexual Offences and Prostitution illustrates this well: "there must remain a realm of private morality and immorality, which is, in brief and crude terms, not the law's business."

As described by liberal theorists, the distinction between public and private realms operates generally and neutrally with respect to individuals. However, in western society women are relegated to the private sphere of home, hearth, and family. The public sphere of workplace, law, economics, politics, intellectual and cultural life is regarded as the province of men. This phenomenon is explained as a matter of nature, convenience, or individual choice. One feminist response to these claims is that the public/private distinction in fact operates both to obscure and to legitimate men's domination of women. The public/private dichotomy is gendered: it is a "metaphor for the social patterning of gender, a description of sociological practice, and a category grounded in experience."It is also a normative distinction, because greater significance and power attaches to the public, male world. The assignment of women to the domestic sphere entrenches their inequality with men, for women are regarded as dependent on men for subsistence. Moreover the privacy of domestic life makes women's concerns invisible and ensures preservation of the status quo.

Some feminist scholars have cautioned against general explanations of the universally observed domination of women by men. Particular cultural and social contexts, they argue, must be taken into account and "universal" analytic categories such as the public/private distinction run the risk of simply being shorthand for biological explanations of women's subordination.

The anthropologist Maila Stivens, for example, points out that it is very difficult to define the private domain in agrarian societies in Southeast Asia. She observes the complete gendering of all levels of social life right across the traditional public/private division and argues that we should expand our notion of politics rather than analyze all societies within the confines of a particular western construct of the public/private distinction.

But the distinction remains western only if the content of each sphere is defined by western experience, if women are regarded as always opposed to men in the same ways in all contexts and societies: for example if women's social inferiority is universally attributed to their role in bearing and raising children. What is important to observe universally is that it is not the activity which characterizes the public and the private, but rather the actor: that is, women's subordination to men is mediated through the public/private dichotomy. What is "public" in one society may well be "private" in another, but women's activities are consistently devalued by being construed as private. In any event, the western "version" of the public/private dichotomy lies at the heart of public international law, a discipline still largely informed by western values and structures. In this sense, international law is a medium for the ideology of the distinction to be exported from the developed to the developing world: it thus replicates the "reforms" imposed by many colonial administrators which often weakened the position of women in colonial societies.

Feminist concern with the public/private dichotomy in western legal thought has two different aspects: the way that the law has been used to exclude women from the public sphere from professions, from the marketplace, from the vote; and a more basic form of the dichotomy, between what is considered the business of law and what is left unregulated. Analyzing the distinction in this latter sense can be particularly useful in the area of international human rights law.

Why is lack of regulation of particular areas of social life significant for women? Some feminist jurists argue that "law's absence devalues women and their functions: women are simply not important enough to merit legal regulation." But it is important to also recognize that a deliberate policy of non-intervention by the state does not signify noncontrol or neutrality. Thus lack of regulation of rape in marriage supports and legitimates the power of husbands over wives. Further, regulation of areas such as employment, taxation, social security, and crime have significant, if indirect, impact on the private sphere and reinforce a particular sort of family unit a nuclear family in which there is a division of labor between men and women. Lack of direct state intervention in the name of protection of privacy can thus disguise the inequality and domination exercised in the private sphere." In western domestic legal systems, the distinction drawn between public and private supports the sexual violence on which patriarchy is based: it creates a "space into which the law's ordinary protection against violence will not be allowed to penetrate." The most pervasive harm against women tends to occur right within the inner sanctum of the private realm, within the family.

Like national legal systems, international law is constructed within a "public" world, although national and international "public" spheres are often differently defined. International law operates in the most public of all public worlds, that of nation states. Thus the United Nations Charter makes the (public) province of international law distinct from the (private) sphere of domestic jurisdiction; the acquisition of statehood or international personality confers "public" status on an entity with consequences, for example, for jurisdiction, representation, and ownership; the law of state responsibility sorts out (public) actions for which the state is accountable from those "private" ones for which it does not have to answer internationally. The development of human rights law has altered one set of boundaries between public and private in international law to allow the law to address violations of designated individual and group rights. This development, however, has not challenged the much deeper public/private dichotomy based on gender: rights are defined by the criterion of what men fear will happen to them. As in domestic law, the non-regulation of the private sphere internationally legitimates self-regulation, which translates inevitably into male dominance.

First Generation Rights

The very epithet "civil and political" to describe those rights that make up the traditional "first" generation of international human rights law suggests the defining nature of a public/private dichotomy in their content. These are rights that the individual can assert against the state: the public world of the state must allow the private individual protection and freedom in particular areas. The primacy traditionally given to civil and political rights by western international lawyers and philosophers is directed toward protection for men within public life, their relationship with government. But these are not the harms from which women most need protection.

The operation of a public/private distinction at a gendered level is most clear in the definition of civil and political rights, particularly those concerned with protection of the individual from violence: the construction of these norms obscures the most pervasive harms done to women. One example of this is the "most important of all human rights," the right to life set out in Article 6 of the Civil and Political Covenant and forming part of customary international law. The right is concerned with the arbitrary deprivation of life through public action. But protection from arbitrary deprivation of life or liberty through public actions, important as it is, does not address how being a woman is in itself life-threatening and the special ways in which women need legal protection to be able to enjoy their right to life.

From conception to old age, womanhood is full of risks: of abortion and infanticide because of the social and economic pressure to have sons in some cultures; of malnutrition because of social practices of giving men and boys priority with respect to food; of less access to health care than men; of endemic violence against women in all states. Although the empirical evidence of violence against women is overwhelming and undisputed, it has not been adequately reflected in the development of international law. The great level of documented violence against women around the world is unaddressed by the international legal notion of the right to life because that legal system is focused on "public" actions by the state.

A similar myopia can be detected also in the international prohibition on torture. A central feature of the international legal definition of torture is that it takes place in the public realm: it must be "inflicted by or at the instigation of or with the consent or acquiescence of a public official or other person acting in an official capacity." Although many women are victims of torture in this "public" sense, by far the greatest violence against women occurs in the "private" nongovernmental sphere.

The pioneering work of the Women's Rights Project of Americas Watch (WRP) on violence against women in Brazil underlines how arbitrary the distinction between "public" and "private" action is in the context of violence against women. The WRP documented a structure of discriminatory non-prosecution, and indeed sometimes overt acceptance, of three significant forms of violence against women: wifemurder, battery, and rape. With respect to wife-murder, the defense of "honor" in the murder of an allegedly unfaithful wife was successful in some regions in 80 percent of cases in which it was invoked and in other cases operated to reduce sentences significantly. Husband-murder, by contrast, was treated considerably more seriously. Although over 70 percent of reported cases of violence against women in Brazil take place in the home (compared to 10 percent for men), domestic violence has typically been treated either as a matter outside, the criminal justice system, or more recently as a minor, peripheral problem. The WRP also reported the common non-prosecution and non-punishment of rape in Brazil, and the difficulties created for rape victims in proving their case.

One reason for the wide scale toleration of violence against women in Brazil was the explicitly and implicitly held view that it was a "private" matter, not within the proper scope of the criminal justice system. The public/private distinction operates here at an international legal level as well in the context of attributing state responsibility: can a state be held accountable in international law for the actions of private individuals given that the traditional international legal rules confine state responsibility to activities by, or at the instigation of, its public officials? The WRP Brazil report pointed to the discriminatory pattern of state responses to crimes of violence based on the gender of the victims, and founded Brazil's international responsibility on its violation of the international norm of nondiscrimination.

However, if violence against women is understood, not just as aberrant behavior, but as part of the structure of the universal subordination of women, it can never be considered a purely "private" issue. Charlotte Bunch has pointed out that such violence is caused by "the structural relationships of power, domination and privilege between men and women in society. Violence against women is central to maintaining those political relations at home, at work and in all public spheres." These structures are supported by the patriarchal hierarchy of the nation-state. To Catharine MacKinnon's proposed test of "whether a policy or practice integrally contributes to the maintenance of an underclass or a deprived position because of gender status" the answer in this context must be a resounding yes. The maintenance of a legal and social system in which violence or discrimination against women is endemic and where such action is trivialized or discounted should therefore engage state responsibility. Rethinking the traditional notions of state responsibility is a vital project in women's human rights law. In 1992, the Commission on the Status of Women adopted a Draft Declaration on Violence Against Women. This is a valuable development in women's international human rights law because it makes violence against women an international issue. The Draft Declaration, however, also illustrates a consistent problem in this field. Apart from a preambular statement, the Declaration does not clearly present violence against women as a general human rights concern: it appears as a discrete and special issue rather than an abuse of, for example, the right to life or equality. If the relevance of the Declaration to the interpretation of "general" human rights were made more explicit, it may more strongly influence the mainstream human rights bodies and encourage them to view violence against women as within their mandate and not just the province of the specialized women's institutions.

Apart from the right to life and freedom from torture, other rights in the traditional civil and political catalogue also have been interpreted in a way that offers very little freedom or protection to women. The right to liberty and security of the person in Article 9 of the Civil and Political Covenant, for example, operates only in the context of direct action by the state. It does not address the fear of sexual violence, which is a defining feature of women's lives. The right to freedom of expression has been defined in some national contexts as including the right to make, distribute and use pornography, which contributes directly to the level of violence against women. And the right to privacy can be interpreted as protecting from scrutiny the major sites for the oppression of women: home and family.

Second Generation Rights

"Second" generation rights, economic, social, and cultural rights, might be thought by their very nature to transcend the public private dichotomy and thus offer more to women's lives. Certainly, the fact that these rights do not neatly fit the "individual versus state" paradigm has contributed to their more controversial status and to weaker methods of implementation at international law. But the definition of these rights as set out in the Covenant on Economic, Social, and Cultural Rights indicates the tenacity of a gendered public private distinction in human rights law. The Covenant creates a public sphere by assuming that all effective power rests with the state. But, as Shelley Wright has pointed out, "For most women, most of the time, indirect subjection to the State will always be mediated through direct subjection to individual men or groups of men." The Covenant, then, does not touch on the economic, social, and cultural context in which most women live. For example, the definition of the right to just and favorable conditions of work in Article 7 is confined to work in the public sphere. Marilyn Waring has documented the tremendous amount of economic activity by women all over the world which is rendered invisible precisely because it is performed by women without pay and considered within the private, domestic sphere. Article 7's guarantee to women of "conditions of work not inferior to those enjoyed by men, with equal pay for equal work" thus sounds rather hollow in light of the international myopia with respect to the extent and economic value of women's work. The right to food, set out in Article 11 of the Covenant, is even more clearly relevant to the private, domestic: sphere and yet has been elaborated in a way that offers little to women.

Moreover, the notion of cultural, and religious, rights can often reinforce a distinction between public and private worlds that operates to the disadvantage of women: culture and religion can be seen as spheres protected from legal regulation even though they allow oppression of women by men. While the right to gender equality on the one hand, and religious and cultural rights on the other can be reconciled by limiting the latter, in political practice cultural and religious freedom are accorded a much higher priority nationally and internationally.

The international community does not yet recognize the fundamental gender inequity perpetuated by the current interpretations of economic, social, and cultural rights. For example, in his final report, the Sub-Commission on Prevention of Discrimination and Protection of Minorities Special Rapporteur on the Realization of Economic, Social, and Cultural Rights, Danilo Turk, discussed barriers to the observance of these rights. He identified problems ranging from structural adjustment policies, to income distribution and deficient political will but did not deal at all with the more basic issue of the relevance of these rights to women, half the world's population. Failing to take gender into account means that economic, social, and cultural rights will offer very little to women.

Third Generation Rights

"Third" generation rights cover collective or group rights. They have been championed within the United Nations by developing nations in particular and they have been only cautiously accepted by the mainstream international human rights community because of their challenge to the western, liberal model of individual rights invocable against the sovereign. The philosophical basis of group rights rests on a primary commitment to the welfare of the community over and above the interests of particular individuals. From one point of view, it might seem that such rights would be of particular promise to women, whose lives typically have the quality of connectedness with others, centering more around the family, the group, and the community than the individual. The theoretical and practical development of third generation rights has, however, delivered very little to women. The right to development, for example, is both defined and implemented internationally to support male economic dominance. So, too, the right to self-determination, allowing "all peoples" to "freely determine their political status and freely pursue their economic, social and cultural development" has been invoked, and supported, recently in a number of contexts to allow the oppression of women. The complex and often contradictory position of women in nationalist movements and in the decolonization process has been well documented. As Halliday has observed, "nationalist movements subordinate women in a particular definition of their role and place in society, [and] enforce conformity to values that are often male-defined." However, the oppression of women within groups claiming the right of selfdetermination has never been considered relevant to their validity or to the form self-determination should take: in this sense the right is relevant only in the most public of contexts: male political life. The right to self-determination attaches to "peoples," entities defined ethnically or culturally, even if half the persons constituting the people have little or no power in that community.

By failing to take the phenomenon of male domination of women in both the public and private worlds into account, the right to selfdetermination and the very notion of statehood can in fact reinforce oppression against women through its complicity in systemic male oppression and violence. An example of this is the strong United States support for the Afghani resistance movement after the 1979 Soviet invasion without any apparent concern for the very low status of women within traditional Afghan society. And the victory of the Mujahadeen was accompanied by the withdrawal of social and educational possibilities for women. Another example is the immediate and powerful United Nations response after Iraq's 1990 invasion of Kuwait, justified in part in the name of the self-determination of the Kuwaiti people. None of the plans for the liberation or reconstruction of Kuwait were concerned with that state's denial of political rights to women. Although some international pressure was brought to bear on the Kuwaiti government during and after the invasion to institute a more democratic system, the concern did not focus on the political repression of women and was, in any event, quickly dropped. The achievement of self-determination in Kuwait has benefited only an elite cadre of men, those permitted to participate in government and public life. It has had indeed a negative impact on women in the private sphere: a recent Middle East Watch report documents the widespread physical and sexual abuse of Asian women domestic workers in Kuwait since its liberation and the Kuwaiti government's frustration of attempts for legal redress.

Summary

Women's international human rights must be developed on a number of fronts. Certainly the relevance of the traditional canon of human rights to women is important to document. The instruments and institutions of the "first wave" of international law with respect to women must also be supported and strengthened. The potential of an individual complaints procedure under the Women's Convention, for example, should be seriously explored. At the same time, rights that focus on harms sustained by women in particular need to be identified and developed, challenging the public private distinction by bringing rights discourse into the private sphere. But, most fundamental and important, we must work to ensure that women's voices find a public audience, to reorient the boundaries of mainstream human rights law so that it incorporates an understanding of the world from the perspective of the socially subjugated. One way forward in international human rights law is to challenge the gendered dichotomy of public and private worlds.

10

Domestic Violence as an International Human Rights Issue

Introduction

The evolution of the traditional human rights movement for the purpose of showing both why that movement has neglected the problem of domestic violence and why such neglect can no longer be justified in light of comparable issues that the movement now addresses. I will then outline the type of evidence that in my view is needed to treat the problem of domestic violence as a human rights issue, while noting the ways in which this proof often differs significantly from the evidence required for more traditional human rights inquiries.

Finally, I will discuss the experience of the Human Rights Watch Women's Rights Project in collecting this evidence. In doing so, I will note a troubling void that we have observed in the work of local human rights and women's rights organizations. By highlighting this void, I hope to help spawn the factual research needed to address the problem of domestic violence more effectively as a human rights issue.

Narrow Reading of International Human Rights Law

International human rights organizations, including Human Rights Watch, have neglected the problem of domestic violence against women. In discussing international human rights organizations I will limit myself to two: Human Rights Watch, because it is the organization with which I am most familiar, and Amnesty International, because of its defining role in the field. One cause of this neglect was their narrow reading of the broad language of the International Covenant on Civil and Political Rights (the Covenant). I will limit my legal discussion to the International Covenant on Civil and Political Rights, because this treaty is the most influential within the traditional human rights movement, and because it addresses problems of violence more directly than the Convention on the Elimination of All Forms of Discrimination Against Women. The Covenant contains powerful, expansive phrases, with obvious potential relevance to the fight against domestic violence particularly violence that amounts to murder, and arguably also lesser assaults. For example, Article 6(1) provides: "Every human being has the inherent right to life. This right shall be protected by law. No one shall be arbitrarily deprived of his life." Article 7 provides that "No one shall be subjected to torture or to cruel, inhuman or degrading treatment." Article 9(1) provides that "Everyone has the right to...security of person." All these guarantees are arguably implicated by domestic violence.

Political Motivation

Despite the broad potential reach of the Covenant's guarantees, international human rights organizations, particularly in their early days, treated these provisions as if they applied only to the victims of politically motivated abuse (and even then only if the abuse was at the hands of a government agent). It was as if the sweeping language of these provisions "Every human being," "Everyone" were replaced by the far narrower phrase, "every dissident."

Part of the reason for this narrow reading of the Covenant is historical accident: the large human rights organizations were born out of a concern with politically motivated abuse. Amnesty International was founded to protect people who had been imprisoned for their peaceful political beliefs. The classic prisoner of conscience was a man or woman who had been detained because of his or her nonviolent political opposition to a government. Human Rights Watch, in the form of Helsinki Watch, originated in an effort to protect human rights monitors who had begun to emerge in the former Soviet Union and Eastern Europe following the signing of the Helsinki Accords in 1975. These "Helsinki monitors" arose in response to Principle VII of the Final Act of the Conference on Security and Cooperation in Europe, which proclaimed "the right of the individual to know and act upon his rights." In each case, dissidents were the main focus of concern.

There may have been good reasons for this focus, given the limited resources available at the time for human rights work and the need to create a public consciousness about (and sympathy for) human rights. But justification for this narrow interpretation of the human rights cause cannot be found in the Covenant's text.

Although both Amnesty International and Human Rights Watch have gradually expanded their mandates beyond the classic prisoner of conscience, the paradigm of a government seeking to still dissent remains powerful. For example, while the fight against torture and extrajudicial execution encompasses those detained because of common as well as political crimes, the political prisoner remains a principal concern. Campaigns waged against violations of physical integrity still tend to feature dissidents rather than common criminal suspects. In recent years, however, international human rights organizations have begun to move beyond an exclusive focus on prisoners of conscience. For example, Human Rights Watch has documented summary executions by the police of common criminal suspects, with substantial reports devoted to this topic in Argentina, Brazil, and Jamaica. Amnesty International has engaged in similar work. Torture in countries like Turkey and India, where it affects vast numbers of common criminal suspects, has also received heightened attention. In addition, Human Rights Watch launched a Prisoners' Rights Project, which monitors prison conditions faced by those held for common crimes as well as political offenses, and has reported on prison conditions in some dozen countries around the world.

Of course, there is often a political dimension to abuses against alleged common criminals, in that the victims are usually poor and the abuses tend to serve as a method of social control. But the victims generally are targeted not because of their political views indeed, these often are not known but because of their social status and presumed aspirations. Yet the broad language of the Covenant clearly encompasses these governmental abuses, and it has become increasingly accepted that they should be part of the international human rights mandate.

By the same token, the lack of a traditional political motivation behind domestic violence against women should no longer preclude its consideration by international human rights organizations. Like violence against presumed common criminals, violence against women can be said to have a political dimension in that it arguably serves as a form of social control by reinforcing the subjugation of women. But even that political dimension should not be necessary to address the issue. If international human rights organizations no longer ask the political views of a victim of execution, torture, or inhuman prison conditions, why should they care that domestic violence has little if anything to do with the political views of its victims? A woman killed by her husband for a supposed offense to his "honor" is deprived of her life in as "arbitrary" a fashion (to use the language of Covenant article 6(1)) as a common criminal suspect who is summarily executed by the police.

State Action Versus Inaction

A second conceptual obstacle to the treatment of domestic violence against women has been the focus of the human rights movement, and human rights law, on violations by the state. Anyone can commit a common crime, but only a state and its agents can commit a human rights violation under international law. Since the perpetrators of domestic violence are by definition private, they cannot be treated as appropriate subjects of international human rights law unless the state can in some sense be held responsible.

The necessary theory of accountability can be found in the traditional human rights movement's gradual acceptance of the argument that the state can be held responsible under international human rights law for its inaction as well as its action. The trend toward broader acceptance of this analytic approach was sparked to a significant extent by the effort to grapple with the phenomenon of death squads. Although in places like El Salvador and Guatemala there was strong evidence linking death squads with governmental forces, the international human rights movement did not rely exclusively on a theory of government agency. It also used an argument of complicity, by contending that the government should be held responsible simply because of its systematic failure to attempt to halt the death squads.

Human Rights Watch used a similar theory of government complicity to address private violence against landless peasants in the course of rural land disputes in such countries as Brazil and Paraguay. Although at times the violence is committed by state agents, often it occurs at the hands of private militias in the employ of large landowners who have no direct relationship with the state. To hold the state responsible for this otherwise private violence, we have highlighted the state's systematic failure to enforce criminal laws against this category of violence. The state's abdication of its duty to protect its citizens from crimes of violence amounts to a tacit endorsement of that violence. That complicity provides the requisite governmental dimension to consider the violence a human rights issue. The same theory of state responsibility by omission rather than commission can be seen in Human Rights Watch's treatment of a range of other abuses, including sectarian violence, violence against labor activists, violence against political opponents, slavery, and forced labor. When the Egyptian government turns a blind eye toward private violence against Copts, or the Romanian government does the same toward private violence against Gypsies, Human Rights Watch has not hesitated to hold the government responsible under international human rights law. Similarly, we have condemned as human rights violations:

- the systematic failure of the government in Miami to prosecute those responsible for violent attacks on moderate voices in the Cuban-American community on issues relating to the Cuban government;
- the systematic failure of the governments of Guatemala, El Salvador and South Korea to prosecute those who, at the behest of large private employers, have attacked union organizers and labor activists;
- the systematic failure of the Mauritanian government to act against private citizens who continue to enslave blacks;

- the systematic failure of the Brazilian government to move against large private landowners who employ forced labor.

Implicit in this approach is that a state has some duty to protect those within its territory from private acts of violence and illicit force. When the state makes little or no effort to stop a certain form of private violence, it tacitly condones that violence. This complicity transforms what would otherwise be wholly private conduct into a constructive act of the state.

While the Covenant does not explicitly establish a state's duty to combat private violence, its broad language is fully compatible with this duty. For example, the right not to be "arbitrarily deprived of [one's] life" could be read as imposing a duty on the state to address both official and private violence. Since the international human rights movement has been willing to hold the state responsible under the Covenant for its complicity in various other forms of private violence, there is no reason why it should refrain from using the same analytic approach to address domestic violence. Just as the state's systematic failure to act against private violence directed at landless peasants, labor activists, or disfavored religious or ethnic minorities can give rise to a human rights violation, so this theory of liability by omission can be used to treat the state's systematic failure to confront domestic violence against women as a human rights issue.

For example, in studying domestic violence in Brazil, the Human Rights Watch Women's Rights Project devoted considerable attention to the courts' and prosecutors' persistent acceptance of the "honor" defense the illegal but widely used claim that instances of domestic violence can be justified or excused because the actions of a man's wife or lover allegedly offended his honor. The continued existence of this defense made the state complicit in the phenomenon of "honor" killings because it signaled a tacit official acceptance of the practice.

Limits of State Liability by Omission

Even if one accepts that a state can be held responsible under international human rights law for its failure to address certain categories of violence, the limits to such liability must be defined.

When does a state's failure to stop private violence constitute a human rights violation, as opposed to a mere policy failure?

Theoretically, one could treat each act of private violence as a human rights violation, in that the state has failed to prevent it. But such an absolutist approach to the intractable problem of private violence would trivialize the special stigma behind the label "human rights violator."

Rather, in my view, the limits to state responsibility for private violence must be found in the same notion of complicity that made such violence a human rights matter in the first place. The more vigorous a state's efforts to prosecute violent criminals, the less it can be said to condone, or be complicit in, their crimes. Once this link of governmental complicity is broken, private violence ceases to present a human rights issue.

In this sense, the theory of complicity used to transform private violence into a matter of state responsibility is a relative one. Unlike the absolute duty imposed on the state to prevent acts of unlawful violence by its own agents, a state's duty under international human rights law to prevent private violence extends only so far as a private actor can be said effectively to have become a state agent. It is a human rights violation for a state to commit even a single act of torture, for example. But a single act of domestic violence is not a human rights violation unless the state can be said through its systematic inaction to have condoned the violence.

Unsatisfied with this limited notion of state responsibility, some women's rights activists have suggested an alternative theory. They argue that, unlike other common crimes, domestic violence is inherently an issue under international human rights law because it systematically subordinates women. Victims of ordinary assaults range across all segments of society, the argument goes, but domestic violence is directed primarily at women, with the aim of maintaining male supremacy and depriving them of a range of political, social, and economic benefits. Because of this systematic subordination, these advocates contend, domestic violence constitutes a violation of international human rights law in and of itself. That is, the state has a duty to eradicate domestic violence not simply as it has a duty to counter common crime but akin to its absolute duty to eradicate torture or summary execution by government agents. Or, put another way, they argue that the state must go beyond simply not condoning domestic violence (the standard with respect to most private violence) to ending it (the standard for violence by state agents).

There are two main problems with this approach. First, it fails to distinguish domestic violence from a range of other forms of violence that also systematically subordinate a class of people. Violence in the context of land disputes systematically subordinates landless peasants. Violence against labor activists systematically subordinates workers. Forced labor and slavery systematically subordinate still other categories of people. The list could go on. As the number of classes of victims who can claim systematic subordination at the hands of violent private actors grows, so do the forms of violence that must be considered in and of themselves to be violations of international human rights law and thus to trigger the state's duty of eradication (as opposed to the lesser duty simply not to condone). In the process, the defense of human rights under international law is gradually transformed into an exercise of crime control.

This transformation would have disastrous consequences for the cause of international human rights law because it would devalue the special stigma attached to a violation of that law. If a state's violation of international human rights law had no more stigmatizing effect than the police's failure to prevent a common crime, human rights would be reduced from a series of fundamental legal guarantees limiting the scope of government to mere policy prescriptions.

Second, the effort to distinguish a class of people who merit special protection by the state whether because of their systematic subordination or any other characteristic should give pause because it breaches the universality that underlies international human rights law. An important strength of most, if not all, international human rights law is that its guarantees apply universally. Rights generally exist equally for all. Any theory that creates special rights for a class of people undermines this universality and risks setting a precedent for exempting classes of people from the full protection of international human rights instruments that can easily be abused. Given the long and continuing history of women's suffering under non-universal systems of rights, women's rights advocates should be particularly reluctant to breach this principle of universality.

I do not deny that the rhetoric of human rights can be a useful political tool for those seeking special protections for women. Speaking in terms of human rights can be highly effective in rallying political support for one's cause. But that rhetorical use of human rights discourse to impose special obligations on the state with respect to women is quite different from the universal meaning that human rights concepts should retain under international law. It is one thing for an organization devoted exclusively to the protection of women to use such rhetoric for political ends. It is quite another thing for an international human rights organization, which must be devoted to protecting the rights of all people, to forsake the principle of universality particularly when, as I will show, an alternative approach exists for defining the limits of a theory of state complicity in private violence.

Nondiscrimination

If the Covenant's provisions are not absolute with respect to domestic violence, what do they demand? The substantive provisions of the Covenant provide no clear answer. What steps must a government take against domestic violence to avoid becoming complicit and thus transforming the problem from one of common crime to a human rights issue? Is it enough simply to outlaw the practice? Is it enough to make an occasional arrest, launch a periodic prosecution, or secure a sporadic conviction? Human rights advocates would argue that such desultory efforts are not enough for a state to avoid being held complicit in domestic violence, but the provisions of the Covenant that protect the physical integrity of the person provide no textual guidance on this matter.

The antidiscrimination provisions of the Covenant are more helpful in this regard. They impose an independent duty on the state not to discriminate on a number of specified grounds, including gender, in the protection of various rights. Failure to fulfill this duty constitutes a human rights violation independent of the substantive rights at stake. The advantage of adding this argument to the theory of state responsibility by utter indifference is that it permits evaluation of a state's efforts to eradicate domestic violence well beyond the stage when it is doing nothing. While a discrimination-based theory of state respon sibility does not dictate the precise level of effort to be devoted to combating domestic violence, it does provide important supplemental standards in comparative terms. That is, in the case of the state that is doing the bare minimum in combating domestic violence to avoid charges of complicity, a discrimination theory allows one to insist on greater diligence as a matter of international human rights law. It provides justification for the demand that the state's efforts to combat domestic violence are at least on a par with its efforts to fight comparable forms of violent crime. Of course, if a state's inaction in the face of violence is nearly complete, there is no need to make an argument in terms of discrimination. The state's complicity in itself allows domestic violence to be treated as a human rights issue. But once a state moves beyond the stage of obvious complicity, a discrimination-based theory of state responsibility permits an additional argument: a state can be said to condone a particular form of violence because it pays inadequate attention to prevent it in relation to comparable forms of violence. The textual basis for a discrimination-based theory of liability can be found in several provisions of the Covenant:

- Article 2(1): "Each State Party to the present Covenant undertakes to respect and to ensure to all individuals within its territory and subject to its jurisdiction the rights recognized in the present Covenant, without distinction of any kind, such as race, color, sex, language, religion, political or other opinion, national or social origin, property, birth or other status."
- Article 3: "The States Parties to the present Covenant undertake to ensure the equal right of men and women to the enjoyment of all civil and political rights set forth in the present Covenant."
- Article 26: "All persons are equal before the law and are entitled without any discrimination to the equal protection of the law. In this respect, the law shall prohibit any discrimination and guarantee to all persons equal and effective protection against discrimination on any ground such as race, color, sex, language, religion, political or other opinion, national or social origin, property, birth or other status."

These provisions require, in essence, that whatever efforts a state makes to combat private violence, it must proceed in a nondiscriminatory way. Or, in terms more directly applicable to the problem of domestic violence, whatever level of resources a state decides to devote to enforcing criminal laws against private acts of violence, it must ensure that crimes against women receive at least as thorough an investigation and as vigorous a prosecution as crimes against men. Lesser attention constitutes not only a violation of the antidiscrimination provisions of the Covenant but also evidence of the complicity needed to make out a substantive violation.

There is an additional advantage to relying on Covenant Article 26 in particular as an alternative theory of state liability, in that it allows one to sidestep the potentially thorny issue of whether the Covenant applies to domestic violence short of murder. Some of the Covenant's guarantees with potential relevance to domestic violence are contained in provisions that have no other relevance to private conduct. For example, the "security of person" guarantee found in Covenant Article 9 is crafted onto a section that otherwise addresses only arrest and detention.

A discrimination approach avoids potential difficulties in arguing that these provisions also apply to private actors. Even if they do not encompass private assaults, the nondiscriminatory provision of Article 26 (unlike similar provisions in Articles 2(1) and 3) is not tied to particular rights secured by the Covenant, but mandates the "equal protection of the law" in all respects. Thus Article 26 can be used to address not only discriminatory enforcement of other human rights guarantees but also discriminatory enforcement of any criminal law. Discriminatory enforcement of laws applicable to domestic violence thus would constitute a human rights violation because of the unequal protection of the law even if domestic violence is deemed not to violate the physical-integrity guarantees of the Covenant.

Documenting Discrimination

Unfortunately, the type of comparative fact-finding needed to make out a case of discrimination can be considerably more complex than the inquiries traditionally undertaken by international human rights organizations (though arguably much less complex than proving empirically that a particular form of violence is responsible for the subordination of a class of people). For most fact-finding conducted by international human rights organizations, the case speaks for itself. As noted, it is enough to document an instance of torture by a state agent to establish that a human rights violation has occurred. In the case of overt complicity in private violence such as a state's authorization of an honor defense like Brazil's this remains true. But to make out a case of discriminatory non-enforcement of the criminal laws beyond such overt complicity, it is necessary not only to establish that there has been an unprosecuted crime, but also that the lack of prosecution is due to a prohibited form of discrimination. This comparative element introduces a new dimension requiring a broader analysis of the criminal justice system than is needed for traditional human rights factfinding.

Nonetheless, many of the tools used in traditional human rights documentation can also be employed to prove discrimination. The most readily available and the one principally relied on so far by the Human Rights Watch Women's Rights Project is anecdotal testimony, taken from either victims or their lawyers. We describe particularly compelling cases of domestic violence that the criminal justice system has not adequately addressed. Implicit in this approach is the argument that, if even the egregious cases of domestic violence are not prosecuted, one can hardly expect better results in run-of-the-mill cases. It still is necessary to show that these cases of non-prosecution are not aberrational that they reflect a pattern that is fairly attributable to the state rather than to the exceptional behavior of isolated functionaries. But by assembling a variety of such cases, the pattern needed to establish state responsibility for the prosecutorial neglect of domestic violence can be demonstrated.

We have also relied on "expert" testimony taken from actors in the criminal justice system to establish a pattern of discrimination. Judges, lawyers, prosecutors, and police officers can describe their experiences across a range of cases to assess how the criminal justice system generally treats domestic violence. Sometimes they can provide compelling anecdotes of their own. By introducing a broader view of the criminal justice system, these accounts can provide an important supplement to the case-oriented testimonies of victims and their advocates to show whether domestic violence is treated with less seriousness.

A particularly useful form of evidence is statistical. If it can be shown through statistics that domestic violence is systematically prosecuted less often (or less rigorously) than comparable acts of violence, a strong case of discrimination can be made. But gathering such statistics has been difficult, since few governments maintain systematic data on their criminal justice system. And even countries that do maintain such statistics may neglect to collect data on the gender of the victim, the relationship to the offender, or the locale of the crime. That such data should be collected and maintained should be a standard recommendation of those who examine the state's response to domestic violence.

Role of Human Rights and Women's Rights Organizations

In most human rights inquiries, local human rights monitors play a critical role. With their superior knowledge of a country's legal and political system, they can provide invaluable guidance to the research of an outside organization. Judgments made without such consultation are inevitably inferior. Given the complexity of investigations into systematic discrimination, the need for informed local consultation is all the more important. Yet our experience in enlisting local human rights monitors in our inquiries into women's rights issues has been mixed at best.

Aware of the importance of local expertise on the issues under investigation, we have made the existence of a well-developed women's rights movement an important factor in our initial selection of countries for investigation. For example, our decision to examine domestic violence in Brazil[1] and violence against women in custody in Pakistan was deeply influenced by this consideration. In each case, local women's rights advocates played a critical role in initiating the investigation, providing us with an overview and analysis of the problem we were studying and directing us to victims and "experts." Indeed, these advocates themselves were highly valuable "experts" whose experiences and views were repeatedly reflected in our final reports.

Unfortunately, these two experiences appear to be atypical. In most countries that we have examined, we have encountered a gaping lack of reliable, systematically collected evidence about the scope and nature of domestic violence and other women's rights issues. This void is attributable, in different respects, to both the traditional human rights movement and the women's rights movement.

I have already discussed how international human rights organizations have only gradually moved from their narrow focus on the state's treatment of dissidents to a broader sense of state responsibility based on a duty to redress violence by private actors. A similar evolution can be found at the local level. In countries where politically motivated, state-sponsored violations of human rights continue to be the primary human rights issue, these organizations may continue to work within the classic paradigm. In other countries where politically motivated abuses have diminished, many local organizations have begun to expand their mandates to address non-politically motivated abuses or even state-tolerated, as opposed to state-sponsored, abuse. An evolution of this sort is particularly apparent in recent years in certain countries of Latin America. However, even in countries in which local human rights organizations have completed this progression, we have found a marked failure to address domestic violence, as if violence against women is somehow outside the human rights domain.

This neglect is particularly unfortunate because local human rights organizations have developed fact-finding skills that would be extremely useful in demonstrating systematic discrimination against women in the workings of the criminal justice system. The ability to conduct detailed and accurate case studies is hardly innate; it requires experience in locating and interviewing witnesses, and in producing reports that can stand up to public scrutiny. Since such case studies are routinely produced by the traditional human rights movement, local human rights organizations would be well equipped to conduct similar investigations for women's rights issues. Moreover, although neither local nor international human rights organizations have as much experience examining the systematic workings of a criminal justice system as they do in documenting particular cases, these organizations' familiarity with pertinent laws and their contacts with lawyers and judges can be quite useful for such studies.

By contrast, most of the women's rights organizations that we have encountered have not had the opportunity to develop skills in human rights fact-finding. Given the frequent lack of domestic (let alone international) consensus behind norms of nondiscrimination on the basis of gender, it is natural that the women's rights movement in most countries has devoted itself to such tasks as political organizing and public education. But as important as these efforts are, they are quite distinct from the detailed factual documentation that is necessary to establish a human rights violation (case studies also can be used quite profitably for political organizing and public education). As a result, we have found that local women's rights groups generally have not been able to fill the fact-finding void left by the failure of local human rights organizations to address women's rights issues.

This is obviously an undesirable state of affairs. We have attempted to fill this void ourselves by conducting our own fact-finding. But as I noted, this can never be a fully adequate substitute for the active involvement of local monitors. Aware of the importance of local monitoring efforts, we have sought to use our own investigations and reports as a catalyst to the work of others, with the hope that we might stimulate an understanding of the sort of inquiries needed to treat women's rights issues under international human rights law. We encourage others to do the same, since an important goal of both the traditional human rights movement and the women's rights movement must be an introduction of human rights fact-finding to the problem of women's rights.

Ideally this will come from two directions: human rights organizations will begin to see women's rights issues as an integral part of their mandate, while women's rights organizations will begin to supplement their advocacy with attention to fact-finding and the collection of well documented data. At a minimum, one of the two types of organizations must move to fill the void. Until that happens, the problem of domestic violence and other women's rights issues will never move beyond the political domain to the realm of human rights where they also belong.

❑❑❑

11

Proving Sex Discrimination in Court

Introduction

The worker's lawyer must produce evidence sufficient to prove that gender was a determining factor in the employer's decision that adversely affected his client not necessarily the only factor, but a factor that made a difference in the employer's decision.

Proving an employer's discriminatory intent is never easy. Employers have learned to mask acts of employment discrimination with the appearance of business propriety. As the Supreme Court has observed, employers neither admit discriminatory animus nor leave a paper trail disclosing it. Thus, few employment discrimination cases turn on direct or "smoking gun" evidence of sex bias. Employers do not place memoranda in their files that openly admit to an employment decision based on a worker's gender. Even the least sophisticated of employers is careful not to leave a trail of discriminatory conduct, and it would be rare indeed for a corporate executive to take the witness stand and freely affirm he acted adversely to the interests of a female worker solely because of her gender.

Employment discrimination suits involve numerous complex procedures that make establishing a case difficult, since they allow employers to create barriers that block or divert plaintiff workers from achieving their litigation goals. In addition, these procedures do not readily lend themselves to resolving employment discrimination cases. The complexities of corporate decision making often cannot be adequately analyzed in the adversarial framework of the courtroom. But the litigation process nevertheless insists on an either/or explanation a discriminatory motive either was or was not the basis of a particular employment decision. Moreover, in employment discrimination litigation, "unambiguous villains and victims are increasingly more difficult to identify." How then does a sex discrimination complainant while avoiding employer-initiated barriers and contending with unwieldy legal procedures prove that a discriminatory intent, rather than a legitimate business reason, motivated an employment decision that adversely affected her employment status?

Direct Evidence of Discrimination

The legal procedures used in proving sexual-harassment claims often vary from those used in proving other types of sex discrimination cases. The elements of proof required in a sexual-harassment case are more closely allied with those common to other types of litigation, such as those involving tort claims. The claimant in a tort case must prove she suffered an injury or damages directly as the result of the negligent or deliberate act of the defendant, or as a consequence of the defendant's failure to act in circumstances in which the law requires him to act. The claimant in a sexual-harassment case generally establishes her case by proving she suffered an injury or damages directly as the result of a sexual act unlawful under the precepts of Title VII committed by the defendant in the workplace. The complainant nearly always relies solely upon direct evidence in proving she was the victim of sexually harassing conduct.

Unlike sexual harassment cases, direct evidence of sex discrimination, more often than not, is unavailable to the plaintiff. Due to current legal and social sanctions, people generally repress demonstrations of overt sexism and bias. Thus, even if an employer is aware of his own gender bias, he is unlikely to express it openly. Even if fellow workers were to observe discriminatory acts committed by their employer, and thus could offer the court direct evidence of those acts, they may be reluctant to come forward to testify on behalf of the complainant for fear of jeopardizing their own careers. As a result, cases that turn on direct evidence of sex discrimination are the exception. Debbie Moore's sex discrimination case against Alabama State University was one of the exceptions.

After Moore had worked in the university's admissions office for eight years, the university promoted her to admissions staff assistant, second in command to the director. Later, when the position of admissions office director became vacant, Roosevelt Steptoe, the university's vice president of academic affairs, asked Moore to assume increased responsibilities, and for a time she shared the duties of the admission office director's position with another employee.

Moore had every expectation that she would be awarded with further promotion, and she eagerly awaited advancement to admissions director. Her application for the director's position, however, was rejected by a committee appointed to screen and interview candidates. Moore alleged that Steptoe's bias against women led him to interfere with the application process, thus undermining her candidacy.

Steptoe played a major role in the university's hiring process; he appointed the committee that screened and interviewed applicants for the director's position, and after receiving the committee's recommendations, he made the final decision. Moore focused on two incidents she claimed epitomized Steptoe's bias against female workers. While walking across campus on one occasion, Moore was confronted by Steptoe who, noticing Moore's pregnant condition, commented, "I was going to put you in charge of that office, but look at you now." Later, Steptoe told Moore he would not consider her for the director's position because she was married with a child, the director's job entailed far too much traveling for a married mother, and, in any event, a woman should stay home with her family.

Moore sued the university for sex discrimination. The primary trial issue focused on Steptoe's comments regarding Moore's pregnancy and her duties as a mother. Did these comments constitute direct evidence of a discriminatory bias against Moore? For statements of this type to be considered direct evidence of discrimination, the law requires that the plaintiff demonstrate that the comments are capable of only one interpretation that they reflect a discriminatory attitude correlating to the discrimination complained of and that they were made by a person involved in an employment decision affecting the worker. The court ruled that Steptoe's comments did indeed qualify as direct evidence of discrimination. The comments were made by an official with decisionmaking authority, neither statement was subject to multiple interpretation, and "neither required any leap of logic or inference" to conclude that an act of discrimination had occurred.

Remarks based on sex stereotypes like those expressed by Steptoe may or may not depending upon the circumstances be considered direct evidence of sex discrimination. In one case, a supervisor, in an angry outburst that followed his detection of a deficiency in a woman's job performance, shouted that he did not want any women working in his office. Although inappropriate and illustrative of a negative view of women in general, the remark, in and of itself, was insufficient to be considered direct evidence that established a discriminatory intent regarding that particular worker. In other circumstances, such a remark could very well be perceived as constituting direct evidence of a discriminatory motive.

Indirect Evidence of Discrimination

Since direct evidence of sex discrimination is often not available to assist the worker, the lawyer representing a sex discrimination claimant must search out indirect or circumstantial evidence of sex bias. Soon after enactment of Title VII, the Supreme Court established ground rules for evaluating indirect evidence of discrimination. These rules were based on the Court's observation that an employer invariably responds to a charge of discriminatory behavior with the argument that behind the employment decision that adversely affected the worker lay a legitimate, nondiscriminatory reason. If the worker establishes that the purported nondiscriminatory reason was not the employer's actual reason, or that the employer's reason simply is not credible, the court may assume that the employer proffered such a reason only to cover up an unlawful motive. The Supreme Court explained why it was justified in making such an assumption: "We are willing to presume this largely because we know from our experience that more often than not people do not act in a totally arbitrary manner, without any underlying reasons, especially in a business setting. Thus when all legitimate reasons for an [employer's decision] have been eliminated as possible reasons for [its] actions, it is more likely than not the employer, who we generally assume acts only with *some* reason, based [its] decision on an impermissible consideration such as race [or gender]."

Thus, the task of the worker's attorney is to prove that the employer's stated reasons for its actions were pretexts offered only to cover up discriminatory intent and that the employer has concealed its real reasons. The attorney must prove that the employer's expressed reasons are "pretextual" and were offered by the employer only to cover up its discriminatory intent.

One way to prove intentional discrimination is thus to show that an employer offered a false explanation for its decision that adversely affected the worker. A court or jury may infer from the falsity of the explanation that the employer has dissembled or misrepresented the facts to cover up a discriminatory purpose.

Once the employer's explanation, because of its falsity, is eliminated from consideration, discriminatory conduct may well be the most likely alternative explanation, especially since the employer, who is in the best position to assert the actual reason for its decision, failed to do so. Thus, a court or jury may infer the ultimate fact of discrimination from the falsity of the employer's explanation. A federal appellate court has succinctly explained this rationale: "Resort to a pretextual explanation is like flight from the scene of a crime, evidence indicating consciousness of guilt, which is, of course, evidence of illegal conduct." Thus, in a pretext case, the worker is required to prove that the employer has opted not to express its true reasons for acting as it did. She must prove that the employer's reasons are "pretextual," and these reasons would not have been offered by the employer except to cover up its discriminatory intent.

Many sex discrimination suits involve indirect evidence and focus on the motivation that underlies an employer's decision. Are the reasons advanced by the employer for its employment decision credible? Are they its actual reasons, or was the decision motivated by an impermissible factor, such as the worker's gender? Are the reasons asserted by the employer merely pretexts, proffered by the employer to cover up the true nature of its decision, namely, that it was discriminatory? Even if an employer's reasons did, in fact, serve as one of the bases for its decision, was the employer also motivated to make that decision because of the worker's gender? These are the issues that typically confront juries hearing sex discrimination cases.

In a case that relied upon both direct and indirect evidence, Karen Emmel sued the Coca-Cola Bottling Company of Chicago after it promoted five men to newly created upper-management positions. Because she had not been included among those promoted, Emmel charged the company with violating Title VII. Later, when Coca-Cola again passed over Emmel in a set of similar promotions, she filed a second charge of sex discrimination. The two charges eventually were litigated in a federal court, where a jury found in her favor and awarded her substantial compensatory and punitive damages. Coca-Cola then asked the court to overturn the jury verdict, and when the court refused, Coca-Cola appealed.

Here, in summary, is the evidence the appellate court reviewed. Emmel began her career at Coca-Cola as an account manager, rose to district sales manager, and then was promoted to cold drink specialist, a position that required her to maintain exclusive purchase agreements with existing accounts, develop new business, and increase the services furnished to customers. Subsequently, Coca-Cola created five upper-management positions called area development managers (ADMs). Each of the five employees promoted to ADM positions all males had considerably shorter careers with Coca-Cola and much less time in supervisory positions than Emmel. The following year, the company announced the creation of three upper-management "key account executive" positions, and again the three workers promoted to these positions all males had shorter careers with Coca-Cola and less supervisory experience than Emmel.

Emmel based her indirect evidence case on her allegations that she was far better qualified than the male workers selected for these positions. One of the men promoted to an ADM position had just over five years' experience with the company, compared to Emmel's twenty years. Another had two and onehalf years of supervisory experience; Emmel had eight. In addition to longer service and more supervisory experience, Emmel, unlike some of those promoted, had a positive employment history. While Emmel had won managerof-the-year awards, one of the promoted male workers received four disciplinary warnings during the four years prior to his promotion. Emmel had a college degree, while some of the promoted employees did not.

In response to Emmel's position, Coca-Cola asserted that it did not base the selection of the workers for promotion on length of service, supervisory experience, or college education, but rather on a selection process designed to determine who was the best person for the job, and in this process it was determined that Emmel was not the best person for any of the eight positions in question. But at the trial, the jurors rejected the company's explanation, finding that the reasons given for the selection of the male employees were not credible and thus were pretexts, either false or not the actual reasons for denying Emmel a promotion.

The appellate court agreed with the jury's finding of pretext and ruled that sufficient evidence had been offered to support it. Included in the evidence were company memoranda pertaining to the promotions that contained statements undercutting testimony given at the trial by company witnesses. The court also was influenced by the fact that the company's explanation presented at the trial for not promoting Emmel differed from the explanation given to Emmel at the time the company rejected her for promotion. The court commented: "If at the time of the adverse employment action the decision maker gave one reason, but at the time of the trial gave another reason which was not supported by documentary evidence, the jury could reasonably conclude that the new reason was a pretextual after-the-fact justification."

As noted, Emmel did not rely solely on indirect evidence. Her case was a mix of both indirect evidence of pretext and direct evidence of sex bias. Direct evidence of sex discrimination surfaced in a remark made by one of the company's vice presidents at the time of Emmel's rejection for promotion to an ADM position. He told Emmel that she had not been awarded the promotion because company officials were averse to the placement of women in uppermanagement positions. A number of other comments and statements of company executives, each demonstrating a bias against the elevation of women to upper management, also were received in evidence. Based on this evidence, the appellate court ruled that the jury was justified in concluding that a pervasive attitude existed among company executives that women did not belong in the company's upper echelon. Since direct evidence of sex bias as well as indirect evidence of pretext supported an outcome in Emmel's favor, the appellate court declined to overturn the jury's verdict.

Pretext cases that are not buttressed by direct evidence of discrimination are likely to fail unless the evidence of pretext is clear and persuasive. Evidence that an employer treated its workers unfairly or unequally often will turn jurors against an employer, since many, if not most of them, may be reminded of episodes of unfair or unequal treatment suffered during their own work careers. Deborah Kramer produced this kind of evidence in her case against Nebraska's Logan County School District.

Kramer began her teaching career as a substitute teacher in the district and was later certified as a middle school teacher in mathematics, general science, and natural science. Subsequently, the school district assigned her to teach high school science. After she spent two years in that position, the high school principal, Mike Apple, and the school district's superintendent, John Broadbent, recommended to the school board that it not renew Kramer's contract for the following year. The school board then dismissed Kramer on the grounds that she could not get along with school administrators, that her competency was questionable in light of below-average performance evaluations, that she had failed to function as a team player, and that the school district would be better served by employing a more cooperative teacher. Kramer then filed suit against the school district, alleging she had been discriminatorily discharged because of her gender.

At the trial, Kramer offered evidence that Apple had disciplined her more severely than he had disciplined male teachers for similar conduct, and several female teachers testified they also had been treated inappropriately or unfairly because of their gender. Kramer provided the court with copies of written reprimands prepared by Apple that had been placed in her personnel file, but, in direct contravention of school policy, neither had Apple signed them nor had she received copies of them. She also produced evidence that Apple and Broadbent had materially misrepresented the facts when they informed the school board that her performance evaluations were below average, when in fact five out of six of her evaluations were rated average or better. Kramer adduced evidence that fifteen of the seventeen tenured teachers in her school had signed a letter in her support, thus rebutting the "team player" allegation, but Apple and Broadbent failed to present the letter to the school board. Kramer argued that the evidence relating to her competency and to Apple's and Broadbent's unfair treatment of her and other female teachers supported a finding that the reasons given for her dismissal were pretextual, and that Apple and Broadbent, in recommending nonrenewal of her teaching contract, had been motivated by sex bias. The jury agreed and awarded Kramer back pay and compensatory damages.

Another pretext case was that of Pamela Long, an Asian American, holder of a master's degree in accounting and fluent in the Japanese language, who applied to Ringling Brothers Barnum & Bailey for a controller's position in Japan. Long was willing to relocate to Japan and travel extensively, if necessary, and she possessed sufficient accounting experience and computer capability to perform the functions of the controller's position. Ringling, however, was unwilling to interview her. A recruiting firm later informed Long that Ringling had declined to consider her for the position because she was a woman, that Ringling thought a woman would be ineffective in the controller's position on account of the cultural bias against working women in Japan, and, moreover, that it was concerned about a woman traveling alone in a foreign country. Long filed a legal action against Ringling for sex discrimination.

Ringling hired a man for the position, but at the trial, it denied that it had specifically set out to hire a male. Ringling claimed that Long had not filed her application soon enough to be considered for the position, since insufficient time then remained to train her for the position. But evidence submitted at the trial disclosed that when Ringling received Long 's application, the position was still open. In addition, Ringling's witnesses presented conflicting testimony regarding the extent of training required. One testified that a two-month training period was necessary, another that Ringling had no established period of training, and still another that a person with Long's experience would require little training. The court, sitting without a jury, ruled that in view of Long's extensive accounting experience, together with her fluency in the Japanese language, Ringling had more than sufficient time to train her if they were of a mind to. Based on the evidence, the court was persuaded that Ringling's reasons for not interviewing Long were pretextual:

> *The Court believes that Ringling has articulated no more than an after-thefact attempt to legitimize an unlawful discriminatory decision not to interview nor employ Plaintiff. The evidence establishes, in the opinion of this Court, that Ringling wanted a male and that Plaintiff was rejected because she was a woman. Having rejected Ringling's proffered reason for not interviewing nor hiring Plaintiff, the Court reaches the ultimate conclusion that Ringling's decisions were motivated by intentional discriminatory considerations, and that Plaintiff did prove by a preponderance of the evidence that Ringling intentionally discriminated against her because of her sex/gender.*

In another case, a female worker was allegedly terminated for insubordination and absenteeism, but these were not the reasons given her at the time. In fact, not until an unemployment compensation hearing several months after the worker's discharge did the employer mention the insubordination and absenteeism allegations. When the employer again asserted them at the trial of the worker's sex discrimination case, the court noted that since these were not the reasons provided the worker at the time of her dismissal, they were of doubtful authenticity. and the circumstances suggested that they were fabricated after the fact to justify a decision made on other grounds. Based on these and other facts, the court ruled that the reasons given for the worker's discharge were pretextual, and it awarded judgment in favor of the worker.

A fairly high proportion of pretext cases are dismissed at the summary judgment stage of the litigation or after trial, as was true for Jan Johnson, a resident physician at the Baptist Medical Center in Kansas City, Missouri. Her attending physician, or supervisor, was Lawrence Rues, an associate director of the hospital's family care center. After Johnson had been in the residency program for a year and a half, the hospital informed her that she had failed to meet its minimum standards of acceptable performance, and it presented her with the choice of termination or resignation. Johnson chose to resign, and then sued the hospital for sex discrimination.

Baptist Medical furnished the court with substantial evidence of its displeasure with Johnson's performance. Her evaluation forms, for the most part disclosed "needs much improvement" ratings, and recorded faculty comments touched on her weak knowledge base and inability to diagnose and manage patients. Johnson attributed her low marks to Rues and other faculty members she claimed harbored a discriminatory animus toward women. She characterized

Rues as "intimidating, abusive, and judgmental" in dealing with her and other female residents, but as "patient and understanding" when dealing with male residents. Johnson also claimed that certain male residents with performance evaluations similar to hers were not asked to leave the program. The evidence revealed, however, that these male residents had fewer unfavorable evaluations than she. Johnson's support for her other allegations was largely hearsay, and she could offer the court little other probative evidence in support of her positions. Johnson thus was unable to establish a case of pretext, and her case was dismissed.

Pretext appears in myriad forms and is often detected only through the vigilance of the affected worker. Because she is better informed than anyone else regarding the particulars of her own job, she generally is in the best position to evaluate the accuracy and truthfulness of the reasons advanced by her employer to justify its adverse employment decision. Her ability to root out the facts underlying the employer's decision often determines whether a pretext case will succeed or fail.

Disparate Impact

Nearly all of the cases reviewed in this book fall into a category of discrimination lawsuits known as "disparate treatment" cases. "Disparate treatment" refers to an employer policy or practice that treats some workers less favorably than others, sometimes because of their gender. A classic example of a disparate treatment case involved the termination of the Nebraska schoolteacher discussed earlier in this chapter. In *Kramer,* the schoolteacher alleged that her principal had disciplined her more severely than male teachers, and other female teachers testified they had been treated inappropriately or unfairly because of their gender. Unequal treatment and disparate treatment are synonymous, and disparate treatment is the most common form of employment discrimination. The disparate treatment of male and female workers underlies a large proportion of sex discrimination cases.

"Disparate impact," as distinguished from "disparate treatment," comes into play in a sex discrimination case when an employment policy or practice that appears on its face to be neutral or nondiscriminatory falls more harshly upon women than upon men. Employment decisions or practices that appear to be fair in form but are discriminatory in practice disparately impact female workers.

Workers who rely on the disparate impact approach to proving discrimination are generally trying to eliminate employment policies or practices that create barriers to job opportunities and advancement or in some other fashion seriously disadvantage women. As an example, an employer, in connection with certain jobs, may establish height and weight requirements that disproportionately disqualify women from consideration and thus disparately impact female applicants for those positions.

In disparate impact cases, an employment policy or practice may have been adopted without a deliberately discriminatory motive, but it may nevertheless constitute the functional equivalent of an act of intentional discrimination. As one court explained it: "In essence, the disparate impact theory is a doctrinal surrogate for eliminating unprovable acts of intentional discrimination hidden innocuously behind facially neutral policies or practices."

Female workers who rely on the disparate impact approach are not required to prove that the employer was motivated by a discriminatory purpose in initiating or implementing the targeted policies or practices. The motivation of the employer is irrelevant to the outcome of this type of case. If the workers can establish that an employment policy disproportionately affects women because of their gender, the employer must show, if it hopes to prevail, that the policy is essential to its business needs. But even if it is essential, the workers may nonetheless carry the day if they can show that the employer has available to it other policies that it could implement, if it wished, that would impact female workers less disadvantageously. A plaintiff alleging disparate impact in an employer's hiring practices must establish three elements:

1. A significant disparity exists between the proportion of women available for a particular position and the number of women hired for that position.
2. The employer has in place a specific, facially neutral employment practice that affects the rate of hiring women.
3. A causal nexus exists between the employment practice and the disparity.

Once the plaintiff worker has established these three elements, the employer may attempt to justify the challenged practice by showing that it serves a legitimate, nondiscriminatory business objective. But as noted, even if the employer succeeds in establishing such a business need, the worker may still prevail by showing that another employment practice, impacting women less harshly, is available to the employer to satisfy its business objectives.

The disparate impact approach to proving sex discrimination is most often used in broad-based class actions and in connection with EEOC litigation initiated on behalf of a large number of complainants. Nevertheless, an individual worker complainant and her attorney must remain alert to the possibility of taking this approach when circumstances warrant. This is particularly the case when it may not be possible to prove that an employer has intentionally engaged in acts of discrimination.

Employer Defenses

Although a vast number of defenses are available to employers contesting worker claims of sex discrimination, employers assert certain defenses with some regularity, and we will examine two of them, each of questionable validity.

Suppose a female worker is terminated but replaced by another woman. Is she foreclosed from proving that her employer was guilty of sex discrimination by reason of the fact that she was replaced by a woman and not a man? Numerous employers have asserted this defense, usually with little success. Even when a woman is fired and replaced by another woman, she may have been treated differently from her male co-workers. Her employer may have terminated her on account of a single lapse in performance, while it may afford a man working at her side far greater latitude before reaching the stage of dismissal. In these circumstances, who replaces a female worker is largely irrelevant. Thus, even when a female worker cannot claim that her employer replaced her with a man, she may still allege that her employer treated her less favorably because of her gender. That her replacement is a woman demonstrates the employer's willingness to hire women but does not support the employer's claim that the decision to fire the worker was made without discriminatory intent, or that the employer does not discriminate against women in other workplace matters.

Let us take this a step further. An employer discharges a female worker and replaces her with another woman. Moreover, the person who made the decision to fire the worker also is a woman. May the fired women assert a valid Title VII claim? This was the situation Dawn Veatch confronted when she sued her employer, the Northwestern Memorial Hospital in Chicago. Veatch alleged that after sixteen years with the hospital, she was summarily discharged by her supervisor, a woman. The hospital maintained that Veatch should be barred from continuing with her legal action, as she could not assert a valid claim of sex discrimination because a woman made the decision to terminate her and her replacement also was a woman. The court rejected the hospital's position on the ground that the mere fact that one woman fired another does not prove that the decision to fire was free of sex discrimination. The court expanded on that view: "When power and status are distributed unevenly, administrators may sometimes view members of some groups as more easily expendable than others either because of some misplaced notion of inferiority or because some groups with less power cannot protest adverse treatment as effectively." Thus, a supervisor, man or woman, may discern that a decision that adversely affects a female employee may spawn less opposition and create less friction in the workplace than a decision that adversely affects a male employee. Moreover, a female supervisor working in an institution dominated by males may feel extra pressure not to be soft on female subordinates, and this pressure may motivate her to act less favorably toward female workers. Therefore, the mere fact that Veatch was fired and replaced by a woman did not legally bar her from proceeding with her case.

Another strategy, the "same actor" defense, has recently gained popularity with employers in cases where the same person who hired a female worker later fires her. It is based on the rationale that if the same person both hired and fired a worker, it is unrealistic to assume that discriminatory intent was absent at the time of the decision to hire but present at the time of the decision to fire. As one court observed, from the viewpoint of the employer, "it hardly makes sense to hire workers from a group one dislikes only to fire them once they are on the job." The court then established the following rule: "In cases where the hirer and the firer are the same individual and termination of employment occurs within a relatively short time span following the hiring, a strong inference exists that discrimination was not a determining factor for the adverse action taken by the employer."

A case in point involved Evelyn Sasmor, a senior vice president at Harcourt, Brace & Company, who hired Mary Bradley as an information services manager. Approximately one year later, Sasmor terminated Bradley, allegedly because of performance problems. Bradley later claimed in her sex discrimination case against Harcourt, Brace that Sasmor's real reason for terminating her was that she wanted to give Bradley's position to a man. The court was dubious; if Sasmor had preferred a man in the position, why did she not hire a man in the first instance? Bradley attempted to buttress her case by offering evidence that Sasmor appeared to favor Bradley's subordinate, Tom Jackson, but the court was of the opinion that Sasmor's favoritism of Jackson stemmed from his competence, particularly in light of Sasmor's negative view of Bradley's performance. The court then applied the same-actor defense, holding that where the same actor is responsible for both the hiring and the firing of a discrimination plaintiff, and the actions occur within a short period of time, a strong inference arises that there was no discriminatory motive involved in the decision to fire the plaintiff. The court dismissed Bradley's case.

The same-actor defense has its limitations. In the *Bradley* case, if Sasmor hired Bradley with the intention of firing her as soon as she was able to groom Jackson for the position, application of the same-actor defense would lead to an injustice. If an employer hires a woman in the belief that she will comply with certain sex-based stereotypes relating to a woman's role in the workplace, and later fires her because she declines to comply with those stereotypes, the same-actor defense should not be a factor in the case.

When applying the same-actor defense, the length of time between the hiring and the firing affects the strength of the inference that may be drawn that discrimination was not a factor in the worker's discharge. Over a period of time, an employer may develop an animus or bias that did not exist when its hiring decision was made. On the other hand, an employer who is of a mind to treat male and female workers equally is less likely to change, regardless of the passage of time. Whenever the same-actor defense is asserted, all the underlying facts must be explored before any inferences may properly be drawn.

Bibliography

BARRET-KRIEGEL, BLANDINE. The state and the rule of law. Princeton, N.J.: Princeton University Press, c1995.

BOUVARD, MARGUERITE GUZMAN Women reshaping human rights: how extraordinary activists are changing the world. Wilmington, Del.: SR Books, 1996.

CAMERON, MARGARET (2000) 'Young men and Violence Prevention', Trends and Issues in Crime and

CHATTERJEE, M. (2005). Women's Human Rights. Aavishkar Publisher, Distributor, Jaipur.

CONNELL, R.W. (1995) Masculinities. Sydney: Allen & Unwin.

DADHICH, N. (20003). Women, Conflict-Resolution and Culture. Aavishkar Publisher, Distributor, Jaipur.

DESAI, LEELA. (2003). Feminism and Its Strategies, Pointer Publishers, Jaipur.

DEVI. S. (1999). Women's Status and Social Change, Pointer Publisher, Jaipur.

DYCK, ARTHUR J. Rethinking rights and responsibilities: the moral bonds of community. Cleveland, Ohio: Pilgrim Press, 1994 EVANS, TONY. US hegemony and the project of universal human rights. Houndmills: Macmillan Press: New York, N.Y.: St. Martin's Press, 1996.

EUGENE VOLOKH, "Diversity, Race as Proxy, and Religion as Proxy," 43 *UCLA L. REV.* 2059 (1996).

FLOOD, MICHAEL (1993–94) '3 principles for men', XY: Men, sex, politics 3.4, Summer

FLOOD, MICHAEL (1997) 'Responding to Men's Rights', XY: Men, sex, politics 7.2, Spring.

FLOOD, MICHAEL (1998) 'Men's Movements', Community Quarterly No. 46, June.

FORSYTHE, DAVID P. Human rights and peace: international and national dimensions. Lincoln: University of Nebraska Press, c1993.

FUNK, RUS ERVIN (1993) Stopping Rape: A challenge for men. Philadelphia, PA: New Society Publishers.

GEWIRTH, ALAN. The community of rights. Chicago: University of Chicago Press, c1996.

HAYWARD, RUTH F. (1999) 'Needed: A new model of masculinity to stop violence against girls and women', WHO Global Symposium on Violence and Health, 12–15 October, Kobe, Japan.

HIREMATH, R.C. (2005). Women and Gender Issues, Pointer Publisher, Jaipur.

HOWARD, RHODA E. Human rights and the search for community. Boulder: WestviewPress, 1995.

IYER, P. (2006). Women in Developing Countries. Aavishkar Publisher, Distributor, Jaipur.

IYER. P. (2006). Human Rights of Women, Pointer Publisher, Jaipur.

JOHN, ANGELA V. and EUSTANCE, CLAIRE (1997) (eds) The Men's Share?: Masculinities, male support and Women's Suffrage in Britain, 1890–1920. London: Routledge.

KIMMEL, MICHAEL S. (1993) 'Clarence, William, Iron Mike, Tailhook, Senator Packwood, Spur Posse, Magic... and us', in Buchwald, Emilie, Fletcher, Pamela and Roth, MARTHA (eds) Transforming a Rape Culture. Minneapolis: Milkweed Editions.

KIMMEL, MICHAEL S. and MOSMILLER, THOMAS E. (1992) Against the Tide: Pro-feminist men in the United States, 1776–1990. Boston: Beacon Press.

LANDSBERG, MICHELE (2000) 'Canadian Feminists' Uneasy Alliance with Men Challenging Violence', Voice Male Spring (Men's Resource Centre of Western Massachusetts).

LAUREN, PAUL GORDON. Power and prejudice: the politics and diplomacy of racial discrimination. Boulder: Westview, 1988.

LUXTON, MEG (1993) 'Dreams and Dilemmas: Feminist musings on 'The Man Question', in Haddad, Tony (ed) Men and Masculinities: A critical anthology. Toronto: Canadian Scholars' Press.

MESSNER, MICHAEL A. (1997) Politics of Masculinities: Men in movements. University of Southern California: Sage Publications.

SAHU, A. (2007). Women's Liberation and Human Rights, Pointer Publisher, Jaipur.

SPRING, JOEL H. Education and the rise of the global economy. Mahwah, NJ: L. Earlbaum Associates, c1998.

STOLTENBERG, JOHN (1990) Refusing To Be a Man: Essays on sex and justice. CA & Suffolk: Fontana/Collins.

STRAUSS, SYLVIA (1982) "Traitors to the Masculine Cause": The men's campaigns for women's rights. Westport, Conn.: Greenwood Press.

TRIMIEW, DARRYL M. God bless the child that's got its own: the economic rights debate. Atlanta, Ga.: Scholars Press, c1997.

UPRETI, H.C. (2000). Women and Problems of Gender Discrimination, Pointer Publisher, Jaipur.

WALZER, MICHAEL. On toleration. New Haven: Yale University Press, c1997.

WEINER, MYRON. The global migration crisis: challenge to states and to human rights. New York: HarperCollins College Publishers, c1995.

WEISSBERG, ROBERT. Political tolerance: balancing community and diversity. Thousand Oaks, Calif.: Sage Publications, c1998.

WIESEL, ELIE. From the kingdom of memory: reminiscences. New York: Summit Books, c1990.

INDEX

A

American Association of
University Professors
(AAUP), 7
Bar Association Journal, 2
An Outstanding Profession al, 34
Any of these, 52
Appropriate therapeutic Stance
for Treaters, 40
Area Development Managers
(ADMs), 247
Available Resources, 40

B

Biological and Psychosocial
Hypotheses, 148
Bread Winners, 16

C

Care and Justice in Public and
Private, 137
Changing Data, 159
Changing Minds, 159
Charter-Based Bodies, 197
Child-Rearing Potential, 89
Circumstances of Justice, 115
Clarification of the Clinician's
Role, 43
Closed Mind, 160
Collective Ignorance, 68
Columbia Gas System Service
Corporation, 12
Committee on the Elimination
of Discrimination against
Women, 196
Common Counter Transference
Reactions, 45
Denominators, 202
Concomitant Stresses, 53
Confirmation Bias, 159
Consideration of Care and
Justice, 108
Coopersmith, 24
Cross Cultural Dialogue, 179
Research, 150
Cultural Feminism, 175, 213
Customary Property Law, 188
Cute Behavior, 83
Cynthia, 64
Cynthia Jones, 63

D

Decreased Libido, 62
Deft touch, 34
Department of Biochemistry, 36
Dependants, 135

Devalued Female, 158
Direct Evidence of
    Discrimination, 243
Discriminatory Person al Law,
    186
Disparate Impact, 252
    Treatment, 36
Dispute Model, 99
Document Relevant Historical
    information, 43
Documenting Discrimination,
    237
Domestic Protection, 200

E

Education for the 21st Century,
    167
Emancipation of Women, 151
Employee Assistance Program
    (EAP), 42
Employer Defenses, 254
Equal Opportunities, 212
    Rights, 212
Ethnic and Racial Groups, 151
    Identity, 178

F

Faculty Evaluation Advisory
    Committee, 8
Family Planning Programs, 190
Federal Academy of Public
    Administration, 176
Feminist Critiques of Rights, 208
Fiat Iustitia Pereat Mundus, 146
First Generation Rights, 220
Forensic Strife, 1
Formats for initial Evaluation s,
    40
Function of Women's
    International Human Rights,
    205

G

Gender Discrimination Models,
    82
    Make-Up, 29
General Knowledge, 153
Good Legs, 151
Group Dynamics Impede
    Progress of token Women,
    84

H

Helsinki Monitors, 229
Human Rights Committee, 182
    Watch, 231
Hyperinsomnia, 62
Hypersexuality, 62

I

Ideal Workers, 71
Immediate Crisis and Special
    Cultural Challenges, 59
Indirect Evidence of
    Discrimination, 245
Individual Deficit Model, 82
Insomnia, 62
Intergroup Relation ship Model,
    88
Internal Discourse, 179
Internalization of Blame for
    Discriminatory Experiment,
    102
International Covenant on Civil
    and Political Rights, 228
    Human Rights Law, 172
    Protection, 194
Interpretation of Diagrams, 153
Isolated Majority World Ethnic
    Groups, 156

L

Liberal Feminism, 175

M

Madison County Veterans
Service Agency, 32
Managing the initial Referral, 41
Masculine Culture, 69
Massachusetts institute of
Technology, 66
Medical and Psychiatric History,
54
Model Cities Program, 6
of Sexual Harassment, 91
Modes of Resolution, 40
Mommy Tracks, 27
Myopia USA, 148

N

National Bar Association
Magazine, 2
Directory of Legal
Employers, 2
Institute of Health, 14
Science Foundation, 14
Natural Biological Model of
Sexual Harassment, 92
Nature Needs Nurture, 165
New England Journal of
Medicine, 13
Noddings-Type, 145
Non-Governmental
Organization s (NGOs), 177
Therapeutic Stance by
Clinician, 49

O

Olsten Corporation, 37
Organization al Model of Sexual
Harassment, 93
Orientalist Trap, 177
Outcomes of Cross Cultural
Research, 152
Overt and Blatant forms of Sex
Discrimination, 28

P

Physical and Psychological
Symptoms, 61
Pike County School System, 30
Polacco's Salary, 36
Political Motivation, 228
Politics of Cross-Cultural
investigation s, 151
Pravda, 151
Prima Facie Duties, 123
Principle of Judgment, 111
Problems Related to
Clarification of Clinician's
Role, 46
Progress, Challenges and
Prospects, 173
Proving Sex Discrimination in
Court, 242
Psychobiosocial Perspective, 162

Q

Quantitative Reasoning, 153
and interpretation of
Diagram, 154

R

Radical Feminism, 175
Reading Comprehension, 153
Regional Protection, 198
Relevant Legal Issues, 40
Past History, 53
Reserve Life insurance
Company, 28
Resource Manual on Strategies
for Confronting Domestic
Violence, 191
Resourceful at Improvisation,
131
Role of Family in Gender
Discrimination, 28
Rutgers Medical School, 24

S

Second Generation Rights, 223
Selective Seroton in Reuptake inhibitors, 63
Sennello Case, 34
Sex Differences, 170
- Discrimination, 66
- Discrimination in today's Workplace, 39
- Role Model, 85
- Role Spillover Model, 92
- Stereotyping, 34

Sexual Harassment, 82
Slut, 14
Smoking Gun, 242
Sociocultural Model of Sexual Harassment, 95
Socioeconomic Model, 92
Spears Case, 34
Special Coddling for a Special Girl, 83
Statistical Abstract of the United States, 72
Structural Adjustment Programs (SAPs), 184
- Institution al Model of Gender Discrimination, 84

Study Ability, 153
Subsequent Practice, 180
Subtle and Subjective Consensus among the Partners, 7
Swedish Scholastic Aptitude Test, 154

T

Terpstra and Baker Models, 98
The Dead End Division, 49
- Definitive Answer, 152
- Group Relation s Model, 99
- Role Model, 99

Theories of Social and Gender Justice, 76
Throgmorton Case, 34
Traditional Men's Fields, 151
Transforming "Men's" Rights Law, 216
Treatment of Sexual Harassment, 39
Types and Styles of Presenting Symptomatology, 40

U

Unconscious and Unknowing, 68
United States Forgecraft Corporation, 30

V

Vassar College, 24
Villanova University School of Law, 6
Violence against Women, 191
Vocabulary, 153

W

Western industrialized Nation s, 153
Whore, 14
Woman's Voice, 213
Women in Law, 3
- Career Aspiration s, 79
- Ghetto, 214
- Health, 190
- International Human Rights Law, 172
- Libber, 35
- Rights Project, 221
- Work, 72

Work and Education al Environments Experiences for Women 81
World War II, 16